THEORY OF FINANCIAL RELATIVITY

Unlocking Market Mysteries that will Make You a Better Investor

Daniel R. Moore

DEDICATION

In Memory of Michael J. Rider
for his endless pursuit of knowledge
through the study of history

ACKNOWLEDGMENTS

This book would not have been possible without the support of my loving wife, Susan, and my children, Erin and Connor, who provided endless words of encouragement as well as plenty of curiosity while the research, writing and publication of the book was happening.

TABLE OF CONTENTS

PROLOGUE

PROLOGUE

I was born in September 1962 in Oklahoma, the Sooner State. At the time I had no idea how making my arrival into the world in a state known for settlers who showed up early to stake first claim on land would become an appropriate analog for the first 50 years of my life. I did not stake a claim in Oklahoma. I did not stay there long, just two years. I was not born with a silver spoon in my mouth. My father was an Army ROTC cadet while earning his chemical engineer degree at Virginia Tech. His father was a railroad engineer in Appalachia, Virginia and my mother's father worked as the foreman in the coal mines in Derby, Virginia. My father landed in Fort Sill, OK to do a tour of duty after college graduation, and that was where my voyage began. The Sooner State perpetually in my blood, my life has been filled with quests. Pursuits of many things, but the two areas that stand out most are a drive to build secure wealth, but equally, if not more important, knowledge about how to do so. The latter is the reason I wrote this book – to document and share the knowledge I have gained through a very exciting and high growth time period in American history, and stake a small claim to a piece of that history in a way that will let others hopefully perpetuate the understanding and become better investors.

My earliest recollection of an important date in history was watching, on a black and white TV, Neil Armstrong become the first man to step foot on the moon on July 20, 1969. Then there were the Vietnam War reports and stories about POWs I listened to while in first and second grade when I lived in Kingsport, Tennessee. On to the long gas lines during the oil crisis in 1973, which I witnessed from a new location, the Upper Peninsula of Michigan. At the time I had no idea why the gas shortage was happening, only that foreign countries in the Middle East were involved. And even though I was still young, I can clearly recall the Nixon resignation, with Gerald Ford "clumsily" taking over. Then, euphoria overtook our household in November 1976 when Jimmy Carter was elected president. It was an elation that was short lived, however. I was in high school in Asheville, NC during the Carter years. From that point on my memory becomes a lot clearer. Certificates of deposit rates of over 10% at times are firmly in my memory bank. And my parents' mortgage rate was at an equally high level. But they didn't seem to suffer in the process. They bought and sold houses on several occasions during the period, and each time the price of the house increased. Inflation was rampant, but not a lot of people seemed to be that concerned – until the Presidential election approached in 1980. It was a time of fast paced relative adjustment, as I would discover looking back on that point in history in researching this book.

In 1980, I struck out to obtain a college education in the sleepy town of Clemson, SC. The first event, outside of adjusting to the rigors of college level academics relative to high school, was the sweeping in of Ronald Reagan as President. I would learn in finance courses I took in my junior and senior year that the deregulation of interest rates in 1980 made it an important time in U.S. monetary history. During the time I also studied the work done by Milton Friedman and read the book "Wealth and Poverty" by George Gilder, and other economic supply-side literary works. I am a product of the social transformation known as the Reagan Revolution.

After obtaining an undergraduate degree in financial management, I began a second stage of my journey which put me in close contact with inflection points in financial history - boom times and dramatic bust. My first job coming out of college was as a credit analyst for NCNB. For those who do not know the company history, North Carolina National Bank, through mergers and acquisitions allowed by deregulation, became Bank of America when it combined with the California-based institution in 1998. When I joined the bank in 1984 the bank operated only in North Carolina. By 1998, they operated in all 50 states. The short time period I worked at the bank left a solid impression upon me. As a credit trainee, I met on several occasions the visionary behind the expansion strategy of the bank – CEO, Hugh McColl. A man with military training and high ambition, building the largest bank on the planet, or at the very least the U.S., was a quest which he was not going to be denied. But, successful execution of the strategy was not going to be born out of an academic formula. Rather, the vision was simple - build sheer size and scale advantage operationally over all of its competitors using computer technology. Little did I know at the time it was the birth of "too big to fail," and I would revisit my early investment in the bank in 2008 under far different circumstances.

I did not stake a large claim at NCNB, moving on to other territory by obtaining my MBA at Duke University from August 1986 through May 1988. It was a very interesting time to obtain an MBA degree. When I arrived on campus, the stock market was growing much faster than it had in years, and the Reagan years had produced solid, non-inflationary growth. However, a shock to the financial system occurred in the fall of 1987. A sudden flash crash in the stock market left Wall Street wounded just as I was looking for opportunities coming out of graduate school. Although the '87 stock market decline and subsequent recovery was one of the sharpest and shortest in history, it still left a dent on my return to the financial industry upon graduation.

Given the circumstances, I landed at Northern Telecom as a management trainee out of graduate school. To be honest, I was a fish out of water. A highly trained financial professional a thousand times more versed in discounted cash flow than ASICs and equally under knowledgeable in Moore's Law and the likely path for computer technology in the communication industry. But I did have a few assets that I had accumulated along my life path that served me well in the transition. I did an internship with IBM during my junior year of undergraduate studies. Although it was in the finance department, my job during the summer was to write applications to move mainframe programs used by the department to the PC. IBM did not become the monolithic provider of personal computers in the years that followed, but they were on the leading edge of understanding how they would be best utilized. So I got nuts and bolts training on how computers worked – both mainframe and PC based. The training was not just glossy application level point and click application implementation. There was no mouse. There was no internet. There was no easy to read manual. The only available resources were the 4 floppy disk-based programs and accompanying manuals – DOS, Basic, Word and VisiCalc. I became well versed in these programs, and the knowledge gained served me well through the remainder of my education and career development.

Northern Telecom in the late 1980s was a booming company. I learned quickly that the company, based in Canada, was enjoying a major upsurge in growth because of the sales of its Digital Switching product line. The opening for the company into the U.S. was created by the confluence of two events. One was the change out of analog based telephone switching equipment across the United States. The computer age had created technology that reduced the form factor and power consumption of the analog equipment then in use by a factor of 10. The business case for changing out the old equipment was ripe. The second, and probably equally important reason was the landmark Anti-Trust decision presided over by Judge Greene in 1982 which broke up the AT&T monopoly. The consent decree, usually called the modified final judgment (MFJ), required AT&T to spin off seven Regional Bell Operating Companies (RBOCs) who maintained ownership of the access network connection to phone customers. AT&T was allowed to maintain the long distance network and inter-connecting transmission network across the country, which would eventually be a key asset for the growth of both the wireless network and the internet. The MFJ was a key court decision for Northern Telecom, eventually renamed Nortel in the 1990s, because the RBOCs needed a second supplier in addition to AT&T in order to run their business. It also spawned competitors in the long-distance business – SPRINT and MCI – companies which Nortel became the primary telephone switching gear supplier. The laws of staking a first claim in a changing environment whatever the cause might be were becoming a little clearer to me at that point in my life.

My career development at Nortel was blessed in the early 1990s to cross paths with a brilliant scientist and developer by the name of Mike Rider. Mike was distinguished in his development work in many aspects of digital technology at the ground level, deep in the construct of application specific integrated circuits (ASICs) and embedded processors, which feed the form factor changes in the industry. He was also a visionary, probably because he studied history so thoroughly, and could project the learning's of the past to what would happen in the future. His biggest knowledge deficit, and probably what he wanted to learn the most about, was business and finance. As luck would have it, in the early 1990s the biggest challenge for Nortel was how to manage the fortune it had amassed in the transition from analog to digital in the telecom industry and evolve as the half life of the installed base of equipment became shorter and new technology was developed.

In the early 1990s I saw the first practical demonstration of internet technology – online look-up of information using a software application known as a browser on a personal computer. The significance of this meeting was that it took place in the context of a planning meeting for the star multi-billion dollar DMS-100 product line, which I was responsible for business planning in support of product evolution. In white board sessions with Mike, what he foresaw was breathtaking, but also very troubling for the Nortel business model. From a networking technology standpoint, the internet was going to become the switch, and voice was going to become a very cheap application on the net. Voice-based technology, which was the primary revenue generating service for the bulk of Nortel's customers, was going to come under severe price pressure in the next 10-20 years as the switches that supplied the service were busted apart into component pieces of the internet – leaving only a look-up database for connecting two ends of a call connection. Mike just saw one big ASIC called the network, which was once confined and controlled by a central office mainframe switch. So we set out to evolve the platform by turning the technology inside out, allowing the Nortel installed base of network equipment to transform. The change was easy to do technically, but not simple from a business perspective.

The competition for the network prize was fierce, both inside the company and outside. Cisco was the obvious front-running prize winner. Born out of the natural evolution of computing and networking technology, Cisco laid claim to the distributed internet-based network of the future with a fast growing installed base of routers throughout the U.S. and world. Just as I had been in contact with the "too big to fail" banking sector formation in the mid 1980s, in the mid 1990s I found myself in the midst of the "irrational exuberance" associated with the take-off of the internet age and the dot.com boom, and I was armed with a disadvantaged set of assets. The Telecom Act of 1996 was the nail in the coffin for Nortel. At first the Act produced a major upswing in telecom because it deregulated the local telephone business, creating a rash of new competitive local exchange companies (CLECs). All of these companies needed a digital switch in order to enter the telecom exchange business. The RBOCs were required to provide access to their local customers at price advantaged rates. The new CLECs approached Nortel, and not only did the company oblige with product, they also provided "low cost financing." The business strategy was a financial mistake, which in the market downturn post 2000 would bring the company down and eventually into bankruptcy. The CLEC business model was not sustainable, for the simple reason that it was based on the old network model, not the internet. The Telecom Act of 1996 set clear lines of regulated and deregulated communication networking businesses. Voice networking based on Nortel DMS technology was firmly entrenched in the regulated side of the RBOC business model, and investment in that part of the network was put into maintenance mode. Non-regulated activities such as internet access and wireless were the clear winners. I sold my stake in Nortel in 1999 just as the company stock peaked and did not look back. It was one of the best trades of my life.

I landed in Silicon Valley for a joy ride, which I will elaborate upon in a section of this book. But the series of life events that drove me to sell and re-invest in 1999, and then finally sell out again post 2004, provide the real life inspiration for writing The Theory of Financial Relativity. During my tenure in Silicon Valley, it was clear that there were forces acting upon the markets which I had become deeply intertwined from a career standpoint – that had nothing to do with technology value. There was money showing up in the market, "trucks full of money." Where was it coming from? And then, it suddenly vanished. I had studied Adam Smith and the concept of the "invisible hand" in college. However, this force seemed to be more of a magician than an invisible hand. With a bent for financial puzzles, this one seemed worth solving.

When I finally cashed out of California in 2004, selling real estate that had magically doubled in value from the point in time I arrived, and also profitably exiting a technology business that I helped to stabilize in the market correction, I undertook a new challenge. The first part of the challenge was to successfully make a living primarily as an investor rather than a worker or manager. The second part of the test was to solve the confounding problem of explaining what causes major market moves, and become better equipped to take advantage of those moves as they inevitably occur over the course of time. This quest consumed ten years of my life from 2004 thru 2013, and is not over. It involved investing money through very tumultuous market times – but then again, as I have learned in doing the research for this book, market volatility is the norm not the exception.

This book documents ten years of research focused on exploring the forces that underpin major market moves from WWII through 2013. The one thing I learned in the computing industry is that real knowledge is gained at the extremes when dealing with systems. Using this technique, the historical analysis focuses heavily on major market inflection points – when stocks corrected downward significantly, and then recovered. Fourteen (14) market corrections are studied between WWII and 2013, starting with the 1946 downturn. Based on the gathered knowledge surrounding these major market events, a research framework for understanding was created, which I have named the Theory of Financial Relativity. 8 Guiding Principles have been formulated from the research, as well as market signals which can be utilized by investors to warn of both good and bad impending change in the market. The implications for portfolio allocations are also reviewed.

To understand why the market moves, having anecdotal stories of what works at a particular time was not good enough for me. I thank my mentor in the telecom industry for his love of history, for guiding me to reach back into time and review the data within the context of financial market history in order to gain true insight. For this reason, this book is dedicated to him. He passed away in July of 2013 after a five year fight with cancer. I had many discussions with him over those five years in which I would use him as a sounding board for concepts I planned to put forward in the book. The discussions often rambled in many directions, but always circled back to "the only constant is change" and "the laws of physics apply to everybody equally." Colorful metaphors about "when pigs break the sound-barrier" were often used.

The data utilized in this book is not proprietary or created through primary research. The laboratory for the research is the market itself. The majority of the historical data can be downloaded from the websites of the St Louis Federal Reserve (http://research.stlouisfed.org) and the U.S. Department of the Treasury (http://www.treasury.gov and https://www.treasurydirect.gov). The ongoing market statistics are reported continuously on the major business media web pages such as CNBC.com and Bloomberg.com. All the data utilized is consistently compiled when possible to reflect the month-end closing trade value. The analysis and presentation of the data is not intended to be overly complicated so as to make it understandable by many – that is my goal. Enjoy!

PROLOGUE

PART I
THEORY PHILOSOPHY

1 VALUE IS RELATIVE, NOT ABSOLUTE

When you shop for groceries or clothes or almost any consumer good, do you find yourself drawn to higher priced items because you believe that a lower price means an item is "cheap"? When you buy a car, do you feel the need to buy the latest edition or the one with the most features or one that is exactly the right color? In purchasing a home, would you feel uncomfortable buying a foreclosed property?

These emotions are driven by people's belief in their own self worth. If you answered yes to any of the above questions, you are entirely rational in the sense that when you spend money if you feel uncomfortable with the purchase, you are "losing" something more in your mind in terms of self-worth, in exchange for dollars saved. If the dollars saved are not worth all that much to you, then take the comfortable route. Consumer brand-based companies are masters at positioning products which play on people's emotions. And many people, in turn, have been very good at branding themselves, and therefore need the positive reinforcement that spending more gives them.

If you are psychologically geared in this fashion, investing very likely is a confusing foreign language.

A necessary tenet for good long-term investing, as opposed to speculating, is being able to spot good value at a relatively low price. "Buying low" is a difficult concept if you equate higher prices with being more valuable. To make matters more confusing, buying an investment just because it is low priced does not mean it is a good value either.

To become a smart investor, you need to minimize any emotion in an investment decision when comparing alternatives and be able to discern the relative value between multiple alternatives. Investing is accumulating assets that are undervalued today, which over time the value will be maintained and potentially hidden value can be realized. Emotional purchases, on the other hand, are just spending and value is lost almost immediately when a transaction is made.

Learning the Concept of Relativity

According to the dictionary, relativity is defined as a "state of dependence in which the existence or significance of one entity is solely dependent on that of another."

As my kids have grown up, I have worked hard to instill the basic concept of relativity through the purchase of everyday living items. The learning moment is created when they have to make a judgment between the purchase of two seemingly similar items, where the choice can result in either spending less money and possibly getting equal or in some cases more "value," or just spending money to feel good. Teaching the value of money is tough to do, and many times it can come off as looking "cheap," particularly when the kids are in middle school, as my son is now, or in high school which my daughter was a few years ago.

There have been constant battles over getting the latest Apple gadget, or the highest priced shoes. Having worked in telecom in the 1990s, I am very aware of AT&T, Verizon and SPRINT's constant desire to raise the RPS (revenue per subscriber) in an industry that is essentially a commodity. They have been very effective in doing this by making the smart phone a must have status symbol. In the process, texting, which technologically is a cryptic form of communication that is essentially noise on a data network, becomes a high dollar feature offered by the big service providers. Value is definitely in the eye of the beholder. I am constantly asking when the bill is being paid, "whose kids am I putting through college with this purchase?" I haven't won a lot of battles in the smart phone value purchase decisions in the household.

My fear has always been that my kids are growing up in a world where they are taught to spend rather than invest and demand value. So, I constantly use special tactics to get the kids to grow up being more critical in their decisions about what something is truly worth. Purchasing cereal is a very basic way to teach kids the concept of relative value. Our local grocery store always carries a brand name and store brand cereal. When the kids want to try a new cereal, I usually get the store brand in place of the brand name first. They will try it and usually not complain. Then when the brand name goes on sale, the alternative (brand name) comes into the house for a test (but never the brand name first).

Not unexpectedly, I rarely hear a complaint when the next week the store brand is purchased. But on more than one occasion, my kids have actually complained that the brand name was actually worse in taste – and directed that it should no longer be purchased.

My kids are still developing the ability to understand the concept of price relative to value – and this will come as they have to spend their own money to buy things. But, by making sure they test a product without getting attached to it for emotional reasons, I have given them basic training in one of the fundamentals of being a smart investor – review investments side by side on a relative basis, and do not become attached to just one alternative.

Great Investors Seek Relative Value Opportunities

The wisdom instilled in the advice of the most revered investors like Warren Buffett or Benjamin Graham is worth the time to review. The common thread in their advice is to find relative value. Mr. Graham's consul is to research a company and base your investment decision on sound fundamentals, investing when the metrics point to an under-valued situation. Warren Buffett uses much the same formula, with the added perspective that in the long run stocks always out-perform. If you have a well-diversified portfolio, usually meaning about 20 stocks of well managed companies across a broad range of markets, you can outperform the average market return.

No one can argue with the results of these legendary investors. They steadily out-performed the market average over time. To follow this methodology of picking winners in the universe of stocks and bonds, a plethora of information is available to assess the value of traded securities. The internet makes information much more readily accessible to investors, and you no longer are limited to sell-side analyst reports from major brokerage firms to get opinions on value.

The number one rule in picking stocks and bonds – you have to do your own homework. If someone is pushing an investment, many times they have an alternative agenda. Your conclusion about value must be based on your investment objectives and your understanding of what value you will receive from the investment.

To assess an investment, the best source of public data for stocks is EDGAR online, which is the SEC government repository of all public filings by a company, including its 10-K (annual Report), 10-Qs, (quarterly reports) and 8-K (material press releases and other information). Business web-sites also give easy access to financial information about stocks. For bonds, the FINRA site tracks all traded issues in the U.S. market – corporate, municipal and government. Assessing a bond, however, requires an in-depth analysis of the same financial information as assessing a stock. The only difference is you look at the information from the perspective of being a lender to the company rather than whether you want to be an owner of the business.

Due diligence for an individual investment can be extensive, and this book is not intended to dwell on the techniques for digging into the data on individual companies. The most important aspect of security analysis is creating a relative framework for assessing whether a company's stock price is inexpensive (buy) or expensive (sell). This framework should include ratio measures that allow you to compare across a number of investments in the category you are looking at buying or selling. You must look at more than one investment in a particular category in order to get a relative feel for value. All great investors have a knack for understanding the concept that the value of an investment is always relative.

Higher Returns Come with Higher Volatility

I have benefited as an investor over the years from using the perspective that Warren Buffett and Benjamin Graham, and others like them have taken. But personally I have never felt the simplicity in their advice was ever quite the essence of investing. For sure diversified, value based stock selection is good fundamental advice for investors who pick stocks. Stocks over the long-run have done better than bonds. The following chart comparing 60 years of returns of various investments proves the point empirically:

AVERAGE ANNUAL RETURNS FROM 1952 THROUGH 2013

A bar chart titled "AVERAGE ANNUAL RETURNS FROM 1952 THROUGH 2013" with the y-axis ranging from 0% to 14% in 2% increments. The x-axis categories from left to right are: FED FUNDS, 2 YEAR T-BILL, 5 YEAR T-NOTE, 10 YEAR T-NOTE, 30 YEAR T-BOND, 20 YR TAX-FREE BOND, 20 YR BAA1 CORP, DOW *, S&P500 *, GOLD (SINCE 1968). Approximate values: FED FUNDS ~5%, 2 YEAR T-BILL ~5.5%, 5 YEAR T-NOTE ~6%, 10 YEAR T-NOTE ~6.5%, 30 YEAR T-BOND ~6.7%, 20 YR TAX-FREE BOND ~5.5%, 20 YR BAA1 CORP ~8%, DOW ~9.7%, S&P500 ~10.5%, GOLD (SINCE 1968) ~11.7%.

* DIVIDENDS INCLUDED

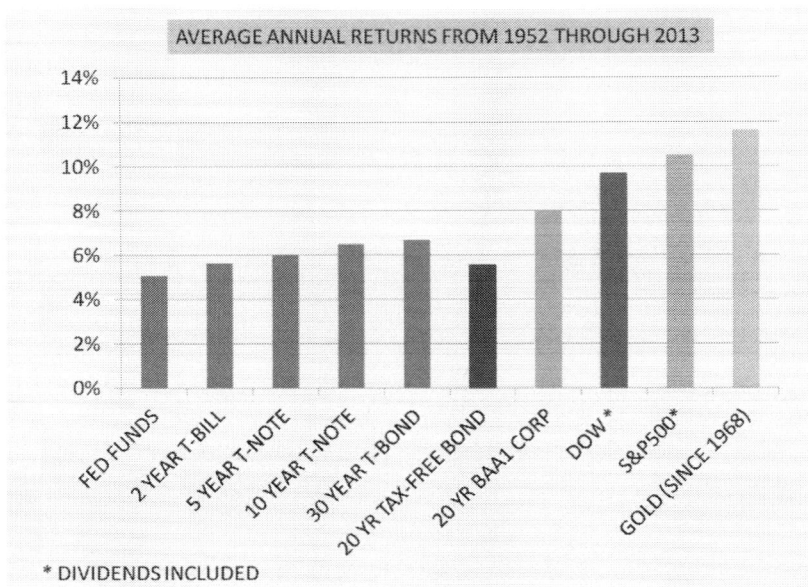

I began studying the market in the early 1980s in college, just as Paul Volcker was breaking the back of persistent inflation with a change in Federal Reserve policy using the growth in money supply rather than pegging of interest rates to manage the financial system in the United States. Interest rates increased dramatically while I was in high school in the late 1970s and college in the early 1980s. Times were tough and the "misery index" political terminology coined by Ronald Reagan became the focal point of the markets and people across the nation. Since I was in college, the best four years of my life spent in poverty, I was able to escape virtually unscathed from all of the changes in the market at the time. Once out of college, I began to build wealth through the market as many in my generation have done. The stock market exploded upward through the 80s, with the exception of the brief dramatic crash in the fall of 1987. Lucky for me again, I was in graduate school at Duke University during the crash, escaping the wrath of the market on my personal assets for the most part.

The 90s were a mix of war early in the decade that weighed on the market, and a major expansionary force driven by internet technology in the latter half of the decade. Post the millennium parties, however, the shine of the market assent definitely and vividly, in my recollection, changed to a dull finish. With the election of George W. Bush and the 9/11 attacks, the market economy switched from peace time to war. From that point forward, the micromanagement of the financial markets by Washington bureaucrats got progressively more evident and aggressive. Active investors through this time period, of which I was one, saw a country driven not so much by technology as in the 1990s, but by oil & gas, the defense industry, and the most memorable sector – real estate. This economic concoction, when combined with substantial consumer and investment banking over-leveraging, led to the liquidity driven market crash in 2008, highlighted by the bankruptcy of Lehman Brothers. Post the 2008 crisis, the investment markets were fixated on the liquidity supplied by the Federal Reserve as the primary driver for increases in the stock market. The market rocketed to new all-time highs in 2013 as the Fed continuously supplied more and more liquidity into the financial market. Many prominent investing figures of our time were lining up behind the momentum led market returns, espousing the long-term advantages of stock investing.

The returns in a well diversified portfolio of company stocks clearly beat the bond market over the long-term. But the road to achieving higher returns is fraught with increased volatility, as the graph below illustrates.

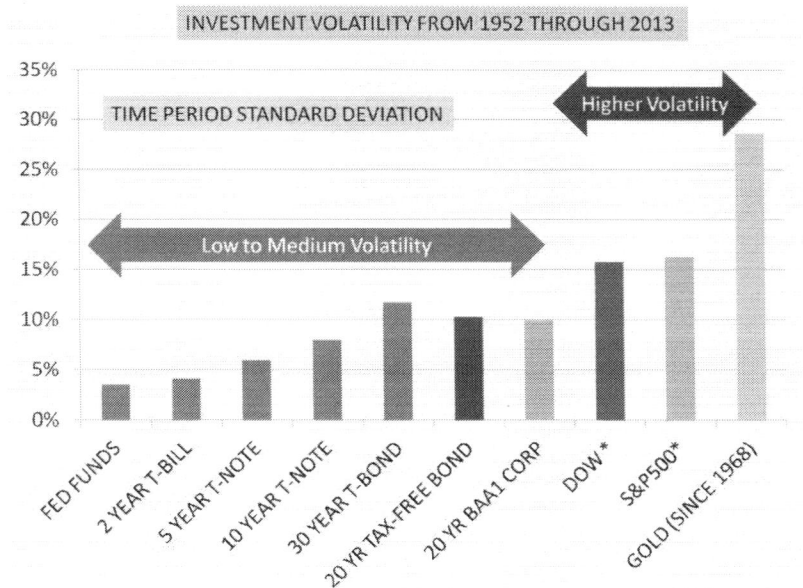

INVESTMENT VOLATILITY FROM 1952 THROUGH 2013

Using the standard deviation of the returns to measure volatility, the stock market is 3-5 times higher in volatility through time than the short-term bond market, and about 1.5 times more volatile than the long-term bond market. Stock returns are very dependent upon capital gains for return and are perpetual, meaning that value is derived from the going concern nature of the companies in the stock market. Buying and selling over time can create wide swings in value in the short and intermediate term, which can cause severe changes in the value of a particular stock, and even the stock market as a whole. On the other hand, bonds by definition have a defined maturity date. As the data show, deriving return from the ongoing interest rate of a bond is far less volatile than assets such as stocks and commodities like gold. The trade-off from being able to withstand the volatility, or "hold the risk," is a key to achieving higher returns. The risk reward trade-off is a fundamental premise in modern financial theory. Theoretically, if an investor wants to lower the volatility in his / her portfolio, by creating a mix of stocks, bonds and alternative assets, the overall volatility goes down, and the risk-return ratio improves to a point where the investor can sleep well at night.

Market Portfolio Theory Incomplete

One critique of the "buy and hold" strategy centers on the fact that investing in this manner does not provide the optimal result. This strategy does produce decent results for disciplined, long-term investors. Over time you have a high probability of getting better returns in stocks if you can buy and hold them through thick and thin. My biggest issue with the theory is that the market is volatile, and the risk taken versus the reward is relatively small. In addition most equity assets are highly correlated with each other. These issues beg the question - why is it so? And, is there a better strategy?

How many people do you know who are disciplined enough to follow the buy and hold stocks long-term strategy? A large portion of market participants do not follow this discipline when it comes to stock investing. Therein lays the missing element in market theory that I have struggled with over the years. Different market participants have different perspectives and strategies, and expect different outcomes. Differing expectations is what makes a market. Investing is a relative game. Some players in the game are much bigger in relative size than others; and certain market participants do not always have the same goals as the rational investor assumed by many theories of modern finance. Two such players or forces as I refer to them in this book, usually have a different goal than the rational investor - the U.S. Government and the Federal Reserve Bank. Portfolio theory assumes the effect of the government and Fed on market returns is systemic, not diversifiable, and therefore should not encumber long-term investment decision making. After all, any action by the government bodies should affect the market as whole equally overtime, right? The data is quite interesting with respect to this question.

At my 25th Duke Fuqua School class reunion, I asked a classmate of mine who was responsible for managing a very large equity portfolio what he thought of the stock market in the spring of 2013. Our discussion ranged across many areas, but one comment that stuck with me, because it came from someone who actively manages equity investments for very wealthy clients, and I am paraphrasing - "over the years I see movements in the markets that are always and everywhere done with a purpose and for the benefit of someone."

It was a rather bold, but not unusual statement – quite distant from the random walk theory learned in one of the classrooms at Fuqua. When I speak with many people about the market, the conversation leads to a perspective that forces are at work driving market value, most of which don't meet the definition of "free market forces." The staunch believers in diversified portfolio theory would call this activity noise, meant only to line the pockets of those who profit from the churn in the market. For the most part, I agree with the noise factor, and being able to deaden the noise is important. But, thankfully because of computer technology and the growing availability of data available for research, a new dimension about the market is coming into focus for me, and I will share some of the more compelling information I have uncovered in the remainder of this book.

My research laid out in this book points to the interaction between Wall Street, Main Street, Washington D.C. and foreign trading partners as an ever present relative force influencing market returns in ways that can and should be gauged through time to produce higher portfolio returns with lower volatility. The first signal that led me to do this research is the volatility data provided in the chart shown earlier in this chapter. Oddly, when the standard deviations of fixed income investments are measured over the 60 year time period, short-term interest rates are more volatile than long-term rates when reviewed only in terms of rates (the chart is stated in terms of total return, the rate deviation only is shown later in the book). This interest rate pattern does not reflect a rational market. It reveals a market responding to human behavior and actions, many of which are only rational when viewed with the context of the political sphere. The non-random pattern is a clear indication that government meddling increases volatility and lowers returns for the unsuspecting, exhibited by chain reaction market collapses that are more than noise. The human action produces predictable events, ones that although I have not determined can be totally avoided, most certainly can be better managed by knowledgeable investors.

Thanks to the growing wealth of historical data now publicly available, the overriding market forces in the market can be examined in more detail for better understanding. The question that is examined in the remainder of this book is whether this dimension of the investment market functions in a particular relative fashion which, if better understood and monitored by investors, can produce superior investment results.

2 WE LIVE IN AN UNCERTAIN WORLD

The Heisenberg Uncertainty Principle is a concept in quantum mechanics stating that of all the things you can measure about an object, some aspects cannot be known at the same time. An object's location, for example, can never be known exactly if you know even a little bit about how fast the particle is moving or in what direction it is moving. The principle also works the other way around - the more you know about how fast a particle is moving and the direction it is going, the less you know about where it is right now.

What on earth does quantum physics have to do with investing? In simple terms, investing involves risk, and risk is measured in relative terms or probabilities, not in absolute values. The last traded price of a security is known with certainty. However, the next price cannot be known with precision.

Referring back to the previous chapter, the Uncertainty Principle on an analogous level is saying that no matter how much you research a particular company, you can never know precisely whether the investment is good or bad. You can run all the numbers and predict the expected direction the numbers will change in the future. You can also observe the traded value of the stock at the current moment in time. But at any point when you enter and place a trade, you affect the future direction. Therefore, you can know the absolute value of the investment right now, but you can only know the probable value of the investment in the future. You can never know with absolute certainty what your investment will be valued at in the future. The future outcome for any individual stock or investment is <u>random</u>.

But all is not lost, and you shouldn't immediately reach for the darts to pick your next investment. Additional work done in the abstract world of quantum physics, that when introduced, makes the investment selection process make more sense.

John Bell, in 1964, introduced the Bell Inequality Theorem. The Theorem postulates that, although the behavior of an individual particle is random, it is also <u>correlated</u> with the behavior of other particles.

Taken to the analogy of the observable investment world, even though an individual investment trades in a random value pattern, its value relative to other market variables moves in ways that is far less random, and even deterministic. In other words, the future of an investment's price cannot be known with certainty, and is far less determinable if viewed only in isolation. However, if put into the context of a market of traded assets, and the market is measured over time, then the predicted value of an asset relative to another asset can be calculated with possibilities.

Speculating Versus Investing

To the untrained eye, the stock market looks like a big gambling casino. In many ways the analogy holds true. The stock exchanges are clearing houses that take a cut of every traded transaction. Every position is held until cashed in. And the reward for the position taken is a seemingly unpredictable outcome, measured only in probabilities and rarely a deterministic event.

The uncertain nature of the market is what leads to its volatility. A characteristic of situations which have a high degree of risk is volatility, born out of differing views of future outcomes. In my mind market uncertainty has led

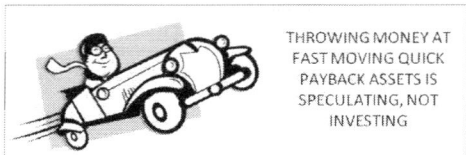

THROWING MONEY AT FAST MOVING QUICK PAYBACK ASSETS IS SPECULATING, NOT INVESTING

to the terminology common among investors when referring to taking investing positions – "playing the market." As the Heisenberg Uncertainty Principle postulates, you can never really know whether what you are investing in is good or bad, so trying is futile. But what you can know is the momentum of direction that the value of a potential investment is moving with a high degree of certainty.

The active churning of positions based on trading momentum is common practice. However, it is questionable whether the routine meets the spirit of investing. It is more akin to an act of speculation. Investing with the idea that you can get out of an investment faster than the next fool is not a good idea. And I have witnessed some tragic outcomes where people believed they were investors, but instead became speculators and lost considerable wealth as a result.

Day trading was a mania in the late 1990's as the stock market churned every higher, particularly in the technology sector. During the time period, many DOT.com companies went IPO without even having a proven revenue stream. Massive amounts of money were raised for companies without any fundamental basis for valuation – only hope for a piece of the action in the future. A large number of these companies like Sycamore Networks, Webvan.com, Pets.com went bust in very short periods of time, while only a few such as Juniper Networks actually survived the carnage. Later in the technology cycle, Google went IPO and proved that a stable dependable revenue source does matter in company survival and ultimate investor return.

I recall the late 1990s and early 2000s vividly because I worked in the technology sector at the time – as a new product Business Director for Nortel until 1999, and then until 2002 as a Business Development / Capital Fundraising Vice President for Caspian Networks (initially known as Packetcom), a major Venture Capital project in Silicon Valley led by US

SPECULATING IS A MOMENTUM GAME, USUALLY WITH FINANCIAL CAUSUALTIES

Venture Partners and New Enterprise Associates. My most vivid recollection of this time is that all sense of market balance and relative value was lost amongst many market participants. All the major financial players in the market had a sense that things were out of control, but as long as someone was willing to ante-up, the momentum game continued. The result of layer upon layer of good money chasing unviable investments eventually led to a dramatic unwinding of the market, post year 2000, at first particularly concentrated in NASDAQ registered tech investments. However, just as sub-prime was not contained in 2007-08, the entire stock market eventually followed the downward trend. Momentum style investors were big casualties in this market downturn. I recall several individuals who were fully invested in Nortel Network stock during this time period. Nortel was a darling on the Street in the late 90s. The stock rose from the teens in the early 90s to over $100 per share in 2000, driven by speculation that demands for technology to build out the internet would be astronomical. Many investors doubled down on their investments with margin, riding the momentum wave to large paper profits.

When reality set in post September 2000 and the market took a dramatic turn down, the paper profits quickly disappeared. By 2002, Nortel's stock was valued at less than $1. In some cases, novice investors were blind-sided by the quick change, having to sell to cover margin calls on positions set at high basis values. Sometimes, the sell covered only the margin call and taxes. The investor in the stock got nothing in return.

Speculation of this nature is not investing. And buying on margin to purchase momentum investments, and in many ways any asset that can make wide swings in traded asset value, is gambling. This same scenario played out in the real estate industry in the major market crash of 2008. In the 2008 market many investors used their home as the margin account, leveraging the home value with cheap money generated from second mortgages and cheap re-financings. The difference in this case was that a lot of this leverage was spent on consumer goods, leveraged into second and third home purchases, and even found its way into the purchase of stocks.

Markets Unattached to Relative Value

The time frames leading up to 2001 and 2008 were without question periods when the market participants lost complete sense of relative value. Financial theories I learned in school were totally useless in these situations other than the fact that I knew that the markets were not "healthy." The one saving theory that provided some protection was "diversification." But diversified portfolio theory said hold your long positions because you cannot time the market and cannot do anything about systemic market risk. The momentum players, on the other hand, were all reading the signs of deceleration. These traders are religious adherents to the Uncertainty Principle, and they most likely logged out of the market as it began to turn over. A momentum trader's philosophy is that it is futile to try and know the real value of a market security at any point in time, but you can definitely determine what direction it is moving with a high degree of certainty. When the market turns over, run for cover.

What was the better strategy – just stick to your portfolio principles or rebalance to cash like the momentum players? If you knew the probability of what would happen, and could place a value on the upcoming 50% downward market move; without question, investors armed with the knowledge would trade a large segment of their portfolio to cash, or other stable store of value. Indeed, many did choose this strategy, as evidenced by the fall in yields

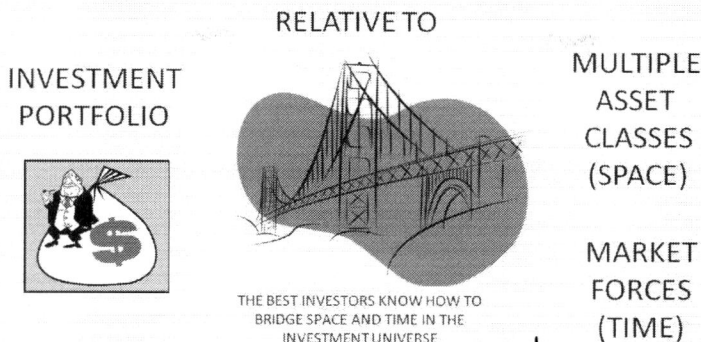

RELATIVE TO

INVESTMENT PORTFOLIO

MULTIPLE ASSET CLASSES (SPACE)

MARKET FORCES (TIME)

THE BEST INVESTORS KNOW HOW TO BRIDGE SPACE AND TIME IN THE INVESTMENT UNIVERSE

in the Treasury market as the market traded down. Hence, a deep and very predictable liquidity crisis ensued.

Were the market participants that rebalanced prior to the 2008 market crash just lucky? Or was the event predictable – correlated in some fashion to market indicators that were clearly evident in time for savvy investors to make necessary steps to protect their portfolio and even take advantage of the situation. The Bell Inequality Theorem predicts that events such as the 2008 Crash, as well as many market moves throughout history, are predictable, not random events. The theorem, when analogously applied to a financial market, postulates that although the trading pattern of an individual stock or bond has a random component, it is also highly <u>correlated</u> with the behavior of major market forces and the value of similar assets.

> YOU MUST KNOW WHERE YOU ARE IN THE INVESTING UNIVERSE
> * RELATIVE TO CHOICES IN THE INVESTING <u>SPACE</u>
> * RELATIVE TO MARKET FORCE OVER <u>TIME</u>
> AND DECIDE IF A CHANGE WILL MAKE YOU RELATIVELY BETTER OFF

This concept of correlation of market value to driving market forces is the fundamental premise on which the Theory of Financial Relativity is based. The correlations create a framework from which knowledgeable investors can gauge the downside risk, or upside potential of investments within their portfolio at every moment in time. Armed with this intelligence, the possibility of doing better than simply diversifying away risk of random movements of securities in a portfolio becomes a real possibility.

3 FINANCIAL RELATIVITY PRIMER

The stock market for traded securities changed substantially from 1980 through 2013. The advent of mutual funds and index funds led to an explosion in financial products that an investor could buy and sell in his or her account to obtain a diversified portfolio across multiple asset categories. The universe of investments could be bought and sold in a split second, and the computer age led to its own set of problems relating to algorithmic trading and "flash crashes" caused by the misuse of low latency, high speed computing technology.

The growing market of traded, liquid assets is at the core of the Theory of Financial Relativity. These various markets form a growing and increasingly large universe of traded assets which move in random fashion in isolation, but trade in a more predictable correlated fashion when analyzed and understood relative to general market forces. Understanding and spotting these relationships can uncover value gaps and opportunities for investment gains as the market marches through time and conditions change. Having these insights make an investor better equipped to protect wealth during the inevitable downturns that occur in the market over time.

Information is the key ingredient in the new age of computerized investing. A plethora of data spews from market sources every millisecond of the trading day. This fact, however, does not mean that actionable information is produced. Being buried by a sea of data can be a real problem. The key for successful application of the Theory of Financial Relativity is discerning the most relevant sources of data. Valuable data can be used to predict future market events. By tracking this type of data through time, it can be turned into actionable correlated <u>information</u> that can either be used to assess the probability of future market changes, or in some cases actually signal a major market event.

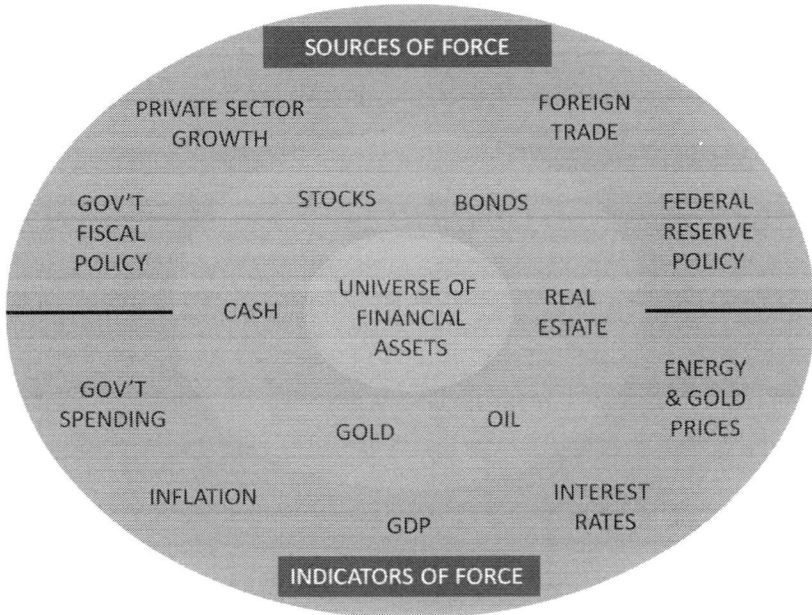

In researching this book, the most relevant economic and market statistics and data was tracked from 2003 to 2013 in conjunction with the active management of a significant financial portfolio. Additionally, the data being tracked was augmented with historical data reaching back to the Depression Era and WWII to create a basis for understanding how the market traded over a much broader scope of situational variables. From the knowledge gained from this research a framework emerged which pointed to 4 significant and measurable forces as the major contributing causes of relative change in U.S. stock market value –private sector growth, Federal Reserve policy, U.S. Government fiscal policy, and foreign trade. Within this context, the movement in market asset values of stocks, bonds and commodities was correlated to the major market forces. These indicators of force are analogous to buoys for boaters or mile-markers for the highway traveler. They provide relative measures from which to assess both where you are in the uncertain investing world, and more importantly to assess where you are going, not only in the momentum sense, but relative to the entire investment universe.

The list of indicators of force in the model framework shown in the figure above is not all inclusive. But these indicators peculated to the top of the list as the highest correlated metrics of force applied by the four major agents of change in the research. These indicators, and insight into why they provide such valuable information, will be explained in detail in future chapters. They include:

Gross domestic product (GDP) - the market value of all officially recognized final goods and services produced within a country in a given period of time.

Interest rates - the rate that is paid by borrowers for the use of money that they borrow from a lender.

Consumer Price Index (CPI) –the measure of the average change over time in the prices of consumer goods and services that people buy for day-to-day living.

Energy and Gold - the change in price over time for a barrel of West Texas Intermediate crude oil and the traded value of Gold per ounce.

Federal Government Spending - all outlays by the U.S. government, including transfers to state and local governments.

U.S. National Debt - the total amount of money the United States federal government owes to creditors.

 Federal Reserve Balance Sheet - the total amount of assets held for investment by the U.S. Federal Reserve Bank.

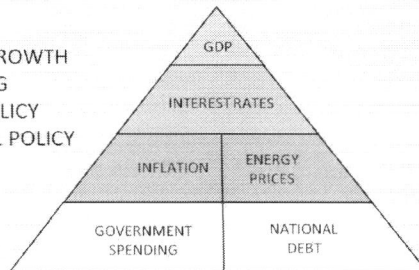

MARKET FORCES
1) BUSINESS AND JOB GROWTH
2) CONSUMER SPENDING
3) FEDERAL RESERVE POLICY
4) GOVERNMENT FISCAL POLICY
5) FOREIGN TRADE

GDP
INTEREST RATES
INFLATION
ENERGY PRICES
GOVERNMENT SPENDING
NATIONAL DEBT

RELATIVE FORCE METRICS

The metrics were tracked to gain understanding of the correlation of each metric to the stock market as measured by either the Dow or S&P 500. In addition, these variables were also studied to understand if they provided informational signals of impending major change in market direction before a correction or during a market rebound after a correction. For instance, the stock market is commonly referred to as both a discounting machine for long-term value, but also a voting machine over the shorter term. Investors vote with dollars by trading assets in the short-term. So, in many cases the rate of change in the market itself becomes a useful market information source. Likewise with respect to interest rates, particularly when it comes to longer-term maturities versus shorter term maturities, and/or, riskier bonds versus risk-free bond classes, the spread between the various maturities can provide an investor useful information about their relative position in the investing universe.

Financial Relativity and the Human Factor

One major challenge I have faced in putting to work many of the financial concepts I learned 30 years ago is dealing with irrational market pricing. The theories all assume a rational market, one in which a hypothetical investor uses rational judgment to value a particular asset. The rational investor based theories do not incorporate what in retrospect could be classified as irrational, excessive risk taking behavior of human beings in the activity of trading market assets. This assumption is actually very odd when you think about it. The very exchanges in which assets are traded are human creations, and the currency in which an asset trade is settled is a human creation as well. No wonder some many market participants view the activity of investing as "playing the market," rather than "managing wealth" or "saving."

The Theory of Financial Relativity is a study of the market to derive the most useful trading market relationships that explain why the market moves, whether the moves are rational or seemingly irrational, such as the ever present occurrences of market bubbles. When humans interact in traded asset forums such as a stock exchange, perceptions of value change through time. The Theory presumes that the aggregate movement of the market is always predictable in the long run– predictable only in the sense that relative value can be determined in relation to the human forces acting upon the market. These forces need not produce a rational market result at any point in time. Whereas the laws of physical science and nature are stated as absolutes which cannot be disproven, the only absolute in the Theory of Financial Relativity is that change is constant, and the perception of value moves relative to the change in force exerted by human behavior. Because people must interact in order to trade assets, because governments are involved in the creation of the currency which is used to intermediate an exchange, value of any traded asset becomes intertwined, correlated, to the movement of the strongest forces acting upon the market. The market forces incorporate the human "atoms" as a very real force in the world of asset valuation.

To many, this part of the investing universe seems very subjective and emotional, even irrational at times due to the elements of fear and greed being constantly introduced into the equation. It also leads many to believe the market is somehow "rigged." But to the savvy investor, opportunity is created when markets are most out of synch, when the relative value of assets in one market is juxtaposed with another. In some instances, it creates the proverbial, "blood on the streets" time to buy, assuming of course you have liquid assets on hand to make purchases. And, since the market is an amalgamation of people interacting, data shows that similar patterns through time happen over, and over and over again. The remaining chapters of this book are dedicated to culling insights into why the market moved from WWII through 2013, and illuminating the explanation through the introduction of a new financial model known as the Theory of Financial Relativity.

"The Theory of Financial Relativity is a system of ideas explaining why investment markets move through time in a predictable rather than random pattern. The ideas are encapsulated in 8 Guiding Principles derived from the correlated effects that dominant forces have on the determination of relative value in the financial market. The principles provide a framework for developing signals that warn of impending losses and potential gains in investment value, extrapolating future market outcomes based on relative market scenarios and rebalancing investment portfolios in response to changes in market forces. The Theory has implications for understanding the persistent pattern of asset bubble creation and dissolution in the financial market."

$$p = mv \qquad 1)$$

$$F = \dot{p} \qquad 2)$$

$$F_{12} = -F_{21} \qquad 3)$$

PART II
GUIDING PRINCIPLES

4 RELATIVE BEST OF TIMES FOR STOCKS

In Chapter One of this book, the data showing how much the S&P 500 outperformed the U.S. Treasury and investment grade corporate bond market from 1952 thru 2013 was shown. Without question, holding an S&P index fund or a portfolio of stocks representative of the index provided a greater return to an investor than the bond market in the period. Investing your funds in this fashion, however, does have costs. The S&P 500 companies only pay a small dividend, on average, around 1.8%. This means that if you do not hold a very large portfolio and you need to access funds, chances are you will have to sell assets in the instances that you need to raise cash. Bonds, alternatively, pay a fixed, more manageable coupon rate that many investors count on for portfolio liquidity.

The two investments also differ greatly in terms of overall volatility, with stocks exhibiting far greater volatility than bonds. These characteristics of the two markets have led most portfolio managers to recommend a mix of stocks, bonds and alternative investments such as gold and commodities to lower the overall volatility of the portfolio and provide a more optimal return. The baseline portfolio could range from 70% stocks, 30% bonds for a 30 year old investor, to 40% stocks, 60% bonds for a retiree.

Diversification is very sound advice for investors, and nowhere in this book will I recommend breaking the rule of staying diversified in your investment holdings. At the same time, however, I cannot find any magical formula for obtaining higher returns without taking some risk with the investments in your portfolio. Balance is important in investing, and knowing your risk tolerance – the type of investments you can hold and still sleep well at night – is important.

But, what is the characteristic about the U.S. stock market that leads renowned investors like Warren Buffett to say with confidence that he knows that "over the long-term stocks will out-perform other investments?" Gaining some insight into how the market returns have fared over time is a starting point for many in understanding the answer to this question. It also points toward the possibility of greatly improving the returns and lowering the volatility of your portfolio if you can master what is unique about the best time to be invested, versus not being invested, in stocks.

S&P 500 Return Distribution Since 1952

Over the 60 years from 1952 until 2013 the S&P 500 provided an average annual return of 8.7% before dividends. This return is calculated based on the month-end close each of 12 months during the year, and compared to the closing price for the same month the prior year. These aggregate returns are then averaged over the 60 year period. This technique for calculating the return is used so that the distribution of returns throughout a time period can be analyzed. The results are pictured in the following graph.

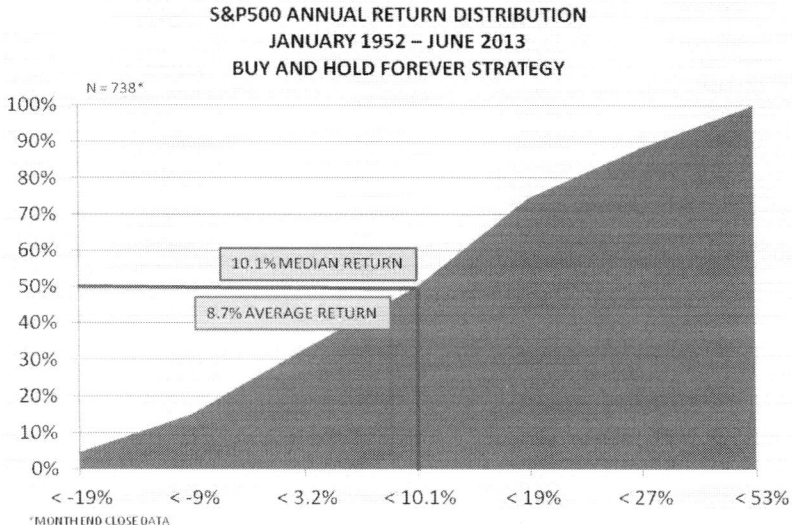

S&P500 ANNUAL RETURN DISTRIBUTION
JANUARY 1952 – JUNE 2013
BUY AND HOLD FOREVER STRATEGY

N = 738*

100%	
90%	
80%	
70%	
60%	
	10.1% MEDIAN RETURN
50%	
40%	8.7% AVERAGE RETURN
30%	
20%	
10%	
0%	

< -19%   < -9%   < 3.2%   < 10.1%   < 19%   < 27%   < 53%

*MONTH END CLOSE DATA

When the time series is reviewed it provides an interesting perspective. Over 50% of the time if you invested at month-end close and held the investment exactly one year, you could expect a 10.1% return or greater plus dividends.

This seems like decent odds. However, 28% of the time the market actually provided a negative return year over year, more than 1 out of 4 times. That, on the other hand, doesn't seem like particularly good odds. In fact, 15% of the time the market experienced losses of 9% or greater. Negative 10% returns define a market correction.

RETURN OF RETURN	PERCENT OF TIME
< -19%	5%
< -9%	15%
< 3.2%	33%
< 10.1%	50%
< 19%	75%
< 27%	88%
< 53%	100%
AVERAGE	8.7%

As shown in the table and graph, some time periods gave investors particularly high pay-offs. Over the time period, 12% of the time the stock market provided home run returns of over 27% year over year.

So, what return will you get over the next year if you invest at the end of the coming month and hold the investment for 1 year? Is it a random pattern, similar to rolling the dice in Las Vegas or playing the roulette table; or, is the pattern part of the boarder correlated financial universe as explainable by the Theory of Financial Relativity? Taking a closer look at the data provides some clues.

Worst Market Returns since 1952

It turns out that when the time series of year over year returns of the market is reviewed in detail, the negative return periods over the 60 years after 1952 are clustered. What this means is that making an investment in stocks, at least at the aggregate market level, is not an event governed by some random act of nature. The realized return on investment, although the absolute magnitude is highly uncertain, can be forecast to either be positive or negative with some degree of certain simply by knowing whether the

GOOD NEWS
• AVERAGE RETURN OF 8.7% BETTER THAN COMPARABLE BAA1 BOND

BAD NEWS
• NEGATIVE RETURNS (<0%) OCCUR 28% OF THE TIME
• 15% OF THE TIME EXPECT NEGATIVE RETURNS OF 9% OR GREATER

previous month-end year over year return was positive or negative. The upward bias in market returns, followed by punctuating downward market moves, leads to a predictable pattern in stock returns through time.

The graph below was created based on an algorithm which reviews the year over year return of the S&P 500 through time since 1952. The green shaded time periods are the optimal time periods to be invested in the stock market – time periods in which the year over year returns are overwhelmingly positive.

On the other hand, the darker red shaded areas are periods in which an investor with perfect foresight would choose not to be invested in the stock market.

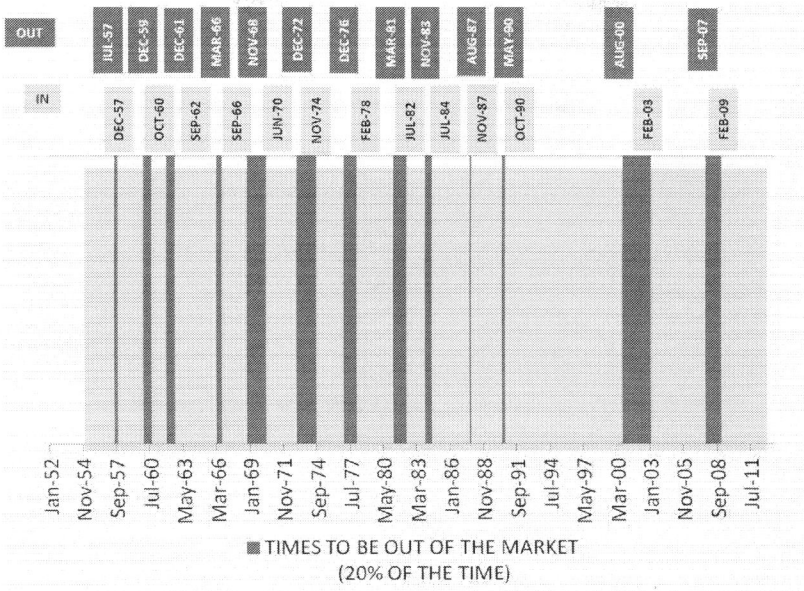

■ TIMES TO BE OUT OF THE MARKET
(20% OF THE TIME)

The resulting graphic of this time series of data is fascinating. It shows that obtaining more optimal results in the stock market would not require significant churning of stock investments. In fact, the hypothetical model suggests that simply getting out of the market when year over year returns go negative, and then knowing when to re-enter means being invested in stocks 80% of the time instead of 100%. And the number of times you would make this type of portfolio shift over 60 years would have been a total of 13 times, on average every 4 years up until 1980, then stretching out to longer intervals post 1982.

The compelling aspect of the information contained in this data is that the evidence points to the fact that low return time periods for the stock market are not random. If achieving a positive or negative return on an investment in the market were random, they would be far more erratic and less serially correlated. The progressive nature of the returns is likely partially based on the market being driven by correlated expectations of future returns – momentum traders hooked on the sense of certainty generated from past results as predicted by the Heisenberg Uncertainty Principle. But an equally likely reason the returns are not random is the effect of outside forces such as the Federal Reserve and U.S. Government, which can be shown to predictably impact the direction of the returns over time.

Return Improvement by Avoiding Market Downturns

How much would the return on your stock portfolio improve if you were able to avoid the series of correlated negative returns which come with the 13 significant downturns identified in the graph since 1952? The data is shown in the following graph:

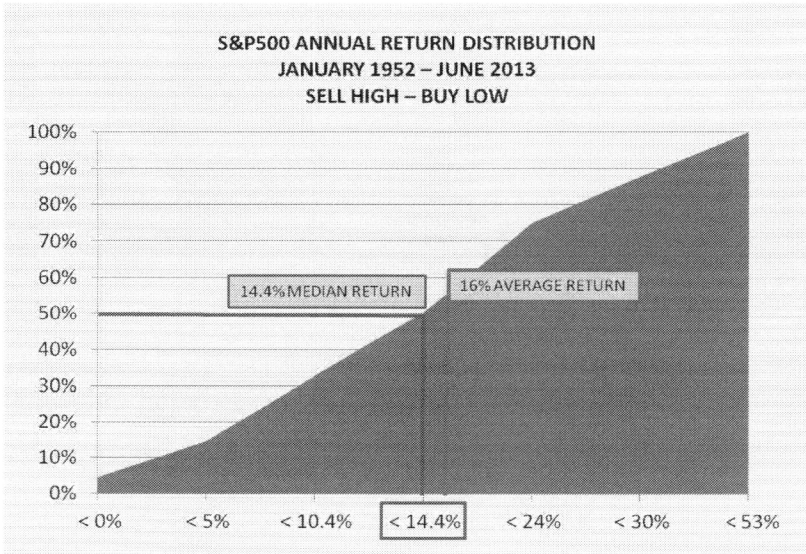

S&P500 ANNUAL RETURN DISTRIBUTION
JANUARY 1952 – JUNE 2013
SELL HIGH – BUY LOW

Rather than an 8.7% average return plus dividends, the return escalates almost two fold to 16% per annum. As illuminated in the table above, the probability of seeing a negative year over year return drops to 5%, and 67% of the time your S&P index fund would have returned month-end, year over year returns of over 10.4%.

Market Timing versus Relative Portfolio Management

Jack Bogle, Chairman and Founder of Vanguard Funds, is often quoted as saying market timing is futile. His argument is that no one can precisely know when markets are going to peak and enter a correction, recession or even worse phase. Even if they could do so, from Mr. Bogle's viewpoint, you cannot correctly tell when to re-enter the market.

This perspective is interesting in that I am sure he is right for at large majority of investors. The idea of being able to forecast accurately a market peak and reversal seems like a daunting task. However, making portfolio adjustments when the stock market meets certain criteria for being too expensive, or likewise if it reverses after a major sell-off is not market timing. These are portfolio rebalancing or rotational actions that should not be shied away from. Market timing is trying to play individual stocks, or options - timing an overbought or oversold situation and trying to make a quick buck on the market ensuing volatility. I do not recommend being caught up in trading market noise. The research in this book is focused on the major market moves, and the correlating forces which come together to create the fall, and then in the timeframe six months to up two years later, provide a suitable re-entry point. Major market moves for investors who are investing for long-term wealth creation need to be managed. The actual technique used to manage the situation may involve rebalancing or hedging.

Not making adjustments in your stock holdings during major market turning points can destroy OVER 50% of your long-term capital gain potential. The surprising thing in the data is that the average stock market return is not significantly above that of a BAA1 20-30 year bond over the 60 years studied. The BAA1 bond produced returns since 1952 of 8.0%, with far lower volatility than the stock market. The standard deviation of returns on the S&P 500 over the time period was 16.42% versus 10.7% for a 25 year BAA1 bond portfolio. Knowing this information, many investment managers have taken to leveraging bond returns to provide equivalent returns to the stock market with less volatility, and higher on-going cash flow.

In other words, the average return being touted as the best path for most investors is advice that is bound to provide mediocre results and liquidity issues in major market downturns. Understanding the market better, and the signals it sends when it is ready to roll-over or reverse during these major market moves, is the crux of becoming a better investor.

PRINCIPLES OF FINANCIAL RELATIVITY

#1 Nominal GDP is the Nucleus of Financial Relativity in the U.S. financial market.

#2 Interest rates are the yardstick by which Financial Relativity is measured.

#3 Higher levels of U.S. Debt relative to GDP depress real GDP and inflation.

#4 Inflation and asset bubbles are financial market imbalances always and everywhere linked to government fiscal policy excesses.

#5 The Fed is the Regulator of Financial Relativity with the power to create and extinguish market imbalances.

#6 Oil price spikes are a foreign force "shockingly" correlated with stock market corrections.

#7 Gold valued in dollars is an absolute reflection of the magnitude of market force between the U.S. and its export trading partners.

#8 Major stock market corrections are triggered by the Fed tightening monetary policy to remedy an inflation or asset bubble imbalance and restore global market relative balance and order.

The 8 Guiding Principles of the Theory of Financial Relativity are the foundation for providing real insights into why the market moves. These principles have been synthesized from the study of the major market corrections and subsequent rebounds from WWII through 2013. The next seven chapters of this book contain the research underlying these principles.

5 NUCLEUS OF FINANCIAL RELATIVITY

If you follow business news, you have very likely heard a report similar to the following:

"The government reported today that the U.S. Gross Domestic Product grew by 4%. The stock market responded to the news, trading...."

An assumed relationship exists between the stock market and the measurement of the country's GDP that pervades the reporting of the economic statistic. The implied relationship is so ingrained in the parlance that one might assume it is an unequivocal law of nature that the two are seamlessly intertwined. What is the basis of this implied relationship, and what value does it actually have for investors? These are important questions worth answering.

Correlation with Uncanny Resemblance

The U.S. GDP reached $16.633 Trillion in the 2nd quarter of 2013. At the beginning of 1957 the U.S. GDP was $464.4 Billion. On a relative basis, the DOW in January 1957 traded at 45. In June of 2013 the DOW closed the month at 1606.

Coincidence, you ask? The two indexes after 56 years have maintained a relative relationship with GDP that is almost perfectly 1:1. As the graphical view shows below, the relative relationship between the U.S. stock market major indexes and the country's GDP are indeed highly correlated through time.

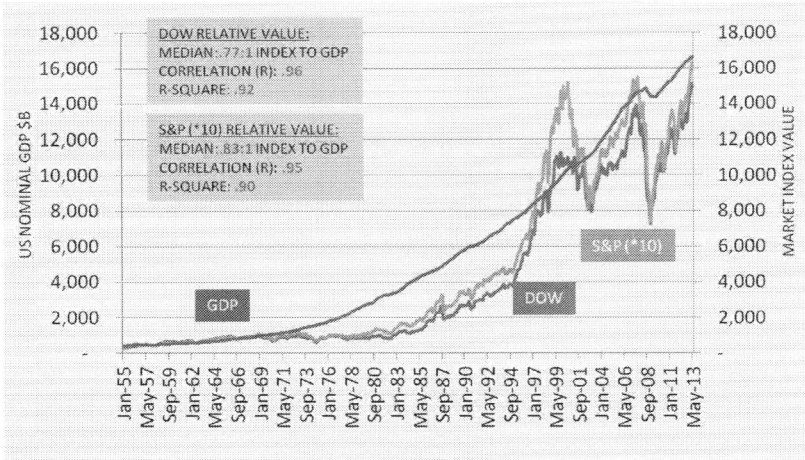

In the case of the DOW, the correlation is .96, meaning that an extremely high degree of the change in value of the stock market is explained by the change in growth of the U.S. GDP. The S&P 500 shows a similar correlation of .95. The R-Square of each index to GDP is also very high.

Obviously this relationship is not an accidental happening. Both the GDP measurement and the stock indexes are created by human beings. The financial market is not driven by natural recurring forces like the rise and setting of the sun, or the law of gravity. The stock index is constructed based on a broad representation of publicly traded companies in the stock market. The index when constructed was established with a value which had a set relationship with GDP. Over time, factors which affect GDP also affect the value of the companies in the index. Thus, the two constructed measures move in relative correlated fashion. GDP is the most favored economic measures tracked by stock investors because it has a predictable relationship with the major indexes. It is a very sound nucleus from which to assess the fair value of the S&P 500 or the DOW.

GDP is a Relative Milepost, Not a Predictor

Understanding the relationship of the stock market to GDP, however, is not as simple as taking the country's latest GDP level and multiplying by a relative factor to predict the appropriate value for the stock market. Although the data show a high correlation of stock index value and GDP, during extended periods stocks traded above the average or median relationship to GDP, and vice-versa. In fact, if the month-end closing value of the S&P 500 (times 10 to create a base one factor) is measured relative to GDP over time since 1955, a distribution curve can be plotted. The curve is normally distributed with a median value of .83. This means that since 1955, 50% of the time the S&P 500 traded at a level which was above .83 times GDP, and 50% of the time it traded below this level.

S&P500 (*10) RELATIVE TO GDP SINCE 1955

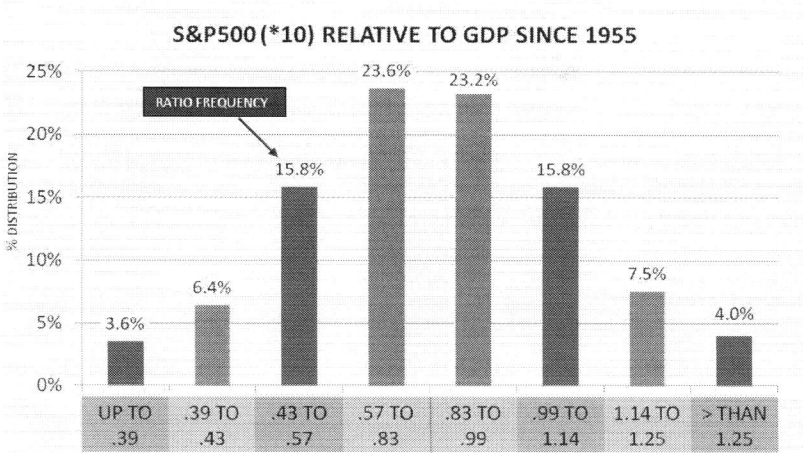

The distribution shows that over time the relative relationship was in the range of .43 to 1.14 78.5% of the time. Also, less than 7.6% of the time the relationship was lower than .39 times, or greater than 1.25 times GDP. Through time, "mileage does vary," but the statistic does revert to and from the mean with a definitive range. If the same time series is reviewed for the DOW, the resulting distribution is very similar. The DOW distribution of values shows a median value of .77 times GDP, but otherwise is distributed in a relatively similar range as the S&P 500.

Because the range in the relationship of GDP to the stock indexes shows a wide variance, using GDP as a simple predictor of the stock market is not advisable. Other factors must be considered. In addition, GDP data provided by the government is not available in a timely fashion to have any meaningful short-term trading value for investors. You are much more likely to be able to predict the upcoming quarter GDP using the current stock market value, than visa-versa.

FREQUENCY ANALYSIS
S&P (*10) TO GDP
1955 TO JUNE 2013

RANGE	# OBS	% FREQ
UP TO .39	25	3.6%
.39 TO .43	45	6.4%
.43 TO .57	111	15.8%
.57 TO .83	166	23.6%
.83 TO .99	163	23.2%
.99 TO 1.14	111	15.8%
1.14 TO 1.25	53	7.5%
> THAN 1.25	28	4.0%
	702	100.0%

However, what makes GDP the nucleus of Financial Relativity is that significant and measurable forces are working in a manner which through time have a meaningful impact on the economic statistic. GDP is like a mileage counter, and effort exerted by private market participants seeking to "maximize profits" or government bodies seeking to drive public "good" blend together in an attempt to push the recorded result upward. In order to keep your bearings in the sea of data in the market, GDP is a very rational centerpiece from which to base relative value assessments. The correlation of GDP to the stock market, and the upward bias of the measurement form the foundation for first Guiding Principle in the Theory of Relativity:

1st PRINCIPLE OF FINANCIAL RELATIVITY
Nominal GDP is the Nucleus of Financial Relativity in the U.S. financial market.

Forces at Work Beyond the "Invisible hand"

When reviewing GDP relative to the stock market from the 1950s through 2013, the data exhibits a mechanistic, micro-managed quality, which shows an imperfect resemblance to the spirit of capitalism as neo-classical economics predicts. In the neo-classical framework, capital markets are a forum for human interaction, where assets are traded and value is set every minute of the traded day. Adam Smith's epic work in the "Wealth of Nations" has been generalized to depict the capital market as having an "invisible hand" - a force that drives consumers to choose freely what to buy and each producer is allowed to choose freely what to sell and how to produce it. This force in turn creates a market that settles on product distribution and prices that are beneficial to all the individual members of a community, and hence to the community as a whole.

Milton Friedman has likened Smith's Invisible Hand to "the possibility of cooperation without coercion," and promoted this ideal as the best model for the U.S. economy to obtain maximum growth in his Nobel Prize winning work. The invisible hand may indeed be a factor in the average 6.6% GDP growth since 1955, and the corresponding 6-7% compound annual growth rate in the stock market, plus dividends. However, the data do not reflect a laissez-faire driven U.S. economy. The cyclical volatility in the stock market data relative to GDP contained in the following table is the area to focus your attention. The data is punctuated by indications of human systems and bureaucratic meddling skewing market returns over time to "coerce" the market to perform in some way.

Stocks Relative to GDP Growth Rate	1955-2013	1955-1969	1969-1993	1994-2000	2000-2013
GDP AVERAGE	6.6%	6.5%	8.3%	5.8%	4.1%
GDP MEDIAN	6.4%	6.5%	8.2%	6.1%	4.3%
	Correlated	Above	Below	Above	Below
S&P500	7.3%	10.3%	6.2%	21.1%	0.5%
Note: S&P500 CAGR before dividends which can add up to 1.8% to returns depending on fees Returns are calculated before taxes					

The cycles in the data are correlated with election cycles, and changes in the guard between the Democrat and Republican Party. Just look at the data in the table above from 1994-2000, Clinton years, versus the year 2000 until present day that incorporate 8 years of Republican rule, and then 4 years of the Obama administration. This pattern is consistent across the entire timeframe. Unambiguous correlations also exist in the data to actions driven by government policy targeted to drive both economic expansion and contraction. These actions include changes in government tax policy and deficit spending activities, as well as the Federal Reserve rotating from active and passive policy roles through time.

The Theory of Financial Relativity does not posit that any of these outside forces on the aggregate market are rational. In fact, the Theory takes a broader perspective. The Theory accepts the premise that when individuals looking out for their own self interest interact in society with socially engineered systems, odd behaviors when judged from an individual perspective result. The Theory seeks to incorporate the impact of this interaction into a model for understanding the resulting impact on the financial market. Within this context, the primary variables that impact the nucleus of the Financial Relativity can be simplified into the following measures of force:

- **Interest Rates** – Reflecting the market cost of money. Rates are separated into the categories of "risk-free" rates which can be highly controlled by U.S. Treasury and Federal Reserve policy, and interest rates much more affected by the market for risk assets such as long-term corporate bonds.
- **Federal Reserve Policy** – Influencing the market cost of money and indirectly the value of all financial assets as well as the cost of borrowing.
- **Government Policy** – Impacting GDP growth and inflation primarily through Government Expenditures and the means by which expenditures are financed – taxation or borrowing.

- **Inflation** – An index measure which provides a relative metric indicating the difference between real productive growth and simple market price level increases. Consumer price inflation is constantly monitored and monetarily regulated through Federal Reserve policy which impacts market value.
- **Energy Price Levels** – Impacting sustainability of GDP growth and inflation based on the relative cost, and change in cost of energy over time.
- **Foreign Trade** – Affecting the market through the inter-relationship of U.S. current account deficits and excess dollar based savings accumulated and invested, rather than used in trade, by overseas trading partners.

Simple Example of the Theory Construct

There is a saying, "History does not repeat itself, but it often rhymes." One of the interesting aspects about the data assembled in researching this book is the intersecting correlations of data throughout time. This chapter opened by comparing the relative relationship of GDP to the traded value of the S&P 500 in 1957 versus 2013. The data show that on a comparable basis the stock market and the recorded GDP between the two points in time are relatively the same. As the earlier distribution table indicates this did not happened that frequently over the 60 years. Therefore, the two points in time might have similarities which could be used to assess both the absolute value of the market, as well as the probable directional movement in the market based on the forces at work in the economy in 1957 versus 2013.

Looking back at the 1957 data, GDP growth was 5.9%, and decelerating. Consumer price inflation level was coming off of very low levels of below 2%, and increasing to 3%. Interest rates were historically still very low, having come out of the 1940 time period in which rates were repressed and kept low for an extended period of time. The 10 year Treasury note was yielding 3.5% and rising steadily. Corporate BAA1 long term rates were also relatively low at 4.5%, and rising. Government spending had just declined in absolute terms briefly over the preceding 6 month period, and was in the process of accelerating. The Fed was reducing assets on its balance sheet, and was in the process of raising short-term rates.

In the ensuing months post January 1957, the stock market decreased in value by over 10%.

The summer of 1957 and 3rd quarter of 2013 have many similarities, but by no means are a perfect circumstantial match. In both instances the stock market was trading at an all-time high. The market in 2013 exhibited a rising rate environment just as in the summer of 1957, but only on the long-end of the yield curve. Short-term rates were not rising as in 1957. In 2013, the Fed was expanding rather than contracting its balance sheet, although it was expected to do so at a slower pace in the near future. GDP grew at an anemic pace of less than 3% in the second quarter of 2013, and GDP growth faced the possibility of deceleration due to an impending government shutdown and other economic factors. Consumer price inflation was less than 2%. The prospect for slow growth was very similar to 1957. In the summer of 2013 interest rates on the 10 year Treasury were approaching 3%, and the corporate BAA1 bond long-term rate increased to over 5.5% from below 5%. Additionally, government expenditures were falling because of Sequestration, which was passed into law earlier in 2013.

Based on this data and the likeness to 1957, the Theory places higher odds that the stock market at the end of 2013 would face a correction in the intermediate term. However, key market forces were not yet aligned to produce an immediate market meltdown. What major force was missing, and would the situation become more likely for a market collapse as time progressed? Understanding what to look for is information that will be shared in the coming chapters. More precision comes from a deeper understanding of the remaining principles of the Theory of Financial Relativity.

Fundamental Lessons about the Nucleus of Financial Relativity

In order to become a better investor, you have to be versed with a fundamental understanding of where the stock market derives value through time. Value is created by the trade of goods and services between individuals and businesses. The measure of the transactions is recorded in the on-going nominal GDP statistic for the country. It includes both real productivity based growth in output and inflationary price increases. The relationship of GDP to the traded stock indexes through time is a key part of the lesson about Financial Relativity put forward in this chapter.

LESSONS ABOUT THE NUCLEUS OF FINANCIAL RELATIVITY

- Nominal GDP is the constant dollar measure of all goods and services produced in the U.S. economy.

- GDP has a natural upward growth bias due to population growth and increasing productivity.

- The stock market is strongly, positively correlated to nominal GDP growth.

6 FINANCIAL RELATIVITY YARDSTICK

Ask anyone old enough to remember the late 1970s and early 1980s about interest rates, and almost immediately they will dive into the story about how their first home mortgage had an interest rate of 12%, maybe higher. Or they will remember buying a CD paying 10% interest at their bank. The interest rate structure in 2013 was much different. Ask someone in 2043 their perspective on interest rates, and possibly they will recall the good old days when they could obtain a mortgage for 4% in 2013. However, they might also have disapproving memories about the 0.04% interest rate they were receiving on their Money Market savings accounts, and 0.4% rates they were receiving on their 1 Year CDs.

The cost of money as reflected by interest rates is the most important measurement in the universe of financial assets. By understanding the market for credit, and the resulting interest rates, investors gain a wealth of very important information. Signals about the market direction and sentiment can be obtained. The relative return between various investment options and across markets can be analyzed. Even the implied expectations for the riskiness of an investment, as well as the outlook for inflation can be interpreted. These characteristics make interest rates a cornerstone Guiding Principle in the Theory of Financial Relativity.

2nd PRINCIPLE OF FINANCIAL RELATIVITY
Interest rates are the yardstick by which Financial Relativity is measured.

The cost of money is not static in absolute terms, as becomes clearly evident in the graph below showing the term structure of interest rates from 1941 through 2013.

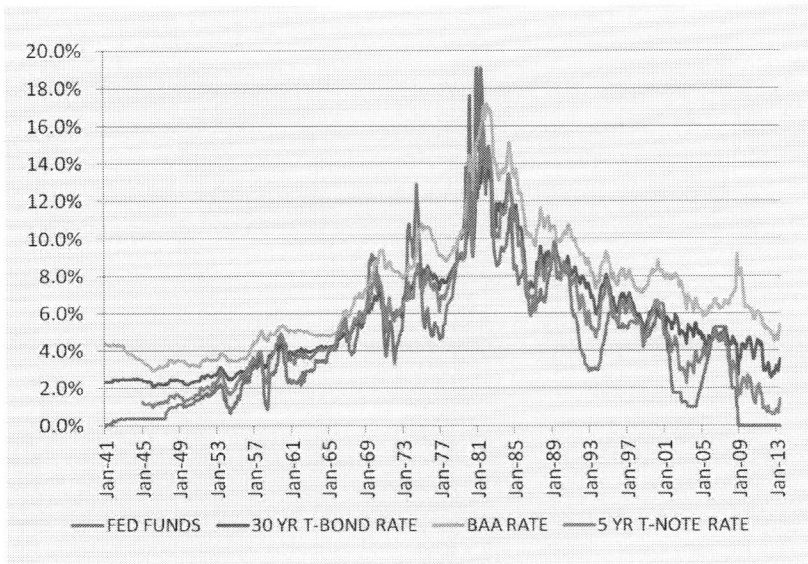

Over the time period interest rates have trended upward from lows set during the Depression Era and 1940s to a peak in 1981, and then back to relative all-time lows in 2013. Several observations about the interest rate market are important within the context of Financial Relativity:

1. The Absolute Level of Interest Rates inversely affects the value of all traded investments through time. The inverse relationship is true both for stocks and bonds. The absolute level of rates, therefore, is the primary variable which should be reviewed in assessing the relative value of an investment as long as the market rate being used for the comparison is consistent in risk and duration.

2. The Rate of Change in long term and short-term rates, and risky asset rates versus U.S. Treasury rates, is rarely perfectly synchronized. This characteristic of the financial market makes the relative spread between rates across maturities and asset classes as important, if not more important, than the absolute level of rates in assessing the directional movement in the market and relative value of specific asset classes.

The term structure of rates is a very important tool in the world of Financial Relativity, and hopefully the examples in this book will make readers more versed in how useful it can become. The remainder of this chapter will focus on how interest rate changes affect the absolute value of the stock market.

The change, however, is not always immediate as you might expect as interest rates go up or down. The stock market is positively correlated to the rate of change in GDP, the nucleus of Financial Relativity, as well as inversely correlated to the level of interest rates. This dual phenomenon means that interest rates can rise, and the stock market can go up at the same time, and vice-versa. The real important aspect of Financial Relativity is that over an extended period of time, the stock market trades at a <u>relative</u> value to GDP which is simultaneously inversely correlated to the level of interest rates. Understanding this core concept in the Theory of Financial Relativity unlocks one of the real mysteries on how the market functions as a discounting mechanism for expected future value, rather than a gambling casino as perceived by many investors.

Interest Rates and Stock Prices

During 2012 and the first several quarter of 2013, there was a raging debate in the business media concerning how much the impact of falling interest rates, primarily attributable to actions being taken by the Federal Reserve Bank over the time period, was having on the stock market value since the market lows of early 2009. Based on the calculation below, the effect explained virtually 100% of the change in value.

S&P INDEX FUND LOW FEE DIVIDEND RATE 1.8%	COMPARABLE 4.52% PERPETUAL BAA1 RATED $100 BOND
JAN-2009 : 826 MAR-2013 : 1598	JAN-2009 : $55.53 MAR-2013 : $100.00
ANNUAL RETURN: 16.5% PLUS DIVIDENDS	ANNUAL RETURN: 15.04% PLUS INTEREST

In the table above, the stock market return from January 2009 to March 2013 is compared to a *hypothetical* 4.52% perpetual bond with an investment grade of BAA1. The BAA1 interest rate was chosen as a proxy for the relative risk of the highly liquid S&P 500. In January of 2009, the BAA1 bond rate closed the trading month at 8.14%. At this interest rate, a perpetual BAA1 rated bond with a coupon of 4.52% would have traded at a price of $55.53. In the ensuing years rates fell, and by the end of April 2013 the BAA1 rate was 4.52%. Based on this interest rate, the value of the hypothetical bond would have been $100, or par value.

Now take a share of the S&P 500 and analyze the returns over the same period of time. As the graphic shows the CAGR of the stock market from January 2009 through the end of March 2013 was 16.5%. The capital appreciation of the perpetual bond over the same period was 15.04%. When the lower dividends are balanced against the higher interest payments on the bond, both investments doubled in value over the time period. The correlation between the change in rates and the change in the value of the aggregate stock market as measured by the S&P 500 was almost a perfect -1. The unique aspect of this time period when the data is reviewed in aggregate is that the stock market in recovering from the lows set in 2009 to levels set prior to the 2008 market crash was very heavily dependent upon the downward movement in interest rates.

The close correlation that was evident during the 4 year time period was broken in May 2013 as long-term rates began to rise, and the stock market continued to rise. Just as GDP is not a mono-variable predictor of stock market value, the market also does not perfectly respond in inverse fashion to the rise and fall in interest rates. However, the data throughout the 70 years between WWII and 2013 show that when the level of interest rates and the GDP level of the U.S. economy are combined, the trading level of the U.S. stock market becomes much more predictable.

Best Relative Interest Rate to Judge Stocks

In my research of the rate structure impact on the value of stocks over time, the data eventually led to the BAA1 seasoned 20-30 year bond index as the most correlated interest rate to stock market performance. Why is the 20-30 year BAA1 rate better for reviewing the stock market than longer-term Treasuries such as the 10 year or 30 year bong? Several possibilities exist. One, corporate bond rates are much more affected by free market forces in determination of the market rate. The U.S. Treasury complex can be very skewed by open market operations of the Federal Reserve Bank and the financing of government spending by the U.S. Treasury. This causes the Treasury rates on a relative basis to not correspond as well with the riskier stock market. Second, Treasuries become safe haven assets during times of market turmoil, and less so during economic good times.

These market tendencies make the inverse correlation of U.S. Treasury rates to stocks less strong over long periods of time. However, the actions by the government and Federal Reserve which influence the interest rate of Treasuries are very much ancillary variables in the determination of the absolute level of the term structure of interest rates – and eventually the BAA1 market rate. The impact of the Federal Reserve policy and U.S.

Government spending are explored more fully in later chapters.

Interest Rate Changes and GDP Growth Effect Stock Market Value

The graph below was created to visually show the distribution in the level of the BAA1 rates from 1955 through 2013.

BAA1 RATE DISTRIBUTION SINCE 1955

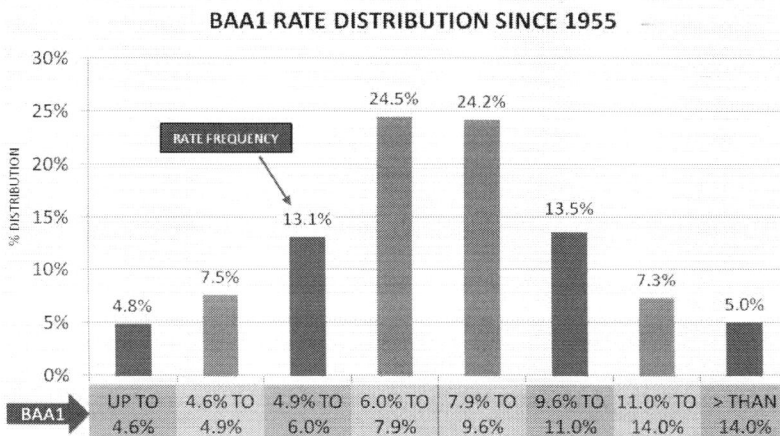

The median BAA1 market interest rate was 7.9%. Almost 50% of the time rates were between 6% and 9.6%, and 75% of the time rates were between 5.4% and 11%. Over the long-term the BAA1 bond rate was in a 560 basis point range 75% of the time, and a 940 basis point range 90% of the time.

With this wide range in rates through time, what is very difficult for many to grasp is just how the movement in the rates impacted stock values. During many time periods stocks rose, but rates went up as well. The key to this understanding starts in the last chapter when the data on the relationship of the stock market to GDP was presented. When the BAA1 rate distribution table is combined with the stock market relative to GDP table, a very clear relationship is illuminated.

FREQUENCY ANALYSIS BAA1 INTEREST RATES 1955 TO JUNE 2013		
RANGE	# OBS	% FREQ
UP TO 4.6%	34	4.8%
4.6% TO 4.9%	53	7.5%
4.9% TO 6.0%	92	13.1%
6.0% TO 7.9%	172	24.5%
7.9% TO 9.6%	170	24.2%
9.6% TO 11.0%	95	13.5%
11.0% TO 14.0%	51	7.3%
> THAN 14.0%	35	5.0%
	702	100.0%

RELATIVE ANALYSIS STOCKS / GDP VS BAA1 RATE 1955 TO JUNE 2013		
BAA1 RANGE	MEDIAN DOW/GDP	MEDIAN S&P/GDP
UP TO 4.6%	1.05	0.85
4.6% TO 4.9%	1.12	1.08
4.9% TO 6.0%	1.04	1.01
6.0% TO 7.9%	0.84	0.95
7.9% TO 9.6%	0.67	0.79
9.6% TO 11.0%	0.44	0.53
11.0% TO 14.0%	0.34	0.45
> THAN 14.0%	0.29	0.39

The table below illustrates that the stock market value relative to GDP is clearly related to the overall level of interest rates. With the exception of the extreme case in which long-term BAA1 rates got too low, shown in the below 4.6% line in the table, lower level of interest rates always correspond to higher trading level of the major stock market indexes relative to U.S. nominal GDP. The strength of this relationship is exhibited in the graph below. The correlation is -.85 for the time period, with an R-square of .72, meaning the correlation level is very significant.

Armed with this knowledge, the fair market value of the stock market becomes much easier to analyze and understand over time. During the high interest time period of the early 1980s, such as the 1st quarter of 1981, GDP was $3.131 Trillion. The DOW, by comparison, was trading at 1005, or .32 times GDP on a relative basis. Interest rates at the time were at a high water mark dating back well before the Great Depression through 2013. The BAA1 rate in March 1981 was 15.34%, the top 5% range in the historical time series data. Given the GDP level and the high interest rates, the .32 times trading value of the stock index to GDP was very close to the historical norm for

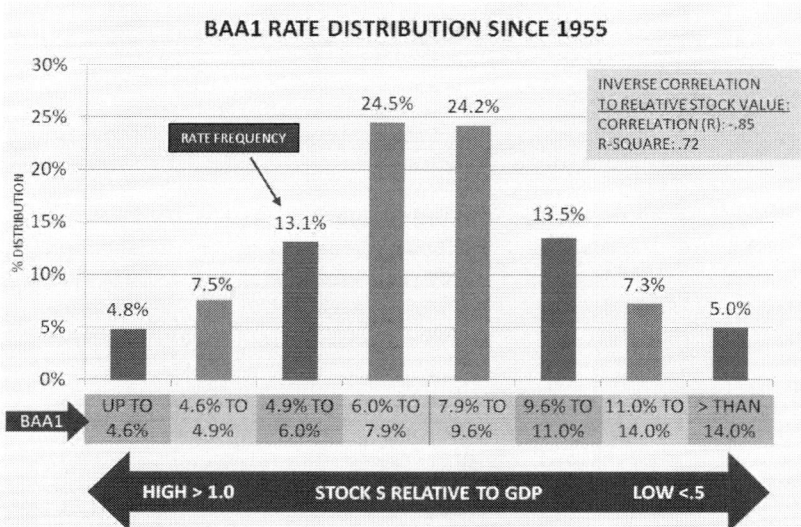

BAA1 RATE DISTRIBUTION SINCE 1955

INVERSE CORRELATION TO RELATIVE STOCK VALUE:
CORRELATION (R): -.85
R-SQUARE: .72

RATE FREQUENCY

% DISTRIBUTION

BAA1	UP TO 4.6%	4.6% TO 4.9%	4.9% TO 6.0%	6.0% TO 7.9%	7.9% TO 9.6%	9.6% TO 11.0%	11.0% TO 14.0%	> THAN 14.0%
	4.8%	7.5%	13.1%	24.5%	24.2%	13.5%	7.3%	5.0%

HIGH > 1.0   STOCKS RELATIVE TO GDP   LOW <.5

44

similar time periods over the 60 years of data.

By contrast, the BAA1 rate in the second quarter of 2013 closed the month of June at 5.41%. The S&P 500 closed the month at 1606 which was .97 times GDP. Based on the level of interest rates and the GDP level, the trading range was only slightly higher than the expected historical trading range of .95 times GDP, in line with what would be considered fair value.

Using the Interest Rate Principle of Relativity

The Financial Relativity Guiding Principles provide a basis for critical analysis of stock value based on changes in the rate structure and GDP as affected by dynamic market forces, whether driven by profit maximizing businesses or government policy. The Theory of Financial Relativity postulates that the market for stock investments in aggregate is valued relative to the on-going value of the goods and services produced in the economy – GDP. However, value is relative, not absolute, through time. The relative adjustment factor is the primary measurement yardstick, the current cost of money. In the case of the stock market, the best relative cost of money is the BAA1 interest rate. So what causes the market to move erratically through time? What if the market is grossly overvalued or undervalued relative to what the Theory of Financial Relativity suggests, what can cause this to happen? Separately, and probably more significantly, why do interest rates swing so widely through time, thereby altering the expected fair value of the stock market?

These are all questions which require a deeper understanding of the influence of the Federal Reserve on the term structure of interest rates, the U.S. Government on the growth rate of GDP; and, the combination of both institutions' policies on the recorded U.S. inflation level. The Theory of Financial relativity appropriately predicts that if the U.S. GDP grows through time, as would be expected simply from the growth in population and natural business activity, then the bias for stock valuations is upward. However, if for some reason growth falls, or interest rates rise much faster than GDP growth, or government subsidy activity skew rates or GDP growth, then the stock market may become relatively overvalued and eventually must adjust in price downward. Likewise, if economic growth occurs and rates fall, if the market doesn't perfectly respond to the change, it will become a better relative buy and eventually there will be a market surge.

Ancillary Forces at Work in the Market

In a free market driven economy, the Theory of Financial Relativity expects that changes in the stock market value would routinely adjust to changes in expectations for GDP growth and the level of interest rates. Interest rates would be set by free market forces and GDP, unencumbered by subsidizes or government coercive forces. In this free market framework, the range of interest rates would likely be much narrower, and the resulting GDP growth rate would likely exhibit a shorter cyclical pattern. The upward bias in the market would not change as long as the population grows and productivity expands.

However, the history of the U.S. economy from the 1980s through 2013 shows a less frequent basis of downward adjustments. When a correction did happen, it was a painful downward move, usually accompanied by changes in monetary and fiscal policy. This implies the presence of monopolistic, subsidizing forces which affect the market level for rates and the short-run growth in GDP. These forces are not new. They have been evident in the data since the Depression Era, and even prior to that time, at varying levels. Through focused study the relative impact of how the policy changes work to impact the natural adjustment mechanisms in market valuation can, and should be taken into account by shrewd investors to avoid the market "bubbles" created by the clearly present ancillary market forces.

Lessons about Interest Rates

The most important lesson about interest rates that investors need to understand is that they provide important market information every minute of the trading day. Rates are also inversely correlated to financial asset value, whether value is increasing or decreasing due to other factors.

LESSONS ABOUT MEASURING FINANCIAL RELATIVITY

- Interest rates are the most observable means of measuring a change in Financial Relativity.
- Useful market information is provided by measuring the rate of change in interest rates over time and the spread in rates between rates of different maturity and risk assets.
- The value of a cash flow generating asset is always inversely correlated to the absolute level of a comparable risk adjusted interest rate relative to its growth rate in cash flow.
- The stock market relative to GDP is highly inversely correlated to the long-term BAA1 interest rate.

7 DEPRESSING NATIONAL DEBT

In the beginning of 2013 the media was fixated on the impending "draconian" automatic spending cuts that went into law March 1st 2013. The cuts were relatively minor at $85B per year on a budget of $4T and scheduled to be implemented over the next 10 years. The stock market showed no visible panic during the fire drill in Washington. Many investors during the time period wanted to understand if they should fear or applaud the spending cuts with respect to their investments. After all, logically if a government service is scaled back, the cuts should negatively impact the country's GDP which simultaneously work against stock valuations – right?

Well, given the 2013 spending and debt levels of the U.S. Government, the evidence pointed to the fact that the opposite was much more likely to actually be true. Since GDP is a major factor in determining overall stock market valuation, government spending and debt at historical high relative levels actually were a burden on U.S. economic growth. Growing debt levels, once they exceed a threshold level, work in a depressing fashion on a country's GDP.

The National Debt Data

Empirical data showing the historical relationship of U.S. Debt to GDP is depicted in the graph below. The data is shown reaching back in time to WWII. After WWII, the U.S. Debt to GDP ratio exceeded 100% due to the massive increase in government spending required by FDR to win the battle. Through time, the country was able to reduce the debt level on a relative basis, and financial conditions changed from the late 1940s through 1960s.

The low point in debt relative to GDP in modern history occurred in the 1970s, which many living today recall as a time period of very high inflation.

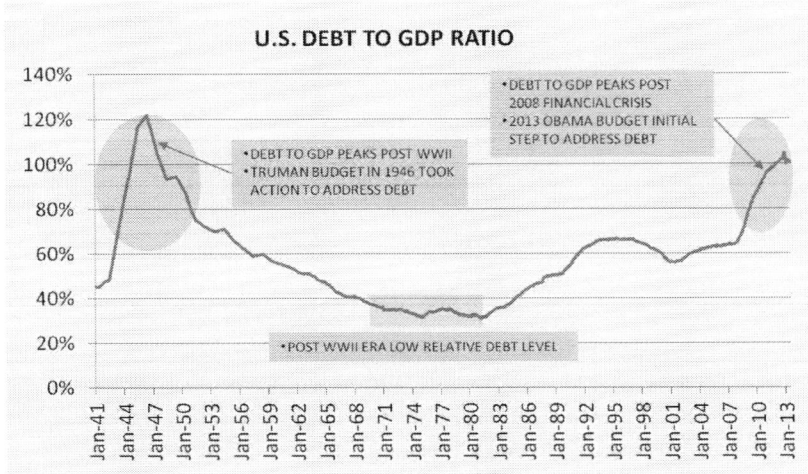

U.S. DEBT TO GDP RATIO

- DEBT TO GDP PEAKS POST 2008 FINANCIAL CRISIS
- 2013 OBAMA BUDGET INITIAL STEP TO ADDRESS DEBT
- DEBT TO GDP PEAKS POST WWII
- TRUMAN BUDGET IN 1946 TOOK ACTION TO ADDRESS DEBT
- POST WWII ERA LOW RELATIVE DEBT LEVEL

In 1980, the government policies shifted with the election of Ronald Reagan. Taxes were lowered and deficit spending began to reverse the declining debt level in the country. Although the goal of Reaganomics was to curb government spending and balance the U.S. budget, it was only partially fulfilled through time. In fact, spending continued to grow at moderate to high levels throughout the 1980s, only slowly declining in growth rate by the end of the 1980s. This was in stark contrast to the path taken to actually balance the federal budget by Truman in 1946. The circumstances regarding the ability of the government to borrow money from the private sector to finance government spending in the two polar extreme cases was seemingly a big factor in the path taken in the two instances.

Moving on to 2013, the country was again in very similar government financial difficulties as post WWII because of the relative magnitude of the National Debt . The Wars in Iraq and Afghanistan combined with very large increases in government spending levels in the 1st term of the Obama Administration caused the National Debt level to explode higher, in much the same fashion as the early 1940s. The end result was a debt to GDP level over 100% at the start of 2013. Steps were taken by the federal government in 2013 to address the excessive debt level that included tax increases as well as spending growth reductions. The budget deficit was also reduced by payments of profits being distributed to the Treasury by Fannie Mae and Freddie Mac, the quasi government housing agencies that were taken into conservatorship during the 2008 financial crisis. As a result of these actions in 2013 the debt to GDP level began to show a slight decline by mid-year 2013.

Why does the Debt Level Matter?

The problem created by excessive National Debt is that as a country borrows more and more money, it crowds out private sector borrowing capacity and the real economy suffers. Academic research by Carmen M. Reinhart and Kenneth S. Rogoff[1], who have studied this issue across many advanced economies through history, supports this conclusion. Since WWII, the real GDP performance illustrates the impact of debt on the U.S. GDP.

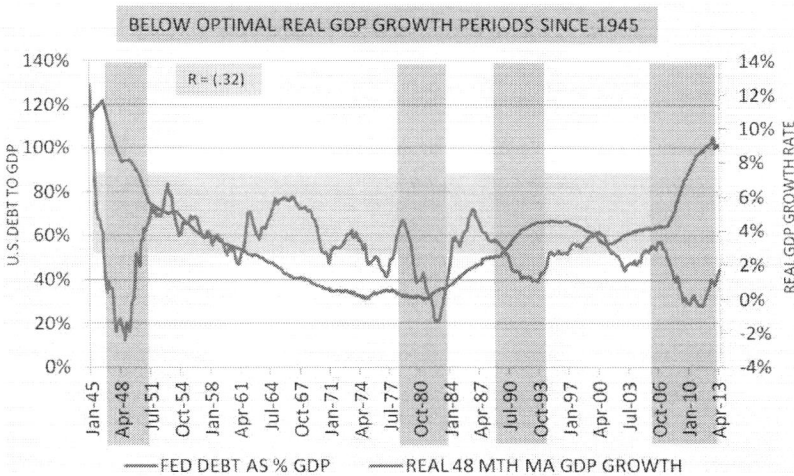

The correlation of real GDP growth to the outstanding level of U.S. Debt to GDP is (.32). What this correlation indicates is that the more the U.S. government borrows in relation to the ability of the country to produce goods and services, the less real growth the country experiences. The graph delineates the time periods (purple) when average growth was sub-optimal during the 68 year time period. Sub-optimal is considered less than 2.5% real growth. The time series data does exhibit some interesting information for investors.

1. The sub-optimal GDP growth time periods are most pronounced at the relative extremes – when the debt to GDP ratio is high and when it is very low. An outlier time period also occurred in the early 1990s.

---

[1] A Decade of Debt, Carmen M. Reinhart, Kenneth S. Rogoff, NBER Working Paper No. 16827, February 2011

2. The correlation is not strong enough to preclude the possibility of other significant contributors to weak GDP growth when the Debt is relatively high. The way that the government acts to deal with high debt levels most likely explains the correlated effect on GDP growth.

3. Pronounced continuous deficit spending and increased debt levels since 1980 showed a pattern of reduced GDP growth in subsequent years (early 1990, Desert Storm; 2003-2012 Iraq War); whereas points in time when the debt level was reduced corresponded with higher subsequent GDP growth (late 1990s – Internet Technology Boom).

A Closer Look at the Long-term GDP Growth Trend

The chart below provides a closer look at the debt to GDP ratio from 1970 to 2013. This starting point for the graphic was chosen because the mid-1970s was the point in time that the U.S. Debt level relative to GDP began to reverse a 25 year downward trend which started after WWII.

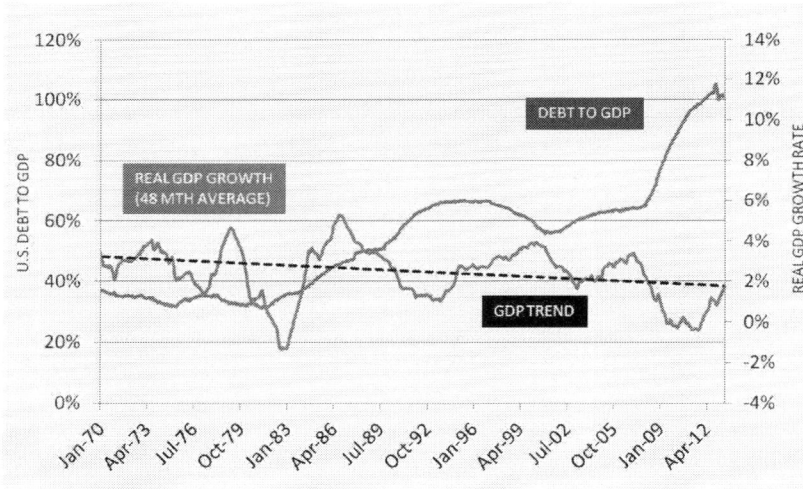

The chart shows that the National Debt outstanding grew from a low of less than 35% in the 1970s to over 100% of U.S. GDP in 2012, and remained at the elevated level in 2013 as this book was being written. From the early 1980's to 2013 the U.S. Debt level increased substantially, to a point where it stood at $16.7T in June of 2013. During the time period in the graphic, the U.S. ran a federal budget surplus only in the year 2000, and was very close to a balanced budget in 1970. During the remaining years in the graphic, the U.S. ran budget deficits. The second line on the chart shows the trend line of real GDP growth from January 1970 thru June 2013. To smooth out the impact of 4 year business and political cycles, a 48 month moving average was utilized.

The GDP growth trend line relative to the overall debt to GDP ratio is an important relationship for investors to understand. The U.S. demonstrated strongest growth during the time frame when debt to GDP ranged from 40% to 70%. When in this range, 2.5%-5.0% real GDP was routine performance, with the exception of the period in the late 70s. In this time period there were other contributing factors to declining real growth, primarily excessive inflation and rapidly rising cost of energy.

Historically the country's ability to produce high GDP once the debt level exceeds 70% of GDP was a problem. The GDP growth went down significantly after 2005 as more debt was taken on by the United States. GDP real growth did not show appreciable gains with major spending programs undertaken in 2009 and 2010.

U.S. Debt Level Impacts Interest Rates

Academic research has focused in recent years on the impact of government borrowing levels on a country's national output. This information is useful, very relevant in the framework of driving national policy decisions regarding the financing source for government spending. But the GDP growth impact of the federal debt is only part of the equation in understanding how government deficit spending impacts market valuation for stocks and bonds. The second important aspect that needs to be reviewed is the relative cost of money, or how interest rates change over time as the government borrows relatively more of the money it spends.

The data in the following chart is quite revealing, and when you think through the information it conveys, one could conclude it is rather obtuse. From the 1940s through 2013, BAA1 rates showed an inverse correlation of R = (.57) to the National Debt to GDP ratio. What this says is that the more the government borrows to fund its spending, the lower rates move. Likewise, the less that the U.S. government borrows relative to what it spends, the higher rates tend to be. The chart also indicates that BAA1 rates were at extreme levels, highest and lowest, at times when real GDP growth was recorded at its worst levels. These time periods were the 1940s, early 1980s and 2008-2009.

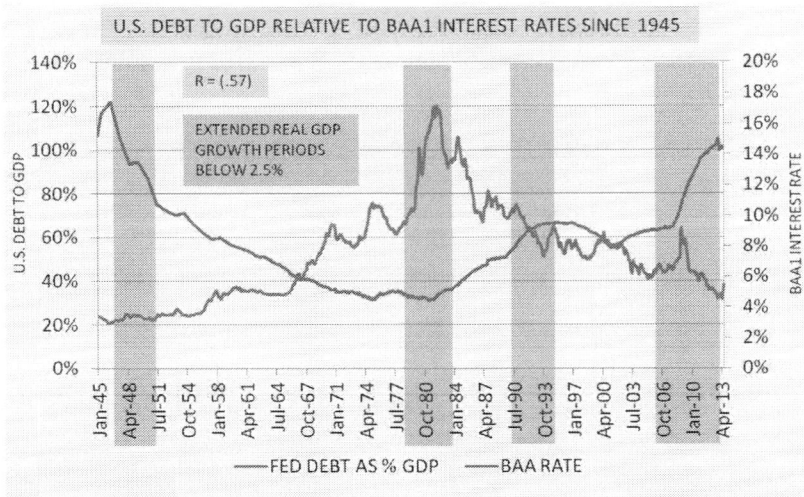

U.S. DEBT TO GDP RELATIVE TO BAA1 INTEREST RATES SINCE 1945

— FED DEBT AS % GDP — BAA RATE

In business lending, the mirror opposite of what this data reflects is more typical. When a company is over-leveraged, interest rates rise to cover the increased risk; likewise, when a company's balance sheet is healthy, credit risk falls and borrowing rates are relatively lower. But in the world of government finance, obviously much more is going on. First, during the time periods of the late 1940s and the recent time period post the 2008 market crash, the term structure of interest rates was heavily influenced by the monopolistic force of the U.S. Treasury in conjunction with the Federal Reserve. The policy during these time periods repressed interest rates. By using the power of the Federal Reserve Bank to drive and keep interest rates low on government borrowing, the U.S. Treasury benefited through lower interest payments on the U.S. Debt. Not controlling the market in this fashion would likely have led to an explosion upward in interest rates. The result predicted by the Theory of Financial Relativity would be mutually assured destruction. The government would not be able to finance its operation, and the stock market would collapse as rates propelled higher as happened most recently in September 2008.

Repressive rate policy may explain the scenario when the government is relatively over-laden with debt, but why did the opposite happen in the late 1970s and early 1980s? The answer to this question lies in the next chapter which explores how inflation is created within the economy, and the resulting changes which occur in the financial relativity yardstick, interest rates, as a result.

Lessons in U.S. National Debt Relativity

The U.S. Debt is critically important to the determination of relative stock market value because it is an indicator of the stored and direction force of fiscal government spending. The lessons that investors should carry with them concerning the impact of government spending on the financial market are summarized in the following table.

LESSONS IN GOVERNMENT RELATIVE FORCE
• U.S. government force is applied to the economy primarily through fiscal spending and regulation, funded by taxes, borrowing or money creation.
• The U.S. government increasingly tax and spent to fund government operations from WWII to 1980, and steadily decreased the Debt to GDP ratio.
• Excessive government spending which is monetized by the Federal Reserve is strongly correlated with inflation.
• Deficit government spending is funding government activity through borrowing rather than taxing.
• The U.S. government increasingly borrowed to fund operations after 1980, raising the Debt to GDP ratio and increasingly borrowed from foreign governments.
• Government spending which is borrowed is inversely correlated with inflation.
• The National Debt to GDP ratio is inversely correlated to real GDP growth and the inflation rate.

The U.S. National Debt is at the center of how money creation is managed in the U.S. economy. However, the directional impact of greater or lower values of debt through time is likely contrary to what many investors realize. As expected, the data show that GDP growth is negatively correlated to higher and higher levels of government borrowing relative to national output. However, the strength in the correlation is not very strong. In fact, the data suggest the country would be well served to manage the debt within an optimal range of 40% to 70% of GDP; when the level far exceeds or is below this level, growth level suffers. The most likely reason that growth suffers when debt is above 100% of GDP is the remedy put in place by the political process to deal with the high relative level of debt.

The more relevant impact of the National Debt on financial markets is the impact on interest rates as the inflation rate falls due the depressing nature of higher debt burdens on the economy. From 1980 through 2013, the stock market experienced significant compounded returns. Correspondingly, interest rates after 1981 fell significantly, including the BAA1 interest rate which is most inversely correlated to stock valuation levels. At the same time the National Debt exploded higher. *The irony of the economic situation that materialized post the 2008 financial crisis was that the primary reason that stock valuations rose to all-time highs in 2013 was the government program to repress rates, which had the negative effect of crowding out private sector growth!* Throughout the time period from 2009-2013 as rates were repressed through extensive quantitative easing, GDP growth was anemic. The Theory of Financial Relativity predicts, however, that Federal Reserve repression of interest rates is not a sustainable long term program, just as it was not in the 1940s. Extended periods of low rates eventually become unmanageable by the Federal Reserve, resulting in pressure on market interest rates to rise. Rising long term interest rates is precisely what began to be experienced in the summer months of 2013, deadened only by a partial government shutdown in early October 2013.

The lessons learned from the analysis of the U.S. Debt from WWII through 2013 provide the foundation for Guiding Principle #3. Both the depressing impact on GDP due to crowding out of the private sector, and the repressive rate structure used by the government to reverse the impact of high debt levels is indicative of self perpetuating democratically elected government bureaucracies. Making decisions that visibly cause or appear to cause domestic hardship is not the natural tendency of the U.S., or any government where leaders are elected by popular vote.

3rd PRINCIPLE OF FINANCIAL RELATIVITY
Higher levels of U.S. Debt relative to GDP depress real GDP and inflation.

The result is a body politic that is ill equipped to do anything but perpetuate spending through whatever means, borrowing as the U.S. began to do excessively post 1980 or progressively raising taxes as it did from the 1950s through the 1970s. This process continues until a crisis point is hit providing political cover to address the underlying problem. In the case of excessive government debt, rather than aggressively address spending as Truman did in 1946, the modern course of action is to use the Federal Reserve to maintain low rates as long as possible for the Treasury and wait for improved GDP growth. The relative effectiveness of the political solution, however, is blunted by the crowding out of the private sector by Federal largess. Eventually if relative economic harmony is not restored through growth, the extraordinary programs instigated by the government will become the trigger point for the next crisis.

8 INFLATION- THE DIRTY LITTLE SECRET

On August 14, 2013 on CNBC the PPI Index change for the month of July was released and there was a debate that ensued between commentators Rick Santelli and Steve Liesman[2]. The argument between the two commentators was about whether the government reported inflation numbers were accurate, or "fudged" in some manner. In short, Rick Santelli's viewpoint was that he did not trust the government calculations. Steve Liesman, on the other hand, took the side that unless Rick could produce better numbers, the Inflation index was accurate and should not be questioned.

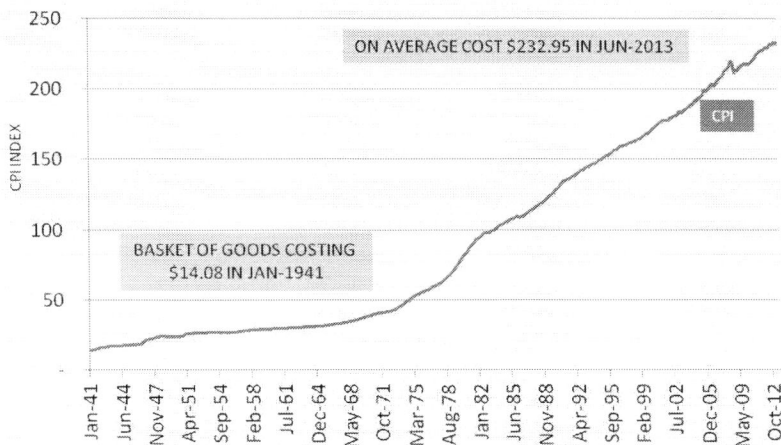

The banter between these two commentators was an interesting exchange.

---

[2] http://www.cnbc.com/id/100962243

Most people I know inherently distrust the U.S. government's reported inflation level. A healthy amount of distrust is probably warranted, but how much? If you review the Consumer Price Index since 1941 you find that a government defined basket of goods which cost $14.08 in January of 1941 increased in cost to $232.95 in June of 2103 or 16.5 times more. The nominal GDP, which includes both real output and inflationary price increases, over the same time period increased 151 times; and, the DOW increased a similar magnitude from 122 to 15,000 or 123 times higher.

Part of the questioning of the inflation statistics may be born out of the potential for the government and the politicians in charge to window dress the statistics to make the economy look better than it really is to the voting public. After all, history is full of examples of governments destroyed when they lost control of their currency. Images come to mind of citizens pushing wheelbarrows full of Zimbabwe dollars to market at the height of the country's hyper-inflation period in 2008. During this time period the official inflation rate was measured in mid-November 2008 at 79,600,000,000% per month.[3] The source of the inflation was a combination of excessive money printing by the country's government to finance involvement in the Second Congo War and corruption of government officials. There was a complete loss in faith in the value of the currency relative to the country's economic output. The Zimbabwe government abandoned the currency in 2009 and began using the U.S. Dollar as its primary currency.

Cost of Living Relative Reality

Luckily for the American people, although the country has experienced its share of wars funded through rapid currency expansion, hyper-inflation, as Zimbabwe experienced in 2008, is not likely. Notable periods in history like WWII, the Vietnam War and Iraq Wars I and II all exhibited increased levels of inflation. These time periods witnessed government actions taken that tested the "faith" in the value of the currency, but the test was passed. Faith in the currency is very important in the robustness of the general economy. Maintaining faith, therefore, requires that the reported inflation statistics by the government be considered accurate.

In terms of the recorded inflation level by the Bureau of Labor and Statistics (BLS), inflation during 2013 when this book was being researched and written was a benign increase of 1.8% year over year in the month of June. This was

---

[3] http://object.cato.org/sites/cato.org/files/serials/files/cato-journal/2009/5/cj29n2-8.pdf

at a time when the Federal Reserve was taking unprecedented actions in the open market by expanding the level of assets it held on its balance sheet from $2T in 2009 to $3.4T by mid 2013, with a projected asset level of $4T by the beginning of 2014. This quantitative easing policy combined with low interest rates on reserves of near 0% as measured by the Fed Funds rate led many at the time to proclaim that inflation was unavoidable. The fact that the BLS was not reporting increases in the consumer price level had to be a result of faulty accounting, or "fudging of the numbers" to use the perspective taken by Rick Santelli.

To get a better view on why the distrust of the government inflation statistics is so pervasive, I decided to take a look at the cost of goods that people are very familiar with, and trace their ascent since WWII. These real life numbers could then be aligned with the index reported by the BLS. The result of this data which is shown in the graph below goes a long way in supporting the rationale in the argument that the government inherently understates what most people would expect as a fair representation of the economic rate of inflation.

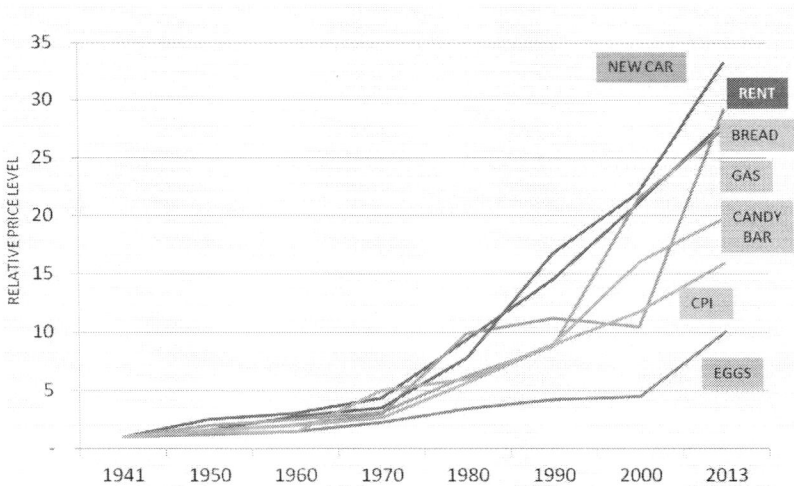

The data is by no means as comprehensive as all of the data tracked by the Bureau. However, the average person spends a very high proportion of what he or she earns on housing, auto transportation and eating. If these expenses represent over 80% of a household budget, the data can easily explain the perception that inflation is much higher than the CPI index reports. For the majority of items an average citizen must purchase in order to live, the cost increased over 20 fold in relative value from 1941 to 2013, with the big ticket items such as rent, auto and gas for transportation showing increases closer to 30 times. The CPI index increase only 15.9 times over the same period of time.

	1941	1950	1960	1970	1980	1990	2000	2013
Monthly Rent	$ 32 $	80 $	98 $	140 $	300 $	465 $	675 $	900
Gallon of Gas	$ 0.12 $	0.19 $	0.25 $	0.36 $	1.19 $	1.34 $	1.26 $	3.50
Average New Car	$ 925 $	1,500 $	2,600 $	3,270 $	7,200 $	15,472 $	20,355 $	30,784
Eggs per Dozen	$ 0.20 $	0.24 $	0.30 $	0.45 $	0.69 $	0.85 $	0.89 $	2.00
Loaf of Bread	$ 0.08 $	0.16 $	0.20 $	0.25 $	0.50 $	0.70 $	1.72 $	2.20
Hershey Bar 1.55oz	$ 0.05 $	0.07 $	0.07 $	0.25 $	0.30 $	0.45 $	0.80 $	0.99
CPI INDEX (June)	14.63	23.88	29.61	38.80	82.50	129.90	172.20	232.94

The usual counter argument by the government is that their statistics assume substitution. This means that if an alternative good or service is available in the economy considered "equal" in relative value, then it can be substituted to arrive at the reported rate of inflation. This subjective comparison framework leaves room for the government to push a more lenient view of price level increases than what most people might expect when reviewing their actual cost of living. The information I have provided in this analysis would not constitute as viable evidence that the government CPI index is understated. However, it does explain why so many people distrust the statistic. Luckily for the U.S., the level of inflation experienced is not anywhere near the magnitude of the problem created in Zimbabwe in 2008.

Price Levels – Relative Upward Bias Generally Assumed

Are you like most people and expect that prices of goods and service will rise in the future? The old adage, "there are two only two things certain in life, death and taxes," probably needs to include a third component – inflation. In general the population has relented to the governing process and accepted that economic policies will result in inflation. Milton Friedman has many famous quotations born out of the 70s stagflation decade in American history, and one that is very telling is:

"Inflation is the one form of taxation that can be imposed without legislation." – Milton Friedman

When you think about the power and responsibilities vested in the highest ranking elected officials in government, one of the most important is the preservation and safeguarding of the value of a country's currency. It becomes a scorecard for President's on which their electability becomes based. The dismal record of Jimmy Carter on this score very much contributed to his inability to be elected for a second term in 1980. The reason that President Carter was so damaged by rampant consumer price inflation is linked to the wit underlying Friedman's piercing quote. The responsibility for keeping the inflation rate under control within the U.S. economy is held in the part of government that oversees the currency – the Executive Branch through the U.S. Treasury. Although not entirely true that the Executive branch of the U.S. government can print money without legislation, it certainly is true that the system in place does not require any new laws for the monetary base to be expanded. In fact, money can be minted at the bequest of the U.S. Treasury Secretary 31 U.S.C. 5112(k) as originally enacted by Public Law 104-208 in 1996:

"The Secretary may mint and issue bullion and proof platinum coins in accordance with such specifications, designs, varieties, quantities, denominations, and inscriptions as the Secretary, in the Secretary's discretion, may prescribe from time to time."

Of course implementing an outright devaluation of the U.S. currency through this action without consensus of the legislative branch is not a likely event currently in the U.S. political system. The idea of minting a $ Trillion coin was debated in the media in the 2011 debt-ceiling struggle as a way for the Executive branch to by-pass Congress in funding government programs. The result was that the deadlocked Congress eventually approved a debt-ceiling increase so that the government could fund programs through increased borrowing. After 1980, funding government operations through debt was the more prevalent option chosen. As will be shown, government borrowing rather than straight taxation from 1980 through 2013 was directly correlated with lower recorded inflation in the general economy. Inflation levels would have been much higher after 2011 if the country had actually minted a Trillion dollar coin to finance government spending rather than increasing the National Debt. Fresh new money would be placed directly into the monetary system without an off-setting withdrawal. This would directly tax the relative value of all assets in the economy, as implied in the Milton Friedman quip, by making all assets proportionally less valuable after the money was minted. Within this conceptual framework lies the essence of how the government becomes the underlying culprit in the bulk of inflation experienced in the economy.

Inflation Root Cause

One of the more challenging aspects of developing the Theory of Financial

Relativity was ascertaining the root cause of inflation. Inflation, in itself, is embedded in the core of Financial Relativity. The constant dollar GDP at the nucleus of the Theory is composed of both real growth and an inflation. The aggregation of both through time creates the measure of nominal GDP which is highly correlated to the value of major U.S. Stock indexes and other assets that derive their value in relation to risk assets like stocks. Inflation as a measure is tracked by the government in several statistical formats, the most common of which is the Consumer Price Index (CPI). So, tracking inflation that occurred in the 70 years of history covered in the book research was not a problem. The real question which investors need answered in order to make better decisions is why inflation occurs in the first place. The result of this quest for understanding provides one of the more interesting findings buried in the data.

A common definition of economic inflation is "too much money chasing too few goods." The simple concept quickly illustrates that if too much money is printed by the government relative to the country's output of goods and services, inflation results.

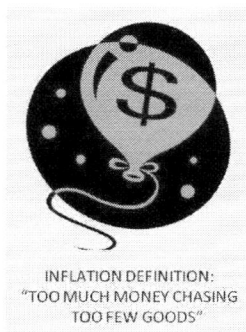

INFLATION DEFINITION:
"TOO MUCH MONEY CHASING
TOO FEW GOODS"

Milton Friedman is known for saying that *"Inflation is always and everywhere a monetary phenomenon in the sense that it is and can be produced only by a more rapid increase in the quantity of money than in output."* Because inflation is created when the level of money in the economy is not supported by economic output, many investors track the growth of the U.S. money supply to project the level of inflation pressure building in the economy. This data is often useful, and M2 growth does exhibit the tendency of higher growth preceding upticks in consumer price levels. Fundamentally, excessive growth in the money supply is the core of why inflation is created. However, money growth is a symptom, not the cause -someone, or some policy had to initiate the change in the money supply.

The perplexing aspect of the simple inflation definition is the difficulty in understanding whether excess money is actually being created in the economy. The money supply must expand if the general measure of economic output is going to expand - mathematically the case otherwise deflation will take hold. The Federal Reserve is mandated to maintain the stability of the U.S. monetary system which has evolved to mean maintaining a target inflation rate of 2% to 2.5% per year. The FOMC must have a good idea of the optimal growth rate in the money supply that will produce low rates of inflation, and their policy actions through time typically keep the money supply growth rate in check. In the 1970s interest rate targeting rather than money supply growth was the general policy, and the result was more rampant price inflation in the U.S. economy.

The symptoms of high price level changes abounded in the 1970s. The prices of consumer goods jumped substantially. A gallon of gas that cost $.36 in 1970 cost

SYMPTOMS:
• HIGHER PRICE LEVELS
• RISING INTEREST RATES
• HIGHER GOLD PRICES

$1.19 in 1980. A car that cost $3,270 in 1970 more than doubled to $7,200 in 1980. And a loaf of bread doubled in price from $.25 to $.50 in the time period.

The yardstick of Financial Relativity responded to the system being awry. Interest rates increased to very high levels not experienced before in the post-Depression Era. The 10 year T-Note was at a decade low of 5.8% in 1971. By March of 1980 the rate reached 12.75%, 695 basis points higher. Even though nominal GDP grew during the decade, it was primarily fueled by inflation. The stock market remained locked in a trading range. The DOW in March or 1970 closed the month at 772. In March of 1980 the DOW stood at 786. The market was not fooled by the deception of higher inflation laden output measures. Higher interest rates were the financial system's way of returning market values to relative reality.

Gold was the one asset that responded positively to the rise in inflation during the time period. Unlike other assets dependent upon dollars to derive value, gold traded as a currency relative to the supply of dollars available. As a result, an ounce of gold which was trading at $35 in 1970 rose to over $600 in 1980, a 17 fold increase. As a relative reaction to the inflationary illness in the U.S. economy at the time, the price of gold from a historical perspective overshot in value. In years subsequent to 1980, the value re-traced to a $300-400 trading range, not to test and break through the $600 range again until April 2006.

Inflation Inflection Point - 1980

What changed in 1980? Some may point to the election of Ronald Reagan.

From a Presidential leadership standpoint, and the fact that he was elected with a mandate to take steps to remedy the inflation ridden economy, Reagan's election was a definite contributing factor. But more precisely, history points to a specific act of legislation know as the *Depository Institutions Deregulation and Monetary Control Act of 1980.*

The Monetary Control Act had three primary objectives - to facilitate the implementation of monetary policy, to provide for the gradual elimination of all limitations on the rates of interest payable on deposits and accounts, and to authorize interest-bearing transaction accounts. One of the major highlights of the Monetary Control Act was the deregulation of interest rates paid by banks. It also opened the Fed discount window and extended reserve requirements to all domestic banks. These actions had the economic effect of allowing interest rates to float with market demand, thereby putting a market generated force in place to dampen the excessive growth in the money supply. The market suddenly had a greater say, through interest rates, in the value of government spending. Historically, the Federal Reserve ceased trying to repress interest rates on Treasuries at low levels beginning in 1981, instead turning to the growth in money supply as the more important regulator of monetary health in the U.S. economy.

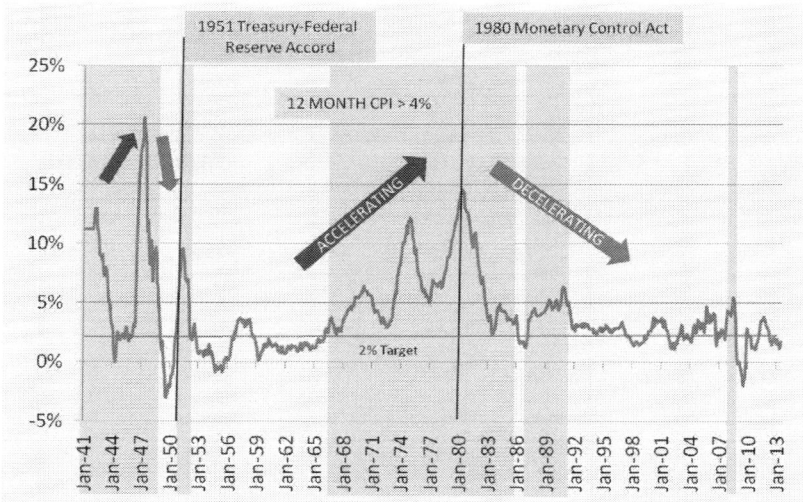

1970s Inflation Contained – Deflation Surfaces in 2000s

The deregulation of interest rates, which allowed free market forces to bid up or down the level of interest rates in the economy in response to inflation expectations, is considered to be one of the important ways that inflation was eventually contained in the 1970s. Inflation did dramatically decline post 1980 as shown in the graphic above. After 1980 through 2013, there were brief time periods in which the general price level in the economy increased at rates greater than 4%, but by and large since 1992 price levels as measured by the CPI trended toward the 2% level. In fact, after the financial market crash in 2008, price levels actually deflated for a brief period. This was the first instance of deflation since the late 1940s, a special case study in financial history that is addressed in a separate section of this book.

What was going on in the financial system? The general population accepted and even expected inflation to occur, but the statistics were not showing upward pressure on prices post the 2008 crisis. The Federal Reserve throughout 2013 actually made public statements that the rate of inflation was too low. Their policy response was record open market purchases of Treasury securities in a stated attempt to keep the money supply growth level high and avoid deflation. They also continued to keep interest rates paid on bank reserves at record low levels of close to zero percent on the short end of the yield curve. Market interest rates in 2013 were at historically low levels on such instruments as consumer Money Market Accounts (.20%), the Federal Funds rate charged banks for overnight lending (0.00-0.25%), and lending facilities such as home mortgages (5.0% for a 30 year mortgage and even less in some instances). Although these low savings rates were in place for the extended periods after the 2008 crash, and the mortgage rates for a considerable part of the time period, there was no relative uptick in inflationary tendency in the economy through the middle of 2013.

The unprecedented actions taken by the Federal Reserve in 2013 is very likely to be a case study in years to come for policy makers. The extreme policy measures being implemented in concert with constrained government spending growth add a great deal to the understanding of how the National Debt is the fulcrum point for managing inflation in the economy.

Government Expenditure Growth Linkage to Inflation

To get a better understanding of how government expenditures affect the recorded rate of inflation, the growth rate in government expenditures is compared to the rate of change in the CPI index since 1952 in the graph below. The time series shows the progressive upward trend in the growth rate of government spending beginning in the mid-50s and sustained virtually throughout until 1980.

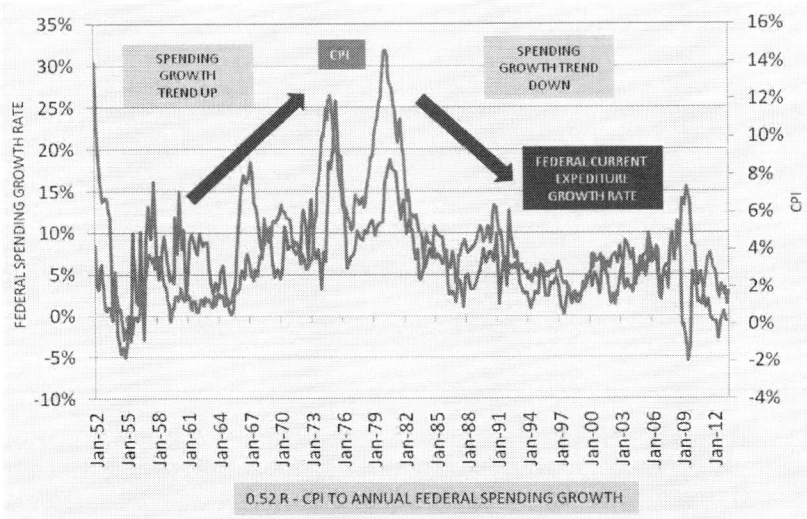

After 1980, although fiscal spending growth continued, it was at a slower pace. The election of Ronald Reagan and the influential change in the budget and spending process at the Federal government is very visible in the statistics. Major upticks in the graph corresponded to the Iraq I and Iraq II Wars and a very discernible peak in 2009 during President Obama's first year. However post 2009 the growth in government spending again slowed. As shown in the table to the right, the growth in government expenditures from 2010 thru mid-2013 was 1.6% annually. This can be traced primarily to the reductions in war time military spending.

GOV'T SPENDING AVERAGE YEARLY GROWTH RATE	
1940s	29.9%
1950s	7.6%
1960s	8.3%
1970s	10.6%
1980s	9.0%
1990s	4.2%
2000s	7.3%
2010-13	1.6%

The CPI correlation to the rate of change in government spending for the time series is .52. The correlation is significant because it clearly shows that points in time that the government spends at a higher rate, increased rates of inflation generally were recorded. This outcome is not unexpected. However, the significance level in the correlation is not as strong as might be expected. This could possibly be due to the erratic government spending growth pattern that results in delayed inflation visibility, and as a result, lower government spending when inflation actually is reported.

Deflationary Influence of the National Debt

The inflation data relative to government spending, however, is imperfect as a predictor of the future inflation level. This pressed my research to a review of other significant relationships between government actions affecting the money supply and the rate of inflation. The more compelling relationship turned out to be an inverse relationship between the relative magnitude of the National Debt and the rate of change in the CPI index.

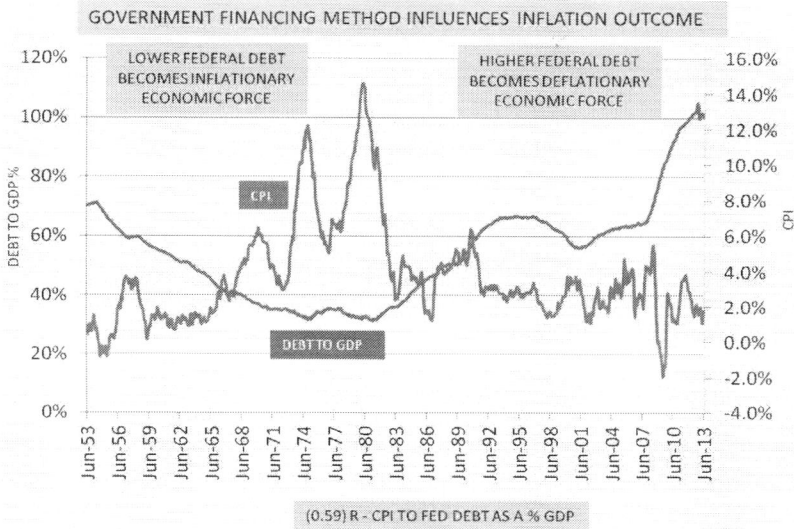

GOVERNMENT FINANCING METHOD INFLUENCES INFLATION OUTCOME

(0.59) R - CPI TO FED DEBT AS A % GDP

As shown in the graph, the more the government borrowed in relation to its national output of goods and services, the lower the level of inflation that was produced from 1953 through 2013. The negative correlation of (.59) means that the method the government used to finance government programs significantly impacted whether the activities were inflationary. It also meant that the outstanding debt balance represented the potential for an inflation explosion if paid off simply by monetization. The reason this phenomenon existed was simple, but also alarming. When the government spends money, it can do so by printing money, by taxing participants in the economy or by borrowing funds from other market participants. In cases where it borrows funds, the act of borrowing withdraws money from the economy at a rate in line with the spending increase. The off-setting actions mean that inflation can be held in check if the government borrowing and spending are in relative equilibrium. However, if it simply prints money to pay off the debt at some future date, then the market imbalance would be exhibited where? – In the term structure of interest rates.

What would Spark a Return of Inflation?

Knowing that government spending tends to increase inflation as the activity leads to excess growth in the money supply, and that borrowing to finance government spending is a countervailing inflation force, the data become much more compelling when the two measures are combined.

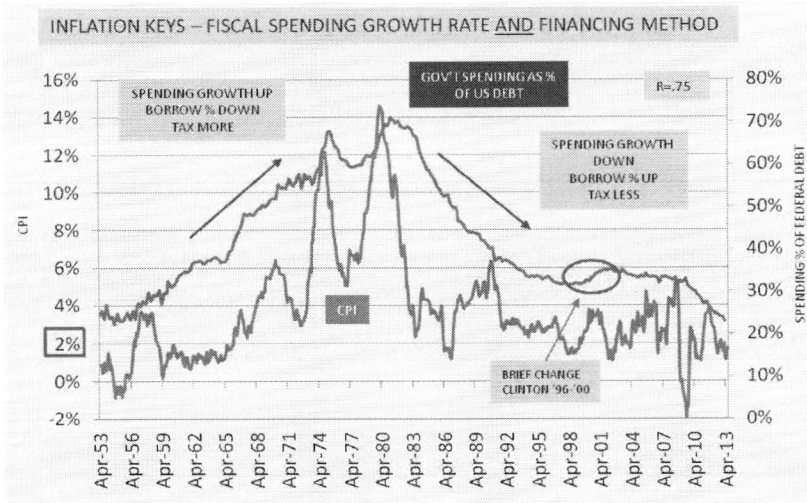

INFLATION KEYS – FISCAL SPENDING GROWTH RATE AND FINANCING METHOD

The data in the chart above shows the total inflation level experienced through time is a function of how fast the government spends money and how much of the spending is borrowed. During the 1960s and 1970s, government spending increased at much higher rates than it did from 1980 through 2013. During the 60s and 70s, however, the source of the money to fund the expenditures was either taxes, or simple monetization of the spending levels. The outstanding federal debt level did increase during the time period in absolute levels; however, on a relative basis to the national GDP, the debt was declining. Combine lower relative borrowing of funds to reduce the supply of money in the economy with more rapid rates of growth in government spending and, voila, inflation is sparked and can run progressively out of control.

Contrast the 1970s situation with what was experienced in the economy post 1980, and more immediately in the 2013 time frame. In 1980, there was a government policy directional change which amounted to taxing less and borrowing more. At the same time there was a downtick in the overall rate of change in government spending growth. After years of this policy being in place, the net result was a steady decline in the inflation level in the U.S.

economy. The surmounting impact of the growing debt load became a deflationary force on the economy.

Reversing the deflationary force is within the power of the policy makers; however, it appears the path is somewhat politically risky. The path involves actions similar to what happened in the 1960s and 70s which caused the debt outstanding to be monetized. What the data show is that the more federal spending that happens without corresponding increases in government borrowing or taxation, the greater the likelihood that inflation will take off. In 2013, the market was on the cusp of creating a higher level of inflation, but it was not germinating. The primary missing component was government spending, which was growing at very low rates. If government spending grows substantially in the wake of extraordinary Federal Reserve easy money actions, inflation in the relative financial universe would most definitely return into the U.S. market with a vengeance. Fears of this scenario may not be far out of the realm of possibilities considering the growth in entitlement spending that the government is currently on the hook to provide a burgeoning segment of the population. Combine the Affordable Care Act subsidized health plan with Social Security for retiring baby boomers, and federal government expenditures over the next decade could grow at a much more rapid pace than is required to keep inflation under control.

1940s Case Study – Government Induced Inflation and Deflation

In order to gain better insight into how a system works, testing it at the extremes to see how it reacts is always a good idea. I personally learned this cardinal rule in computer programming. Every computer program I have ever written that worked just fine under normal conditions exhibited error conditions when rare events were tested. The same is true for the financial system, although in the case of the market, the testing is done with live rounds of ammunition, not under pristine lab conditions.

A unique extreme "test" case of the U.S. financial system occurred in the 1940s which showed in a very short period of time the cause and effect of changes in the rate of growth in government spending as well as the U.S. National Debt. In the first half of the decade, FDR rapidly expanded the level of government expenditures to finance American efforts in WWII. The growth rate in government spending was over 100% in the years of 1941 and 1942. Spending grew from $9B per year at the beginning of 1941 to a peak of $80B in mid-1945. After the war was won, spending was scaled back dramatically. The government spending was funded largely by issuing U.S. Treasuries. The National Debt grew from $50B to an intermediate peak of $249B over the time period.

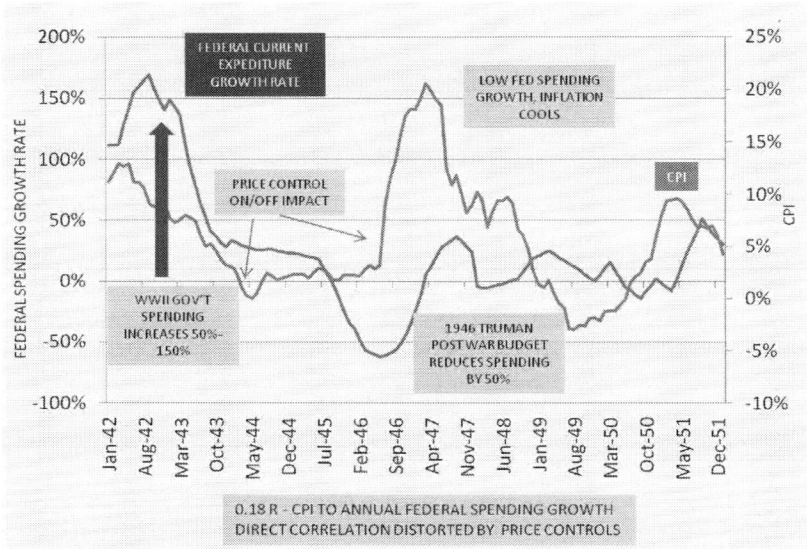

One might expect with massive increases in government spending that inflation would run rapidly out of control. On a relative basis, the government spending rise from $9B to $80B per year is equivalent to the U.S. government in 2013 increasing expenditures from $4T to $34T by 2016. A change of this magnitude is unfathomable in the present day market and political structure. Fears of hyper-inflation being created would be rampant, and probably well founded. Oddly enough, however, as the graph above shows, an inflation explosion during WWII did not happened, at least not immediately. The actual correlation of the change in government spending and inflation over the time period was only .18. However, the reason the correlation is not as strong is attributed to the government actions taken through the time period to arrest the inflationary pressures before the faith in the currency spiraled out of control.

Inflation was high during the period compared with current day standards. The inflation rate shot up over 10% in 1941. However, thereafter, it trended downward and remained in the 0% to 3% range for much of 1943 thru 1945. Historians point to price controls as one of the main contributing factors, and in the price control category one needs to include interest rates on government borrowing. The impact of the very high borrowing level by the

U.S. government and zero bound interest rates controlled through the banking system dampened the ability of consumer prices to increase. Essentially, the government was taking from the economy, through borrowing, as quickly as it was spending, and mandating that the money stay contained in the banking system without multiplying. U.S. citizens at the time patriotically bought war bonds in support of the military conquest. Interest rates during the time period were repressed – rather than rising with the high level of demand for financing by the U.S. government, they actually fell. The equivalent Fed Funds rate during the time was held at a constant .35%. The 5 year T-Note during the time frame fell to a low approaching 1% at the end of 1945. And, the 30 year T-Bond started 1941 at 2.34% and was trading at the same level in June of 1945. The range in movement over the time period was less than 15 basis points. Mathematically the inflation control that was most effective during the time period was the combination of repressive rates which were strictly enforced through the banking system and the government led recycling of money which drained the market of excess monetary liquidity.

In 1946 President Truman implemented a budget which curtailed fiscal spending by 50%, reducing the level of government spending relative to GDP from 36% in 1944 to 14% in 1946. As a reference, government spending relative to GDP for 72 years since 1941 averaged 20.5%.

> **WWII ERA GOVERNMENT EXPENDITURE SUMMARY**
> • In 1941 fiscal spending doubled from $9B TO $18B. GDP was $140B.
> • In 1942 spending increased from $18B to $43B.
> • Spending peaked at $80B in 1945. GDP was $220B.
> • At the peak, fiscal spending was 36% of GDP.
> • The 1946 Truman Budget cut spending to $33B. GDP remained at $235B.
> • The 1946 Budget was 14% OF GDP. Average from 1941-2013 was 20.5%.

The impact on the U.S. economy from the Truman Budget was instructive because just as the rapid increase in government spending the previous 5 years was an extreme hit to the economic system, so too was the rapid reversal. The Truman Budget reduced the level of current government expenditures from $80B per year run rate throughout 1940 to $30B in 1946. This was a remarkable reduction in economic stimulus during a one year period. However, even though the reduction was very large, it was still 3.5 times higher than the $9B in government spending in 1941. On a relative basis, the financial system remained in a state much more highly dependent on government spending than when it started the decade. The government spending influence would become a more permanent fixture in the U.S.

economy in the years that followed.

The effect on the CPI index of the government spending change was a whipsaw reaction. In 1946 the inflation level sky-rocketed. Historians point to the removal of war-time price controls as the primary contributor. But there was another important reversal that investors should be aware of –the borrowing rate of the federal government changed dramatically. The directional change in spending was accompanied by a reversal in the borrowing level of the U.S. government relative to GDP. At the peak of government spending in WWII, the debt to GDP level rose to over 100%, peaking in May of 1946 at 122% and an absolute level to $250B. The debt level of the government was held around $250B until 1950 when it began to slowly increase again. When the debt level began to reverse in 1946 and the price controls were removed, inflation soared for one year. The recorded inflation level peaked at 20.6% year over year increase in March of 1947.

The action to stop borrowing, but continue government spending at relatively high levels relative to pre-war levels could have only one impact – price levels had to adjust upward to reflect the new continuous level of on-going government spending relative to the national output that was not being borrowed. Once the dramatic spike upward happened, however, the inflation level cooled quickly. In fact, the Truman Budget with its austerity measures redirecting spending to peacetime country needs quickly dropped the inflation level to less than 5% by the end of 1948, and then eventually caused deflation in 1949. In a span of 4 years, the government was able to adjust its spending and borrowing level which turned a near hyper-inflation scenario into a deflationary economy. The money in the economy relative to the country's growth over the 4 years was no longer excessive on a relative basis.

To arrest the deflationary tendency, the government began to utilize deficit spending in 1950. They began to spend more relative to the country's GDP while keeping the level of the National Debt growing at a slower pace so that it would not extinguish the impact of newly created money entering the economy. By 1951, deflation turned into inflation again. The pumping up of fiscal spending until inflation ignited became the model for government economic policy for years after 1950. The policy tendency would dead-end in the 1970s when the debt to GDP reached extremely low levels, and government spending growth by contrast reached relatively high levels.

In 2013, on a relative basis the government is at a similar cross-road as the late 1940s, albeit with far meeker GDP growth prospects due to an aging workforce and global competition. But, nonetheless, the relative choice to keep the economy from moving into a deflationary spiral will require a relatively higher degree of spending relative to the pace of National Debt accumulation. The pace of growth in government spending was hotly debated in 2013. Integral in the debates is the issue of raising the country's debt ceiling. Within the context of the Theory of Financial Relativity, the debt ceiling debate is about both the future of GDP growth and inflation. Higher debt levels in the U.S. beyond 70% of GDP are historically a negative force of GDP growth; however, paying down the debt will require much higher real growth in the economy, or higher taxation, which is more prone to cause inflation. A more significant problem concerns whether the economy will experience inflationary or deflationary growth due to the on-going "entitlement programs" the government is on the hook to provide. Ironically, if the Conservatives were to get their way and the debt-ceiling did not rise to allow borrowing to pay for the expenditure increases, the outcome is more likely to be inflationary…the opposite of the intention of the party arguing for the debt-ceiling constraint. The old adage seems to be in play in current history for voters and investors alike, "be careful what you ask for, you just might get it."

Lessons Learned about Inflation

To quote Milton Friedman, "*Inflation is always and everywhere a monetary phenomenon.*"

> ### LESSONS ABOUT THE SOURCES OF INFLATION
>
> - Inflation and asset bubbles indicators of financial market imbalances.
> - Through history from WWII through 2013, inflation was highest when increased fiscal spending policies were coordinated with Federal Reserve monetary easing policies.
> - Inflation is highly correlated with Federal Reserve actions which monetize relatively high rates of change in government spending.
> - Government spending financed through borrowing from foreign trading partners and increasing Debt to GDP is highly correlated with a lowering of the rate inflation.
> - Asset bubbles are created when to many U.S. dollars chase too few investments.
> - Asset bubble inflation is highly correlated with a relative increase in the Federal Reserve holdings of U.S. Debt – reflective of an increase in overall financial system leverage.

The Milton Friedman quote is the essence of how inflation is created, and the preceding table is a summary of the lessons to be taken away from the research presented in this chapter. Excess money in the financial system relative to national output of goods and services is required in order to produce recorded consumer price inflation. Money can be created only at the direction of the U.S. government, and therefore government spending, which is the most direct means for money to enter the U.S. economy, is the most correlated variable to the rate of change in inflation through time.

Monetary induce inflation can be delayed or subdued by the way that the government finances fiscal spending. If the government taxes and spends and lowers the relative level of debt, higher spending levels affect inflation much more directly and rapidly. Monetization of government spending is a more straight forward form of money creation which triggers market participants to raise price levels. Alternatively, if the government borrows a greater portion of its spending increases, the inflationary impact, empirically substantiated by 33 years of data after 1980, is either delayed or subdued.

The actions taken by the government to attempt to control inflation while continuing to increase spending levels are the real intriguing aspect of the financial dilemma the U.S. faced in 2013. Inflation is a negative relative force, and also a component in the nominal GDP measurement. To address inflation, politicians must curtail their own power to play the omnipotent provider for the general population. Constraint is not generally what investors should expect from a politician unless a strong enough countervailing force is evident in the economy. Inflation is a negative force that in 1980 the U.S. government installed an institutional force through Federal Reserve policy to address regardless of the economic pain. However, no one could have imagined that government officials would become perpetually addicted to a financing scheme to store inflationary pressures on the U.S. balance sheet in order to perpetuate a cycle of giveaways and hand-outs.

The countervailing inflationary force from 1980 through 2013 was diminished because the U.S. government increasingly borrowed to finance consumption and ran very high current account deficits. The borrowed funds progressively became reserves on the balance sheets of foreign governments, therefore temporarily extinguishing the consumer price level impact of the higher U.S. money supply. During the timeframe, U.S. foreign policy took advantage of the inclination of third world countries to save rather than spend U.S. dollars. An influx of "relatively" cheap goods into the U.S. market resulted, particularly in technology and other manufactured goods. In other words, the U.S political system simply took the path of least resistance in order to satisfy the consumption demands of the population. It seemed like such a win-win scenario because the act of borrowing and spending and simultaneously reducing the rate of inflation was nirvana.

3rd PRINCIPLE OF FINANCIAL RELATIVITY
Higher levels of U.S. Debt relative to GDP depress real GDP and inflation.

One thing that smart investors know for certain is that when something seems too good to be true, 99% of the time it is bogus. The addictive system of borrowing and spending to perpetuate consumption in the U.S. altered the inflation pattern in the United States most visibly beginning in the 1990s, and becoming more poignant after the year 2000.

This brings me to Guiding Principle #4 of the Theory of Financial Relativity. It incorporates the concept of inflation as being the primary indicator of government excess. The "New World Order" policies instituted with the fall of the Berlin Wall increasingly led the U.S. to finance fiscal spending by borrowing from foreign governments. The irrational behavior in the excessive borrowing by the U.S. government is a perplexing puzzle. *Why on earth would the richest and most powerful country in the world become progressively more indebted to countries that are poorer on a relative basis? Should the wealthy not be the benevolent provider to the less wealthy, rather than the indebted servant?*

In July of 2013 foreigners owned 46.9% of all publicly traded U.S. Debt. The mutated flow of funds over time lowered CPI recorded inflation in the U.S., as the foreign governments dumped excess domestic produced goods on the U.S. economy in order to raise U.S. dollars. However, the pent-up inflationary impact of the monetary base expansion to support the borrowing showed up in other parts of financial system. As a consequence, asset bubbles began to grow and become more pronounced.

4th PRINCIPLE OF FINANCIAL RELATIVITY
Inflation and asset bubbles are financial market imbalances always and everywhere linked to government fiscal policy excesses.

Asset bubbles are always and everywhere a monetary phenomenon, just like CPI inflation. The creation of a true asset bubble can always be linked to government excess.

9 THE FINANCIAL RELATIVITY REGULATOR

The Federal Reserve Bank is an odd duck – a private bank, with government appointed Board Members. Most people assume the Fed is an arm of the government, but it is instead a quasi-government institution that is both private and public. It was created by the Federal Reserve Act of 1913 during Woodrow Wilson's presidency. The impetus for the creation of the Fed is attributed to increasing risk in the U.S. banking system as industrialization began to create concentrations of money and power in the hands of a few individuals, namely Wall Street magnates like J.P. Morgan and John D. Rockefeller. The "money trust," as the Wall Street financiers became known, symbolized the source of financial panics and bank system failures which were increasing at the time. During 1907, there was a severe panic in the banking system that drove public demand for reform. The following year, Congress enacted the Aldrich-Vreeland Act, which provided for an emergency currency and established a commission chaired by Senate Republican leader Nelson Aldrich to study and propose legislation to reform the system.

The result of the Aldrich led committee was a proposal to create a system called the National Reserve Association in 1908, which would be dominated by the private banking industry. It was founded on the concept of a centralized banking model similar to Germany at the time, but as an association of the banks, not dominated by the government. The proposal gained very little public support because of the growing discontent and suspicion that the country was being run and controlled by a few wealthy industrialists, and the Association as proposed would codify what many believed to be true.

As public demand for reform continued to rise, in 1910 Aldrich and executives representing the banks of J.P. Morgan, Rockefeller, and Kuhn, Loeb & Co., secluded themselves for ten days at Jekyll Island, Georgia. The meeting and its purpose was secretive at the time out of fears that the purpose of the meeting, to create a specific plan to gain acceptance of the National Reserve Association proposed by Aldrich, would have no chance of passage in Congress if the group involved in putting together the specifics of the proposed new legislation was made public.

The plan, which was known as the Aldrich Plan, called for the creation of a central bank, the National Reserve Association, with capital of at least $100 million and with 15 branches in various locations in the United States. The branches were to be controlled by the member banks on the basis of their capitalization. The National Reserve Association would issue currency, based on gold and commercial paper, which would be the liability of the bank, not the federal government. The Association would also carry a portion of member banks' reserves, determine discount reserves, buy and sell on the open market, and hold the deposits of the federal government. The branches and businessmen of each of the 15 districts would elect 30 out of the 39 members of the board of directors of the National Reserve Association.

When the legislation was introduced into Congress in 1911, fireworks erupted. Heated congressional debates took place, and many times it appeared the legislation was dead. Democrats were vehemently opposed to the plan because it did not break up the power of the "money trust." It was not until Virginia Rep. Carter Glass presented a bill to President-elect Wilson to amend the Aldrich Plan that the deadlock was broken. The amendment called for a Federal Reserve Board to be appointed by the Executive branch to maintain control over the bankers. The Board provisions in the amendment allowed the legislation to gain momentum for final passage. In December 2013, the Federal Reserve Act was passed, primarily with Democrat support. Even though Republicans voted overwhelmingly against the legislation, virtually all of the Aldrich Plan was intact on final passage.

"In its final form, the Federal Reserve Act represented a compromise among three political groups. Most Republicans (and the Wall Street bankers) favored the Aldrich Plan that came out of Jekyll Island. Progressive Democrats demanded a reserve system and currency supply owned and controlled by the Government in order to counter the "money trust" and destroy the existing concentration of credit resources in Wall Street. Conservative Democrats proposed a decentralized reserve system, owned and controlled privately, but free of Wall

Street domination. No group got exactly what it wanted. But the Aldrich plan more closely represented the compromise position between the two Democrat extremes, and it was closest to the final legislation passed." - American Institute of Economic Research Paper

How the Federal Reserve Creates Money

The Federal Reserve Act of 1913 established the Federal Reserve as the institution with the supreme authority to manage the most important element in the nation's financial system – the money supply. The primary means used by the institution to carry out the task of maintaining the stability of the U.S. money supply can be broken down into three categories. The Fed was given the sole responsibility of issuing and maintaining the appropriate level of the country's currency. They were also entrusted with the power to set a uniform interest rate which would be charged across the banking system on reserves; and lastly, they were charged with the ability to buy and sell assets on the open market in order to either withdraw or put into circulation reserves within the financial system.

FEDERAL RESERVE TOOLS:
• CURRENCY ISSUANCE
• UNIFORM RESERVE RATE
• OPEN MARKET OPERATIONS

"FED SUPPLIES FINANCIAL GRAVITY"

Currency Issuance

The issuance of hard currency into the market is the most basic way that the Federal Reserve can create money. It is not, however, a policy that is typically used to exert change on the money supply. The supply of currency into the financial system is based on the ongoing determination of the necessary demand for currency throughout the banking system. It varies throughout the year, and money enters circulation and is withdrawn on a regular basis. The U.S. Mint designs and manufactures coins for distribution to Federal Reserve Banks. The Board of Governors places orders with the Mint based on the supply and demand needs of their unique districts.

The process of minting money is under the authority of the U.S. Treasury, and a loophole exists in the legislated relationship between the U.S. Treasury and the Federal Reserve that allow for the Treasury to mint coins and place them in the Federal Reserve account without the Fed actually requesting the currency. An action of this nature would constitute a true "printing of money" and would ultimately happen in the unique instance in which the Executive branch of government, led by the President, sought to override the actions of the Federal Reserve concerning the level of the money supply. This issue was raised in the debt ceiling debates in Congress in 2011 with the idea of the U.S. Treasury minting a $1 trillion dollar coin, which would be deposited at the Fed and used to pay off the U.S. National Debt. Such an action would have the impact of expanding the U.S. money supply dramatically, overnight. It would essentially constitute an inflationary across the board currency devaluation. The Trillion dollar coin concept was not chosen as a politically acceptable path for dealing with the country's debt problem in 2011.

The Federal Reserve also oversees what constitutes "legal tender" within the U.S. monetary system. The U.S. currently has a fiat-based currency system similar to many other countries in the world today. For centuries, physical commodities, most commonly silver or gold, served as money. Later, when paper money and checkable deposits were introduced, they were convertible into commodity money. The U.S. abandoned the convertibility of money into a commodity on August 15, 1971. On that day, President Richard M. Nixon signed legislation discontinuing the conversion of U.S. dollars into gold at $35 per ounce. This officially made monies of the United States, and other countries which similarly abandoned gold as legal tender, into fiat money — money that national monetary authorities have the power to issue without legal constraints.

Uniform Reserve Interest Rates

The discount rate is the interest rate set by the Federal Reserve and charged to commercial banks and other depository institutions on loans they receive from their regional Federal Reserve Bank's lending facility--the discount window. The Fed Funds rate is a target rate established by the Federal Open Market Committee (FOMC). The distinction between the two rates is subtle, but important. The discount rate is an actual rate on loans made directly to banks if they need a loan from the Federal Reserve. The Fed Funds rate is an interest rate the Fed sets as the official rate target on overnight lending between banks. In the case of the Fed Funds rate, the Fed is not directly involved in the loan. The Fed must use open market operations to achieve and control the level of interest rates at the target level.

The primary mechanism that the Federal Reserve Bank uses to maintain control of interest rates is by requiring depository institutions (commercial banks and other financial institutions) to hold as reserves a fraction of its deposit liabilities, as well as capital requirements based on the riskiness of the loans that it makes in the market. At the direction of the Fed, or through legislated capital requirements by Congress, banking reserves either expand or contract. When the Federal Reserve policy is accommodative, reserves are encouraged to increase and the result is an expansion in the money supply. The expansion is a function of a bank making loans up to the amount of its excess reserves, creating an equal amount of deposits at another institution. This multiplier effect of deposit creation through lending is how money is created across the financial system. As each bank lends and creates a deposit, it loses reserves to other banks, which use them to increase their loans and thus create new deposits, until all excess reserves are used up.

The reverse of the multiplier effect occurs when the Federal Reserve policy is considered non-accommodative. In these instances, reserves across the banking system are lowered, thereby causing a reversal in the multiplier effect and shrinkage in the money supply.

In modern history post WWII, managing the level of the Fed Funds rate through open market management of bank reserve levels has been the tool most used by the Federal Reserve to manage the growth of the money supply. The Fed periodically makes adjustments in the Fed Funds target through public announcements after the FOMC meets at set times during the calendar year and votes on the direction of open market operations. Although the Fed does not directly transact in the Fed funds market, when the Federal Reserve specifies a higher or lower Fed funds rate, it makes this rate decision stick by reducing or increasing the reserve level it provides to the entire financial system. The adjustment in the short-term interest rate influences the term structure of interest rates, ultimately impacting the lending level in the financial system and correspondingly the level of the money supply.

Open Market Operations

The target interest rate on overnight reserves is not always sufficient in managing the money supply in the manner the Federal Reserve might intend. Witness the financial market situation since 2009. The overnight lending target was dropped to 0% in 2009, and was still at that level as of the writing of this book in 2013. However, the growth in the money supply as measured by M2 did not dramatically increase. From 2009 until mid-2013 the annual rate of increase averaged only 5.7%.

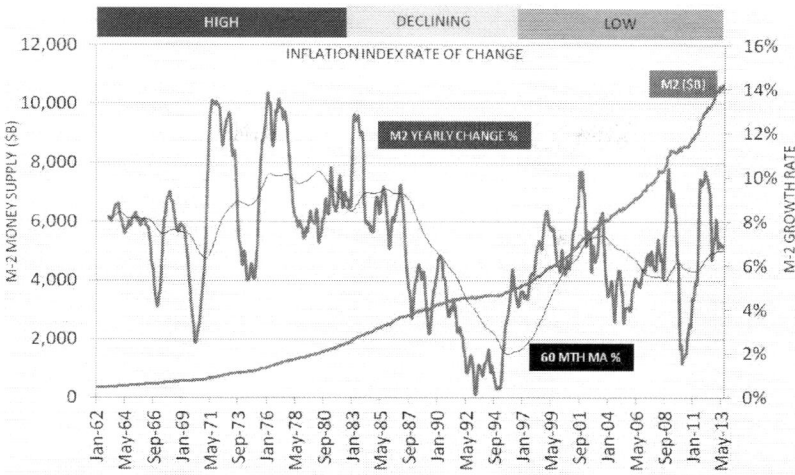

The lack of money supply expansion, even given the extraordinary low interest rate levels in the historical period, may be explained in the stringent reserve requirements that were simultaneously imposed on U.S. financial institutions. During the time period, the Dodd-Frank Act was signed into law by President Obama in 2010. The regulations included in the bill were both onerous and extensive. Direct impact on the money supply was created by tightened capital requirement standards imposed on all lending institutions. In summary, the legislation called for specific and more restrictive floors in capital requirements, and imposed a 15-1 leverage requirement on any institution deemed to be a grave threat to the financial system. The net effect of the regulations was to deter lending, negating the impact of the multiplier effect on monetary expansion, even though rates were being held at such low levels for an extended period. Many loans that the banks made prior to the regulations were suddenly uneconomical given the level of rates and the new capital requirements.

Throughout 2010 to 2013, and likely because the reserve requirements on the private banks became more stringent, the Federal Reserve began to use its third major power in affecting the country's money supply more aggressively – Quantitative Easing. The Fed increases reserves in the system when it performs quantitative easing by buying U.S. Treasury. It has the power to do this simply by electronically writing a check on its own account, and then using the money created to buy Treasuries, Mortgage-Backed Securities, or any asset it deems appropriate in the open market. The seller of the security deposits the funds received from the Fed in a bank, increasing the seller's deposit account. The bank, in turn, deposits the Federal Reserve check at its district Federal Reserve Bank, thus increasing its reserves in the system available to expand the money supply. The opposite sequence occurs when the Federal Reserve sells securities: the purchaser's deposits fall, and, in turn, the reserves in the banking system fall.

The Federal Reserve uses open-market operations to either increase or decrease banking system reserves to encourage lending, and thereby a change in the money supply. Typically it confines its activity to the short-end of the yield curve to affect the Fed Funds rate by buying and selling reserves held by member banks. However, in 2012 and 2013, the Fed began to focus on the level of long-term interest rates to bring those market rates down in an attempt to lower home mortgage lending rates. In so doing, the Fed expanded the scope of its purchase program to a much broader market.

Federal Reserve as Financial Relativity Regulator

With the immense power vested in the Federal Reserve, no wonder it's every move is monitored by the media, the investment community and people across the world. The actions taken by the FOMC on a periodic basis directly impacts the relative value of investment assets through the direct setting of interest rates, the economic growth caused by the increase of lendable reserves in the banking system, and potentially the negative-side effect of inflation that may result from too much money entering the financial system relative to real GDP growth. Keeping a continual check on the policies of the Fed, therefore, is a clear must for investors seeking to manage long-term wealth.

The Fed is a hybrid public-private organization. It serves two masters, the private free market business community as well as the policy desires, good or bad, of the elected government. Because of this dichotomy, the actions taken by the Fed have been anything but consistent through time regarding how it manages the mechanism to create money in the U.S. financial system. In a sense, the policy it pursues is most akin to being a regulator in the financial universe between the desires of Washington, Wall Street and foreign markets. From its position in the multilateral relationship, the Fed is driven to uphold the stability of the money supply as it relates to the registered level of inflation. The modern history accepted target level of inflation is 2%.

The Fed, however, is politically confined to its role as regulator in the system with regard to the cause and effect relationships that result in the financial markets from its actions. The counter-balancing policies of the Fed do result in good and bad financial market outcomes, but private market or government policy actions ultimately are the cause of the good or bad results printed on the GDP growth and inflation scorecard. The Fed's role as custodian of the country's money supply are the reason its actions do not show up as strongly correlated in a direct time relationship with either inflation or GDP growth – although money supply growth is definitely highly correlated with both.

The unique and powerful position of the Fed in the financial market as the "regulator" is the reason for the adage "Don't Fight the Fed." As a result, the timing and impact of Fed policy actions creates important signals of impending change in market valuation.

Successful Fed Relativity Regulation Policy

Open market operations to increase or decrease bank reserves in order to impact the level of interest rates are a normal part of the operation of the Federal Reserve. This activity directly impacts the yardstick of Financial Relativity – interest rates. Monetary policy is used to affect interest rates, usually in order to achieve the Fed's legislated mandate to keep inflation low and foster low unemployment in the country. Because the Fed is such a powerful force in changing the interest rate structure in the financial market, the turning points from "loose" money to "tighter" money or vice-versa become very important times for investors.

Three points in time from 1994 through 2008 when the Fed reversed interest rate policy from accommodative to tightening are shown in the chart on the next page. These points are overlaid with the stock market performance the year before and the year after the increase in interest rates.

The Federal Reserve tightens monetary policy by raising the target Fed Funds rate and simultaneously raising reserve requirements on member institutions. In order for the rate increase to stick, the Fed is usually required to sell assets it holds on its balance sheet (usually U.S. Treasury Securities) at a rate faster than the Treasury is creating public debt. The Fed Funds rate line (black) on the chart shows when the Fed reversed interest rate policy. During the time period the open market action by the Fed is reflected in the quantitative easing (QE) relative measure (blue box). In 1994 and 2004 the data clearly reflect that the Fed had to sell assets in order for the rates to increase. In 1998, oddly the Fed was accumulating assets and rates rose anyway. A very similar phenomenon happened in 2013 and is linked to sales of Treasuries by foreign governments.

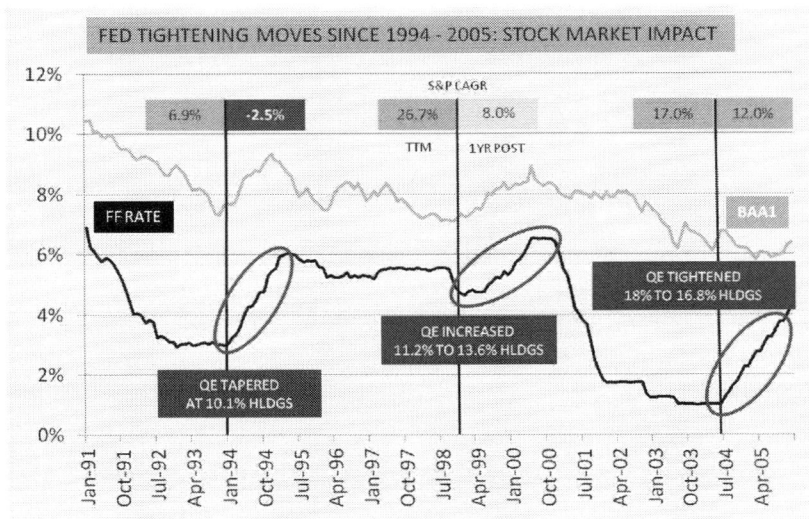

In all three instances in the 1990s and early 2000s when the Fed removed accommodation, not surprisingly, the stock market, as measured by the S&P 500, performed worse the next year. In fact in 1994 the S&P 500 had a down year. However, if you get beyond the 1994 drag on performance, the stock market began to do extremely well from 1996 thru the year 2000. GDP growth in this time period overcame the Fed rate increase; and additionally, long-term rates, primarily the BAA1 which closely correlates with stock market performance began to fall after 1995 even as short-term rate increases peaked. A falling BAA1 rate level is supportive of stock market increases, particularly when the real economy is growing.

The 1999 change in Fed policy was slightly different from 1994. Many investors remember the Greenspan "irrational exuberance" statements in 1996 in reference to the rapid rise in the NASDAQ. But what seems to have been lost in history is the fact that abundant reserves were pumped into the market leading up to the year 2000 to satisfy the market demand for dollar based liquidity, even as the Fed was raising interest rates to tighten monetary policy. The numbers historically reflect the contradiction in Federal Reserve actions, and the market run up in valuation prior to year 2000 is highly correlated to the increase size of the Fed balance sheet in spite of the tightening of interest rates. Subsequent Fed quantitative tightening post the year 2000 can be linked to the un-winding of stock market investment positions, and as history reflects, a substantial market decline.

The reversal of monetary policy in 2004-2005 is generally a good example of when the Fed used quantitative tightening to remove financial system liquidity and simultaneously raised interest rates, and the stock market continued to rise. History reflects that several years afterward in 2008 the economy entered a violent recession, but at the time the policy move worked.

Pre-empting Inflation Prompted Fed Tightening

Each of the turning points in Fed policy had different underlying economic circumstances, and a myriad of variables contributed to the decision to change the rate policy. But five (5) metrics give the breadth of major influencing factors in the policy decision during each instance. The metrics are – the unemployment rate, the rate at which government spending was increasing / (decreasing), the debt to GDP ratio, the inflation rate as measured by CPI, and the nominal GDP growth rate for the year prior to the policy change. In the table below, also included is the GDP growth rate the year after the Fed began increasing the Fed Funds to give a sense of the corresponding change in GDP growth momentum.

PERIOD	UNEMP RATE	GOV'T SPEND	GOV'T DEBT/GDP	CPI	TTM GDP	PERIOD GDP	DOW/ GDP
JAN-94 JAN-95	6.6%	2.2%	66.3%	2.9%	4.9%	5.6%	.57
JAN-99 JAN-00	4.6%	3.6%	61.3%	2.8%	6.1%	5.9%	1.05 UP
JUL-04 JUL-05	5.5%	6.4%	62.8%	3.1%	7.1%	6.3%	.88 UP

The final variable on the chart is the relative value measure of the DOW divided by nominal GDP. From 1941 until 2013 this measure averaged .765, with a median of .764. A higher ratio means the market is generally more expensive relative to other points in history.

The January 1994 timeframe is one of the best examples of a Federal Reserve removal of accommodation followed by a dramatic increase in stock valuations, even though the first year after the policy move was not particularly good for stocks. At the start of 2013 the Obama administration probably wished they were in a similar position—the good old days of the Clinton years. For readers who wonder where the 6.5% unemployment target originated in the Fed policy statements in 2013, note the unemployment rate at the beginning of 1994. The relative financial metrics in 2013, however, were not analogous to 1994. In particular, in 1994 the stock market was relatively inexpensive, the inflation rate was above target, the debt to GDP was in a comfortable range and GDP growth was increasing. The impetus for stock market growth in 1995 was the spawning of the Internet Age, with secondary support provided by a 400 basis point decline in long-term interest rates from over 11% to 7%. By comparison in 2013 rates were on the upswing and reserve requirements were strict, curtailing the potential for lending led economic growth.

The January 1999 and July 2004 time periods were equally good examples of when the Fed was able to transition away from accommodation while the market propelled higher – low unemployment, GDP momentum and a healthy government financial balance sheet. But history shows that a few years later in each instance the market went into "cardiac arrest." Why?

Others have provided rationales, but the data suggest the biggest contributors were continued aggressive government policies in direct conflict with countervailing forces driven from overseas trading partners. The contradictory policy of open market easing while raising rates in the late 1990s is the first case in point. The liquidity pumped into the market at the time was not needed for general market transactions, and as can be seen, did not increase inflation rapidly even though it was above trend at 2.8%. However, it did cause financial asset value inflation (a.k.a. asset bubble) as the stock market reached a relative valuation of 1.05 times GDP in early 1999 and continued to rise. A brief spike in oil prices was a signal of germinating foreign trade tension. The stock market was relatively overvalued, and when the Fed lowered the size of its balance sheet relative to the economy post 2000 stocks went into decline.

The July 2004 to July 2005 time frame is well documented as a period preceding the use of high leverage and excessive speculation in the U.S. residential housing market. It was also a period of war, and government spending was high during the period as a result. Although recorded CPI never got out of control as it did in the 1960s and 1970s or the early 1940s during WWII, the numbers reflect a situation in which the Federal Reserve was monetizing a significant portion of the increase in government spending, which virtually always turns into CPI led inflation. Ultimately the Fed had to respond to the upward pressure placed on the CPI index by tightening even more leading into 2006 – Ben Bernanke's first year as Fed chairman. It turns out that the blunt instrument of monetary policy worked its way through the economy slowly. The quantitative tightening of the Fed balance sheet not only eventually broke the spike up in oil prices in 2007 and 2008, it also caused a severe liquidity crisis in the banking system. The ultimate casualty defining the crisis was the bankruptcy of Lehman Brothers in September of 2008.

The points in time when the Fed choose to "lean into the wind" and raise the target Fed Funds rate in modern history have one very important variable in common – the level and direction movement upward in the CPI index. In all three scenarios, 1994, 1999 and 2004, inflation was approaching 3% and the specter of increasing inflation was viewed as growing. Preempting inflation, usually with a push from disgruntled overseas oil markets, is the most common scenario which leads to tightening of Fed policy.

Dealing with the Devil –Too much Accommodation

The most visible indicator that Fed policy is accommodative and intended to promote money supply growth is a low Fed Funds target rate. At certain points in history, the Fed has become very aggressive with its easing policy. During these time periods, the actual rate of interest paid on reserves by the banking industry, and subsequently passed through on savings accounts to consumers, was below the recorded rate of inflation in the economy. In these scenarios, which are shaded in the graph below, holders of cash lost purchasing power every minute they held dollars.

PERIODS IN HISTORY OF NEGATIVE REAL INTEREST RATES

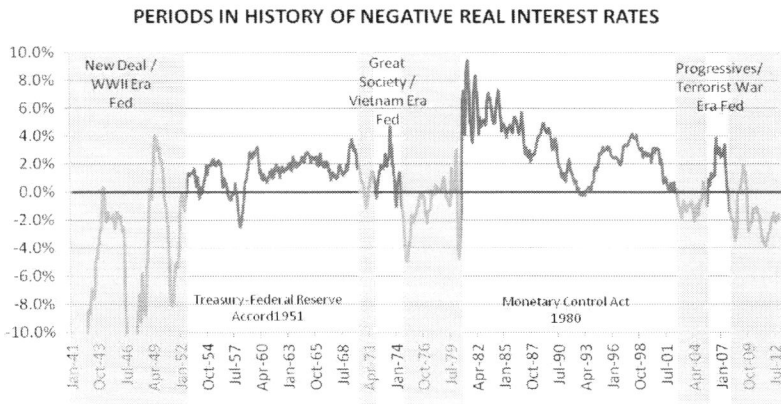

The use of the negative real interest rate policy historically has coincided with periods of conflict and the transition period from war to peacetime. As shown in the graphic above, the three points in time when the Federal Reserve used the policy were during and after WWII, the Vietnam War, and the Iraq War and War on Terrorism Era. However, war is not the only aspect of these tumultuous timeframes. The periods also coincide with major new government domestic spending initiatives. These include the FDR New Deal programs implemented in the 1940s; the Great Society programs instituted in the 1960s during Lyndon Johnson presidency; and the Affordable Care Act created by the Obama administration.

During these three times periods, the hallmark reason that rates were kept low was political pressure that drove Federal Reserve policy to align with the desires of the political party in charge, and the fiscal policy being implemented. This close alignment worked for the public good in the case of the 1940s; however, the 1960s and 1970s were a financial disaster. The jury is still out on the attempt to coordinate monetary and fiscal policy post the 2008 financial crisis.

In order to keep interest rates low during these time periods, the Fed increased the level of reserves in the banking system. They did this through open market purchases of Treasury securities. In the 1940s, the Treasury fixed the rate of interest it was willing to pay on the debt, and the Fed was responsible for seeing that the debt was absorbed by the banking system. For instance, the Fed purchased 10% of the National Debt during the war period of 1941. In doing so, it opened up a tranche of reserves across the entire Federal Reserve banking system which could be used for lending. At the behest of the U.S. Treasury, the new reserves were used to make loans to the U.S. government. Using the money multiplier, the 10% purchase by the Fed resulted in enough reserves across the banks to fulfill the government borrowing needs.

This process of successfully financing fiscal spending is known as "monetizing the government debt," and if the process is done at an abnormal level relative to other market assets and the growth rate of the economy, the Fed is dealing with the devil in terms of the likelihood that inflation will result. In the 1940s and again in the 1960s-70s, the Fed monetization of the U.S. Debt was disproportionately large, and the result flowed through as high inflation. In the 1940s, as the graph below shows, it was the impact of the substantial reserve level increase from 4% to over 10% in Fed monetization that created a massive liquidity increase throughout the banking system. Once the 10% level was reached and stabilized, inflation became a function of how fast government spending increased, which post WWII was curtailed for several years and therefore inflation subsided.

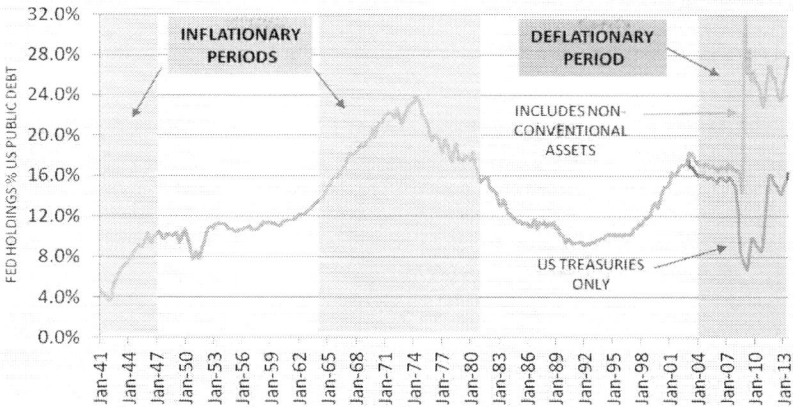

The changing relative rate at which the Fed monetizes government debt is one of the key levers in regulating inflation and deflation – primarily because Treasuries are the risk-free asset most bought and sold by the Fed in open market operations. As a private bank, the Fed can purchase and hold any asset, and its balance sheet composition began to include substantial mortgage-backed securities post the 2008 financial crisis. The excessive purchase of new government debt, or the monetizing of government spending, is the policy action most correlated with creation of consumer price inflation. As the graphic shows, the 10-12% range for Federal Reserve holdings of Treasury debt was typical for the post WWII era in the 1950s. The one instance in 1950 when the Fed attempted to reduce the relative percentage of its holdings of Treasuries resulted in a brief deflationary spiral in the economy. Inflation returned when the Fed resumed purchasing the government debt at a higher relative rate, and government spending increased as well.

The 1960s and 1970s are the poster child of inflation gone awry. Government spending during this time period grew at an above average historical rate, on average 10.6% per annum during the decade of 1970. Why did inflation become such a problem in this period?

The Treasury-Federal Reserve Accord of 1951 freed the Federal Reserve from Treasury control of interest rate levels; however, it retained a co-equal responsibility for management of the National Debt between the two. In fulfilling its debt management responsibility, pressure mounted on the Fed in the early 1960s to make sure the Treasury always received a successful auction at the lowest interest rate possible. During this time, an "even-keel" auction policy began to be followed by the Fed. Based on its debt-management mandate, the Fed would buy securities prior to an auction in order to drive down rates and increase available reserves in the banking system to "accommodate" additional government financing. The auction would be held, and the success of the auction would be determined by how well the rate held up in the market <u>after</u> the debt was distributed. The objective was to make sure the market was on an "even keel" during and after the financing round. This put the Fed increasingly in a political position in which it became unwilling to remove excess reserves once the Treasury issuance was completed. The inability to control the level of reserves in the system as the government borrowed more and more money led to increasingly high levels of inflation during the 1960s.

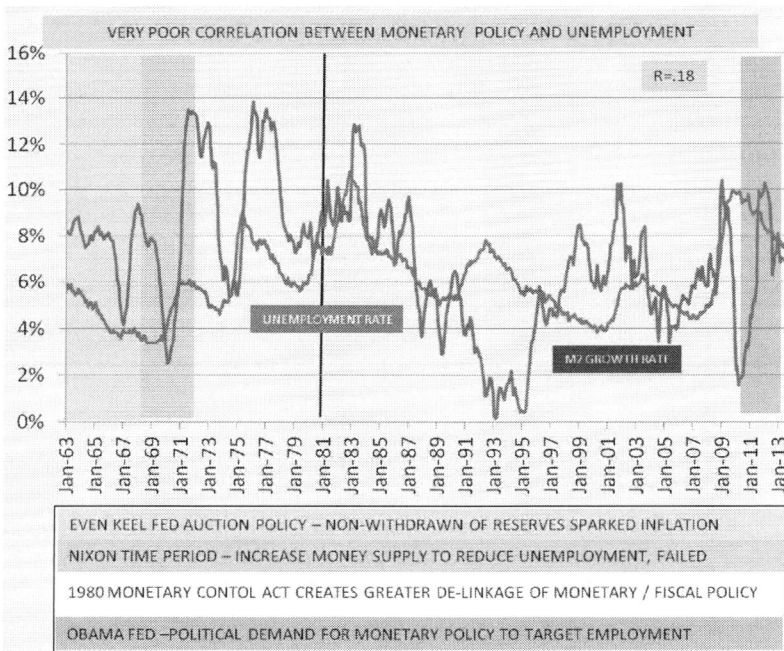

Inflation became an even greater issue when President Nixon entered office in the late 1960s. During this time the academic idea known as the Phillips Curve infiltrated Nixon's administration. The economic concept holds that a trade-off over time exists between unemployment and inflation. The assumption that began to underlie Fed policy at the time was that the government could pursue a policy of trading higher inflation for lower unemployment. This led to pressure on the Fed to coordinate policy and increase money supply growth when unemployment was above the politically acceptable target at the time of 4.5%.

The Nixon approach was an utter failure. In 1972 not only did unemployment not fall as shown in the preceding graph, it increased from 4% to 6%. In retrospect, empirical data is lacking to prove a correlation exists between the change in growth rate of the U.S. money supply and the change in unemployment rate. The correlation was only .18 when data from 1962 thru mid-2013 is analyzed. The low correlation is a very important point for investors. The Federal Reserve is the regulator of Financial Relativity, not the employment watchdog.

In its supreme position in the U.S. financial system, the Fed can impact the cost of money charged by the market on government debt, and thereby greatly influence the downstream rates and valuation of financial market instruments; and, more importantly it can change the level of the country's money supply outstanding, and it does so by changing the level of reserves in the country's banking system by buying and selling government debt. The evidence shows, however, that the Fed cannot change people's desire to work, or someone's need to hire someone to do work by changing the money supply growth rate through quantitative easing. These are societal issues that are most closely aligned with government fiscal policy. Faults in the country's fiscal policy through the ages with respect to the regulatory environment and incentives to work much more closely correlate with the country's employment health. Combine an over-reaching government that was incapable of controlling spending programs with a correspondingly lenient Fed policy, and the result was inflation fireworks in the 1970s.

By the end of 1972 as the election approached for his second term, Nixon chose the political expediency of wage and price controls as the path to reduce inflation pressures. Inflation, however, persisted for the rest of the decade. The Fed was unable to separate itself from the political pressures of the time which held that an anti-inflation Fed policy meant accepting higher unemployment. *The policy action may have sounded politically soothing, but the Theory on which the action was based is not supported by empirical evidence.* The Fed found itself in an irreversible position of over-supplying the financial system with reserves, stoking the inflationary fire ever higher as "too much money was chasing too few goods."

A review of the Fed balance sheet shows that the Fed started to reverse its excessively easy monetary policy when CPI peaked at 12% in 1974. The "even-keel" policy ended as the government began to use an open market auction for debt issuance. The end of 1973 also corresponds to the Arab Oil Embargo which jolted the U.S. financial system. The graph below provides clear evidence that it took major tension driven by foreign trading partners to initiate the reversal of Fed policy. The reversal point can be seen in the graph in 1974 when the Fed balance sheet held almost 25% of the U.S. publicly traded National Debt. Even though the Fed was slowly backing away from its overly accommodative policy, government spending through the Carter presidency of 1976-80 did not subside. Inflation spiked again in the early 1980s as monetary growth continued to run at very high levels. The real counter-balancing Fed policy that arrested inflation did not begin to take effect until post 1980. It corresponds to the point in time that Ronald Reagan became President, and additionally when the Monetary Control Act of 1980 was passed. This point in time marked the end of an inflation ridden time period in U.S. history.

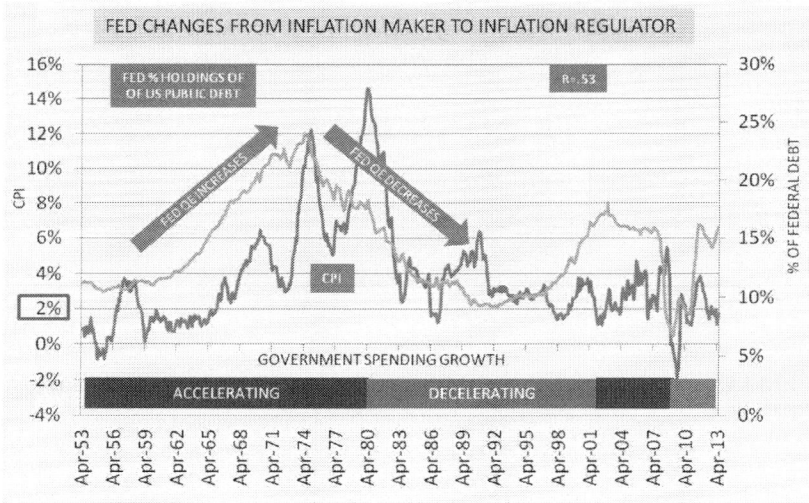

FED CHANGES FROM INFLATION MAKER TO INFLATION REGULATOR

But there was another change in 1980 that accompanied greater Fed independence from fiscal debt management. During that time fiscal policy switched from "tax and spend" to "borrow and spend." Tax policy lowered marginal tax rates paid by Americans across the board in the early 1980s, and liquidity flowed freely into the financial system based on this fiscal policy shift. In a major shift from prior years, post 1980 the Fed maintained a more stringent policy of draining excess reserves from the financial system, reducing the underline relative level of U.S. Treasury holdings on its balance sheet to 10% of outstanding National Debt by the early 1990s. As a result, the inflation level subsided.

From 1953 through 2013, the relative level of Fed holdings of U.S. Debt, or QE, is correlated with inflation at an R-value of .53, which is significant, but not as strong as one might expect. The low correlation reflects the dichotomy in the manner in which the Fed coordinated its policy with the government over time. In the 1960s and 70s the Fed was far too accommodative in its policy and over-purchased government debt. Likewise, after 1980 the Fed was able to maintain greater independence in the regulation of the level of inflation in the economy. The lower R-value is indicative of the Fed primarily working as a regulator, not an instigator of inflation, with the exception of the time periods in which its policy was driven by political expediency.

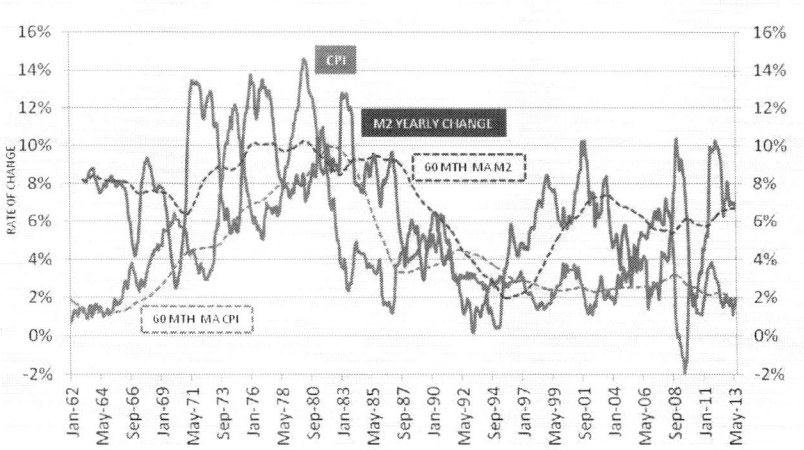

Looking back to the 1960s, easy money supply as shown in the graph above precipitated a high moving average growth rate in the M2 money supply of over 10% from 1976 to the early 1980s. Breaking the back of inflation required a dramatic reduction in reserves in the system by the Fed relative to the outstanding U.S. Debt level, which correspondingly showed up as very high interest rates in the 1970s across the entire term structure of interest rates.

As a result of the Fed policy change in the early 1980s, the rate of inflation subsided dramatically. However, the money supply (M2) continued to grow at a high level reflecting real growth in the economy – the "Morning in America" during the Reagan years. The inflation level from the mid-1980s through

2013 was held in check by Fed policy. To keep inflation low, the Fed rarely allowed the money supply to grow faster than 8%, and the moving average growth in M2 was a full 3% below the level typical during the inflation laden 1970s. The graph also exhibits, however, an increasing deflationary trajectory in price levels in the U.S. economy since 1990.

Unconventional Fed Policies

In September 2008 the Federal Government, and more specifically the Federal Reserve Bank, faced one of the most trying financial crises in post-Depression Era history – the bankruptcy of Lehman Brothers. With the collapse of Lehman severe financial stress resulted as liquidity within the monetary system began to freeze. In response, the Federal Reserve took immediate and unconventional action. At the end of August 2008, the Fed balance sheet showed $865B in asset holdings. By the end of December, the Fed balance sheet had increased to over $2.1T, much of it held in non-traditional assets such as TARP, preferred stock issued by all commercial banks in the U.S. Federal Reserve System specifically to reinforce their capital levels.

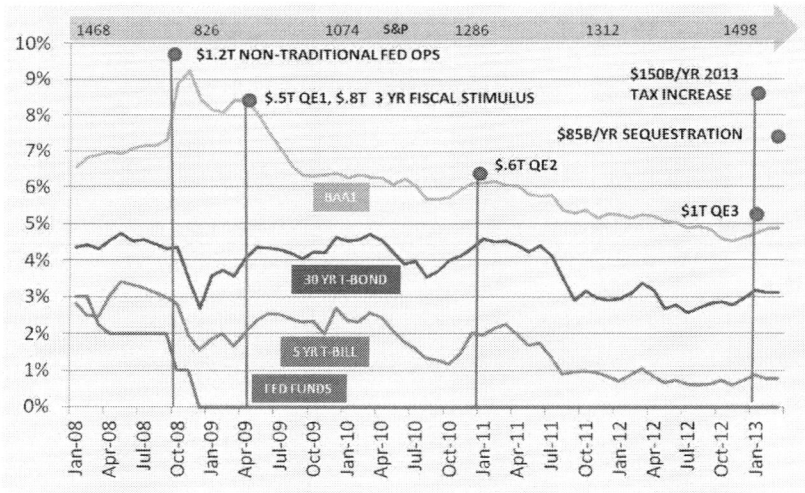

Virtually overnight the Federal Reserve created $1.2T in new reserves across the financial system. The impact on interest rates showed the fear in the financial markets at the time as the BAA1 rate spike to above 9%. Safe haven assets like U.S. Treasuries, alternatively, fell to near record low interest rates not seen since the 1940s. This was at a time when the Fed was not changing its holdings of Treasury securities, holding a relatively stable balance of $480B.

Leading up to the liquidity crisis in September, the Fed actually was a seller of Treasuries – odd, but true, and the tightening action had an exacerbating effect during the crisis. The Fed did not re-enter the Treasury market as a major purchaser until April 2009, when it initiated a quantitative easing (QE1) Treasury purchase program of $500B. This program coincided with an $800B three year fiscal stimulus program passed as the first major action by President Obama after his inauguration in 2009. A new sheriff was in town, and it appeared the Fed was going to act differently than previous decades. A return to the years of coordinated fiscal and monetary policy seemed to be in the works. The level of QE1 matched what was needed to create reserves in the banking sector to accommodate the Obama administration government stimulus program while allowing the Fed to keep interest rates low for "an extended period." The 2009 QE also allowed the Fed to replace the level of reserves it sold off leading up to the crisis.

During 2009 and 2010, the crisis management Fed response worked and the financial system began to recover. By January 2011 the stock market retraced over 70% of its loses, the BAA1 interest rate fell below 2008 levels and the 30 year Treasury bond interest rate was the same as pre-crisis. The Fed balance sheet was also substantially different in composition. Although at a level that matched the beginning of 2009, $2.2T, the balance sheet no longer showed a substantial amount of TARP loans because many banks had paid them off. The capital raised in the banking sector likely came from investors who sold Treasuries to purchase new bank shares issued to cover more stringent capital requirements. The Fed in essence traded its preferred stock in the banks for a greater stake in U.S. Treasuries. The money trail reflects a very interesting revolving door.

As the TARP funds were returned, the Fed redeployed the capital to buy Government Mortgage Backed Securities. The total balance of MBS owned by the Fed at the beginning of 2011 was over $1T. The remainder of its balance sheet was primarily U.S. Treasuries as it tended to its new mission of holding rates low in support of government fiscal policy.

By the beginning of 2011, the major goals that monetary policy could be expected to achieve in dealing with the 2008 financial crisis were reached. The financial system was awash in liquidity and the market was stable. However, the political leadership at the time was not satisfied, and pressures from Pennsylvania Avenue clearly weighed on the policy choices made from that point forward. First there was QE2, a $600B security purchase program taking the Fed balance sheet to $2.8T by the beginning of 2012. The Fed then began to rebalance its holdings to purchase more securities on the long-end of the yield curve in an attempt to drive down long-term interest rates. Then in the later part of 2012, the Fed announced QE3, an $85B per month Treasury and Mortgage Back Security (MBS) purchase program implemented throughout 2013. Once QE3 was fully implemented by 2014 the Fed balance sheet would reach $4T, making it five times larger than when the financial crisis stuck in 2008.

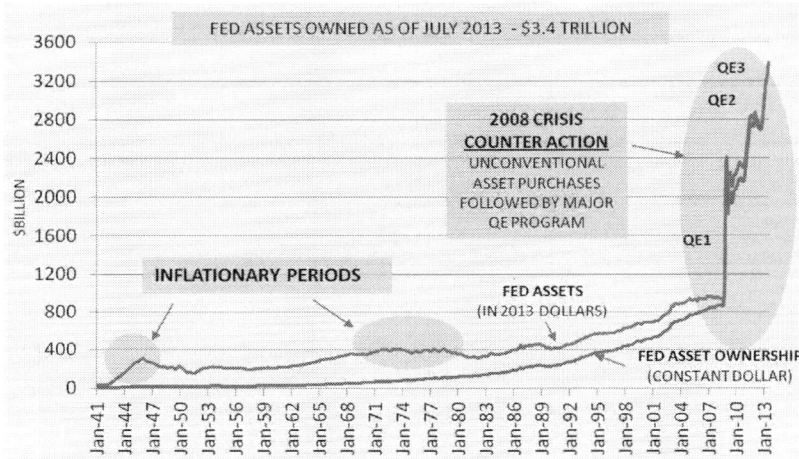

QE3 was a program in anticipation of upcoming fiscal policy changes at the start of 2013. The first was a tax increase of $150B per year and the second was Sequestration, a budget "non-compromise" which put into effect across the board spending level reductions of $85B per year beginning in 2013. Public pressure was being spun in the major media outlets that economic growth was stagnate and inflation was not a problem. Statistically, both were accurate. However, any logic that monetary policy should somehow be the cure for sluggish GDP growth was at best Fed hubris, and at worst purely amateur hour at the Fed. The Fed policy statements as QE3 began to be implemented held a new target. The Fed began to state that it would not begin to remove QE until the unemployment rate reached 6.5%. The Phillips Curve so soundly disproven in the 1970s was retaking the stage.

Déjà vu? Since the beginning of the Obama presidency, the Federal Reserve was increasingly put into the position of coordinating monetary policy at the behest of fiscal political expediency. Some might argue that monetary policy actions were due to the relative inability of Congress during the time period to co-operate with the policies being proposed by Obama's administration. This interpretation is also historically accurate. In any case, major points in history when this happened before, the 1940s and the 1960s and 70s, led to different outcomes.

The situation in 2013 had similarities to the 70s and the 40s. Unfortunately the similarities tended toward the worst of each period. The 2013 fiscal situation was bound by the high level of National Debt, with debt to GDP at over 100%. This was the situation faced in the mid-1940s as the country exited WWII. During the 1940s, compared to 2013, the U.S. did not have an unemployment problem because it was running a current account surplus as trade escalated to rebuild countries ravaged by WWII. Government austerity measures implemented under Truman worked to reduce the debt substantially relative to GDP in less than 5 years because real GDP increased. The 1970s on the other hand were not constrained by the specter of a large National Debt on a relative basis – just the opposite of 2013. This freed the government to enact increasingly higher government spending programs without constraint. Add to the 1970s scenario a complimentary Fed which monetized increasing levels of government spending and inflation ignited and ran out-of-control for the entire decade.

The 1940 Fed Zero-Boundary Rate Policy

The general belief in the market during the timeframe from 2009 through the publication of this book in 2013 was that all of the interventions by the U.S. Federal Reserve and Central Banks around the world would end by inflation running rapidly out of control. However, the policies being pursued by the Federal Reserve Bank when reviewed in conjunction with the U.S. fiscal policy were inflationary primarily for financial assets, not consumer goods and services. Consumer price inflation during the period was a benign 2.1% per annum, while the stock market almost doubled. The combination of relatively constrained spending, increased taxes, and continued borrowing to cover deficit spending at a rate higher than economic growth meant that deflation, not inflation, was the specter being battled - A battle that could only be won if the government stopped borrowing, particularly from foreign nations, to fund its spending habit.

When Ben Bernanke took the reins from Alan Greenspan in 2006 as Federal Reserve Bank Chairman, he was lauded as a scholar of the Depression Era. Beginning with the financial crisis in 2008, almost as if the prologue introducing Ben Bernanke to the public was projecting what was going to happen next, the Fed policies began to draw heavily from policies utilized during the Depression. The Great Depression Federal Reserve was an activist Keynesian policy driven organization, pegging short-term interest rates at or near zero percent for the purpose of wealth re-distribution. The one exception in the period was 1936-37 when Marriner Eccles, then Fed chair, raised reserve requirements on banks from 12.5% to 25% and interest rates were driven up. The result was a plunge in the stock market from 187 to 100, a 47% drop. The decline was championed as a confirmation that a more activist government was required and rates needed to remain low for what would be termed today as an "extended period." Sound familiar?

The conditions which Marriner Eccles confronted in the Fed in 1937 seem oddly similar to the situation that Ben Bernanke lived through in 2008. When Ben Bernanke assumed the Fed Chairmanship in 2006, few people remember that his first decision was to increase the Fed Funds Rate three successive times from 4.5% to 5.25%. This was in effect using a "blunt" instrument at an inappropriate time – but as history will reflect – at a time when speculative market activity and leverage in the mortgage lending market was out of control. The resulting market decline two years later was historic, but by no means a collapse as colossal as the 1929 crash which sent the Dow from peak to through down 83%. The stock market decline in 2008 was 48%, which was almost the identical magnitude drop in value which the history books call a mistake in 1937.

In the wake of the stock market decline in 1937 Galbraith wrote "The 1937 action was the last error of the Federal Reserve for a long time. That was because it was the last action of any moment for fifteen years."

A lot changed in the 15 years between 1937 and 1952. There was WWII, which the War on Terror the early 21st Century did not match in magnitude. Additionally, Social Security and Welfare programs were implemented, and the first checks to social security recipients began mailing in 1941. In 2014 the Affordable Care Act was scheduled to go into full force, and the Medicare and Social Security social programs were well entrenched. During WWII the federal government went deep into debt. The U.S. Debt grew to over 120% of GDP as WWII ended and the troops began to come home. By comparison, the U.S. Debt to GDP ratio rose to 105% in December 2012, up from 66% at the beginning of 2008. In 1946, interest rates were at period level lows on all maturities and the stock market surged through the high set almost a decade before. Voila, 1946 exhibited very similar circumstances to where the U.S. financial market was situated on a relative basis in 2013.

What a perfect model framework for evaluating what happened to cause the "extended period" of low interest rate Fed policy to end, as it did in the years following 1946, and how the stock market responded to the change on a relative basis.

Interest Rate Term Structure – 1941 thru 1957

The graph below summarizes how interest rates changed over the time period from 1941–1957. Pay attention to several aspects of the rate structure.

- In the early 1940s rates trended downward, with corporate rates decreasing the most; government debt during this time was rising from 49% to over 120% of GDP.

- Even as inflation increased rapidly post WWII, interest rates only began to trend upward 18 months after the Truman balanced budgets went into effect in 1946, and then only at a very gradual pace.

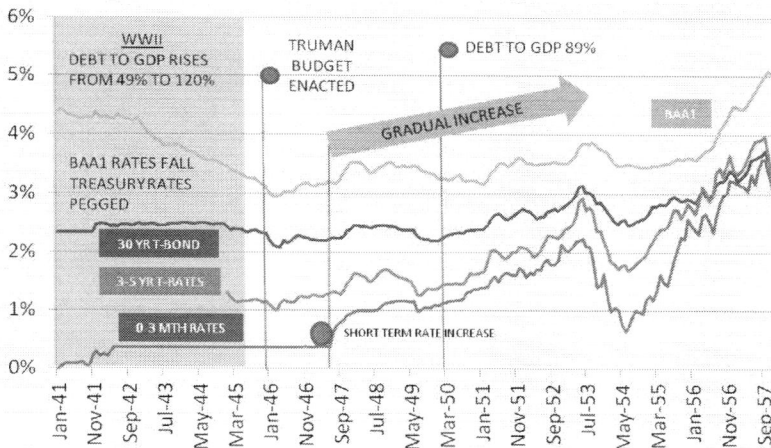

- A perceptible rise across the term structure happened during 1946, from a point that marked time-period lows of .375% on overnight to 3 month funds, 1% on 5 year money, 2% on the 30 Yr Treasuries and 3% on corporate bonds.

- The very short-end of yield curve – Fed Funds equivalent - was allowed to rise to 1.0% from .375% in mid 1947 as the Truman Budget was being implemented and after WWII wage and price controls were lifted. During the year inflation was very high at 18.1%.

- Treasury rates through the time period never dramatically moved higher, <u>even when inflation spiked</u> in 1947 rates changed very gradually.

- It took 6 years for overnight funds to rise 2%; 6 years for 5 year T-Bills to rise 1%, 8 years for 30 year Treasury Bonds to rise 1% and 10 years for corporate investment grade BAA1 bonds to rise 1%.

Throughout the 1940s repressive interest rates were utilized as a government policy of Keynesian re-distribution. Repressive rates are a policy where the U.S. Treasury works in conjunction with the Federal Reserve and Member Banks to auction government debt at rates below the economic rate of inflation. Repressive rates are a government act of price control allowing the government to borrow and not pay high rates as it re-distributes wealth thru government programs.

Fed Power to Repress Rates Reduced Relative to 1940s

Repressive interest rates went into immediate effect as President Obama was elected in 2008. Suppressing the term structure of interest rates was successful up to the May 2013 timeframe. Starting in the spring of 2013, however, rates on longer duration bonds as well as riskier assets began to rise even as the Fed attempted to keep rates low by continued high levels of Treasury purchases. The lack of control in the 21st Century implementation of the repressive rate policy very likely stems from the substantial ownership of U.S. Treasuries by foreigners.

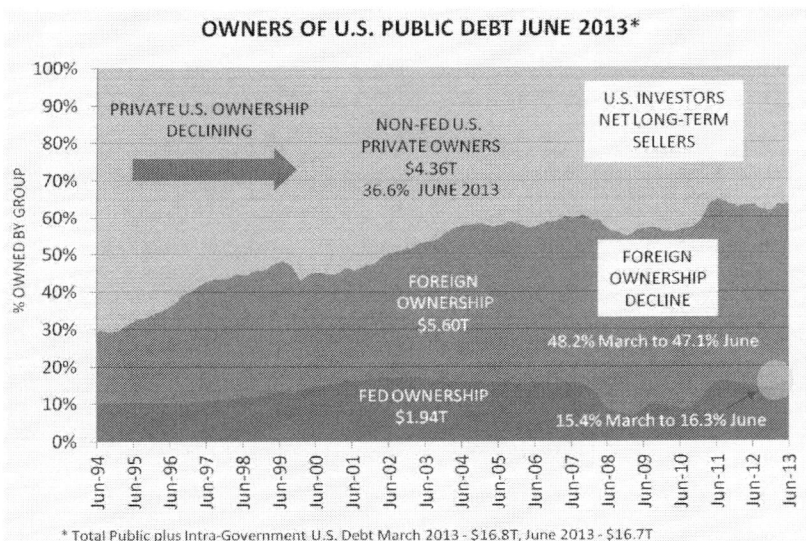

OWNERS OF U.S. PUBLIC DEBT JUNE 2013*

* Total Public plus Intra-Government U.S. Debt March 2013 - $16.8T, June 2013 - $16.7T

98

In the 1940s the ownership of U.S. government debt was almost wholly U.S. based. In 2013 the composite ownership of the publicly traded debt as of June was 47%, declining from a high in 2012 of 48.4%. In the spring of 2013 holders of U.S. Treasuries, both foreign and domestic, began to sell. The foreign owners were selling to generate dollar currency for transactions as U.S. fiscal constraints caused a reduction in the flow of dollars from trade. The selling pressure was exacerbated by retirement savers and investors who could quickly sell long duration investments packaged in ETFs and mutual funds, very different from the market in the 1940s. In 2013, computerized ETF trading can cause interest rates to change more rapidly than the Federal Reserve has the capacity to respond. From May until August of 2013 the 5 year, 10 year and 30 year Treasuries moved up by over 100 basis points.

Stock Market Performance in 1946

In the graph below the performance of the DOW is shown relative to the term structure of interest rates from 1941 through 1951. The graph shows the market reaction as the Federal Reserve slowly began to withdraw monetary easing programs in 1946 in conjunction with the Truman Budget implementation.

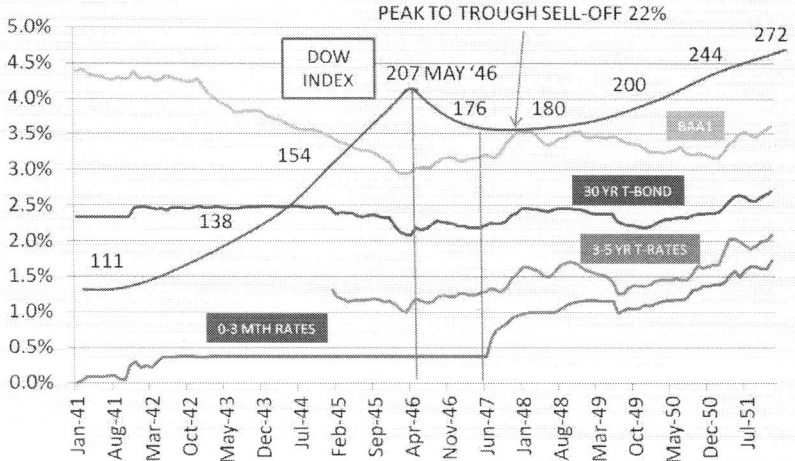

The cyclical rise in stocks induced by the wartime economy and the euphoric run-up at the end of the War came to an abrupt end in May of 1946. The sell-off was a loss of 22% peak to trough. Economic growth as measured by nominal GDP averaged 8% from 1946 to 1950, evenly split between inflation (4%) and real growth (4%). The headwinds of measured government spending and slowly rising interest rates kept stocks from returning to the May 1946 high again until early in 1950. However, the stock market also never broke below the base it formed after the May 1946 correction.

U.S. Treasury interest rates continued to be repressed below the rate of inflation through the entire period until 1951.

What Changed in 1951?

Eventually the Federal Reserve pushed back against the policy of interest rate price controls on new Treasury issues. The discontent reached a head and Truman called the Treasury and the Fed Open Market Committee into his office for a meeting in early 1951. The Treasury, history says, left the meeting convinced that rates would continue to be fixed. However, the argument continued. Finally the conflict was resolved through a negotiated settlement known as the Treasury-Federal Reserve Accord of 1951. The settlement allowed for slightly more Fed latitude in setting rates, and a small tick up in rates, as well as increased rate volatility is visible beginning in early 1951.

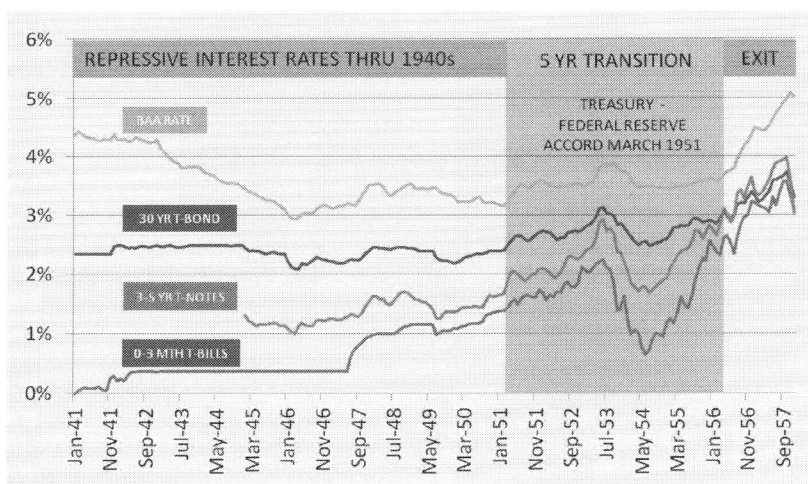

When Eisenhower was swept into office in 1952, more conservative views and a belief in sound money policies became shared between the Treasury and the Fed. At that point the Fed regained a significant part of its independence from policy makers who wanted easy credit and low rates.[4] The one part of its independence it did not gain, however, was its co-responsibility for government debt management. Making sure that the U.S. Treasury got the

---

[4] William Greinder, *Secrets of the Temple – How the Federal Reserve Runs the Country* (New York: Simon & Schuster, 1987), 328.

lowest rate possible eventually left the Fed in a politically untenable position as fiscal spending took off in the 1960s and the Treasury began to demand Fed co-operation in successful debt placement at below market rates of interest.

Lessons Learned about the Federal Reserve

The long-term impact on the financial system from the massive increase in the Fed balance sheet to almost $4 Trillion in 2013 was not known as of the writing of this book. Consumer price inflation in the summer of 2013 was still showing benign readings. The massive injection of reserves into the monetary system had not yet multiplied, causing consumer prices to explode above the target 2-3% level. However, financial assets like the stock market definitely were inflated by the QE measures.

Help in understanding the future impact of the Fed policy can be found in a summary of the lessons about the Fed's role as the Financial Relativity Regulator.

LESSONS ABOUT THE FED REGULATOR FORCE

- The Fed regulates U.S. Financial Relativity by buying and selling U.S. Treasuries and raising and lowering the Fed Funds rate.
- The Fed is mandated by law to take actions to tighten monetary policy when "unacceptably" high levels of consumer price inflation are registered in the economy.
- The Fed is not mandated to respond to financial asset bubbles. Fed policies have the power to create bubbles by excessive monetization of the National Debt.
- The zero interest rate policy is a method of interest rate price control. Supporting below market rates of interest require the Fed to purchase increasing relative proportions of the U.S. Debt, monetizing financial assets in the system.
- Market risk assets reflect financial bubble creation caused by excessive Fed easing policies when interest rates increase in direct conflict with Fed easing policies.
- Tightening Fed monetary policy in response to financial asset bubbles always triggers a stock market correction, the magnitude of which is equal to the amount of relative imbalance in the financial system.

Market data indicated the reason that reserves did not multiply into rapid money supply growth was the regulatory constraints of the Dodd-Frank Act of 2010. The reserves were absorbed by the higher capital requirements for lending. However, when QE3 was being executed in mid-2013, the market began to respond negatively to increased asset purchases by the Fed. Former Fed chairman Paul Volcker began to sound the alarm in May 2013 in a speech to the NY Economics Club. The long-end of the interest rate curve began trending higher in spite of the major quantitative easing program by the Fed. The oil market also began to show an uptick instead of the continued market expectations it would fall.

> **5th PRINCIPLE OF FINANCIAL RELATIVITY**
> The Fed is the Regulator of Financial Relativity with the power to create and extinguish market imbalances.

The financial system was definitely on edge in mid-2013, and there were signals that the Fed was beginning to lose control due to the market distortions its policies were creating. Financial Relativity Principle #5 was beginning to become come into focus as it inevitably does in the financial market.

Principle #5 states that accommodative Fed policies and government fiscal spending programs to encourage economic growth eventually create market imbalances that must be addressed. Typically addressing the imbalances is left to the Federal Reserve and the implementation of tighter interest rate policy. Inflation is generally the most visible indicator of the negative force which the Fed is responsible for addressing. However, the real underlying driver for the eventual Fed response is generally more closely linked to maintaining stability in the value of the U.S. dollar. In almost every case since WWII when the Fed initiated significant interest rate increases, it was done in conjunction with a clear force being driven from the international market, not just in response to domestic inflation. More specifically, it was almost always accompanied by a shock sent from the oil market.

10 OIL'S SHOCKING RELATIVITY

Energy - the lifeblood of the economy. Since the beginning of recorded history, civilizations have risen and fallen based on their access to economical energy resources. Most all investors have an innate sense that the cost of energy in the market is a harbinger of good times or bad. The relative importance of energy in the economy makes it an important element in the Theory of Financial Relativity. In the U.S. financial system, crude oil is the bell-weather. Oil is a primary source of both mobile energy as well as a major part of the petro-chemical business which feeds a myriad of ancillary businesses. Alternate energy sources were under-development with increasing zeal in the second decade of the 21st century. However, demand for existing oil resources continued to expand as well, particularly from nations like China and other emerging market countries. The growing world supply and demand imbalance, as well as the increasing geo-political tension expected to arise from the U.S. attempt to become more energy independent make understanding oil's shocking relativity very important.

In post WWII history, the first major encounter with the economic force wrought by a disruption in supply of oil was encountered during the Korean War. From 1950 through 1953, the U.S. froze the price of oil in order to maintain price stability. In the summer of 1951, Iran nationalized all of its oilfields. An ensuing worldwide boycott removed 19 million barrels of monthly production from world supply. With the lower supply, when U.S. price controls were lifted in 1953, the price rose 10% almost overnight. In 1953, the U.S. entered recession. The rapid change in cost and dislocation in supply of energy were the primary contributing factors.

The shortages created by the Suez Canal crisis produced another economic roller coaster ride in 1956. The blockage of the canal shut off almost 10% of worldwide production as 1.5 million barrels a day were carried through the canal at that time. The heaviest hit region was Europe, dependent upon almost 2/3rd of its oil from the Gulf Region. The U.S. filled a large part of the gap in supply in the 4th quarter of 1956 as the conflict raged. Once resolved, production in the Middle East returned quickly back to pre-crisis levels. The rise and fall of exports, however, was a contributing factor in the 1957 U.S. recession.

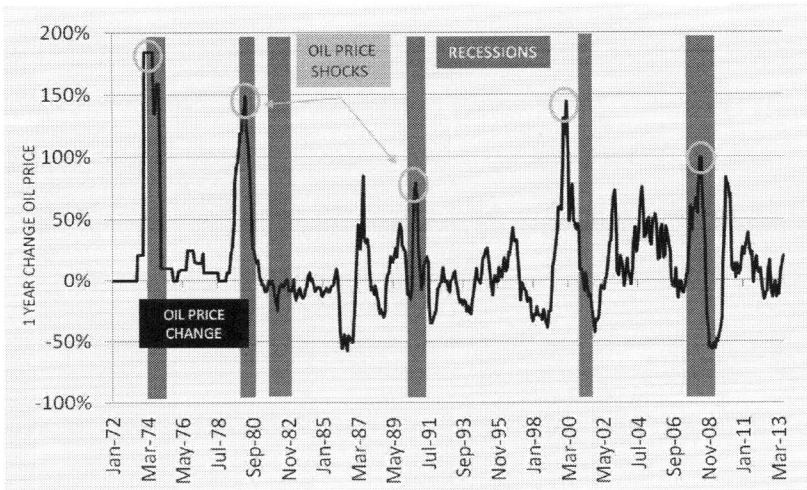

Illustrated in the above graph, oil shocks have occurred in the 12 months leading up to 5 of the 6 recessions in the United States from the 1970s through 2013. In the case of the outlier 1981 recession, it can be argued that it was a direct result of the run-up in oil prices in 1979. The causal relationship between oil price shocks and subsequent recessions is too strong to just be a coincidence. Oil price spikes have historically been a contributing factor to deep economic downturns. The most important issues for investors to understand are the characteristics of a true price shock, and what leads up to the trigger point that inevitably causes a downturn in the nucleus of Financial Relativity – GDP.

Geo-Political Conflicts and Supply Imbalances Trigger Oil Shocks

Oil supply disruptions and the ensuing economic hardship generated by geo-political tensions in the Middle East became a fixture in the post WWII U.S.

economy. The combination of geo-political conflict creating supply disruptions and, more recently, a growing level of worldwide consumption relative to supply were the primary source of the 5 major oil shocks in history between 1973 and 2008. The timing and magnitude in the price level changes in oil are shown in the graph below. The Persian Gulf region conflicts can be traced to all but one of the economic recessions in the period. The year 2000 run-up in oil prices is not historically cited as being driven by conflict or supply disruptions. The period is referenced as a time when Asian demand and consumption began to grow at a faster pace than available supply. It still constituted an oil spike however, as statistically oil prices moved up dramatically during the year 2000.

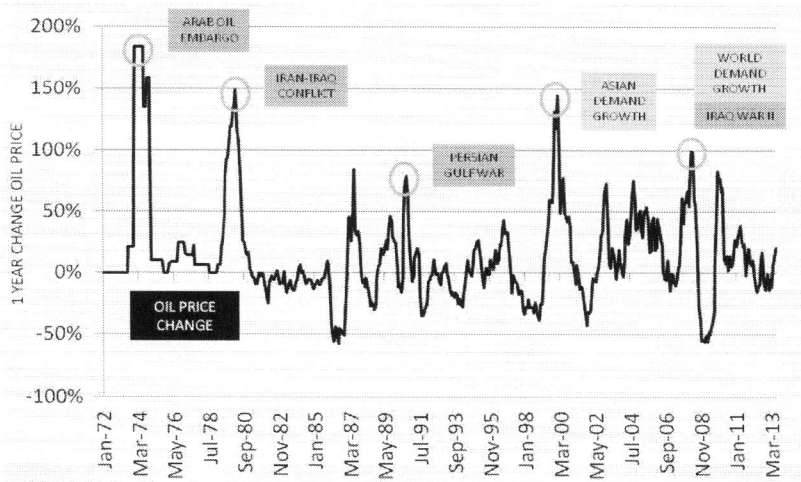

Each of the oil shocks have one aspect in common – the movement up in price established a new all-time high, and the move up doubled or even tripled the price of crude within a 12 month or shorter time period. In all cases except the 1973-74 oil shock there was a negative retracement shortly after the new high was set. The 1974 oil shock was an interesting case study. The pricing power of the OPEC cartel during that time period was very high. Negotiations for an end to the Arab Oil Embargo resulted in Saudi Arabia agreeing to a treaty with the United Sates whereby it would only price oil in U.S. dollars in exchange for military protection of its oil fields.

The Rise of OPEC in the 1960s and 1970s

In the 1970s, the power of the Middle East to create disruptions in supply which could topple the U.S. economy really came into focus. The impetus of the increasing power was the formation of a cartel in September of 1960, well known as The Organization of the Petroleum Exporting Countries (OPEC). The five founding members were Iran, Iraq, Kuwait, Saudi Arabia and Venezuela. These members were later joined by nine other countries. The organization developed a collective vision in the early years after formation, and in 1968 published a 'Declaratory Statement of Petroleum Policy in Member Countries'. The declaration stressed the inalienable right of all countries to exercise permanent sovereignty over their natural resources in the interest of their national development. The statement was a push-back on the Western world at the time as there was a growing view in these countries that the developed world was not paying a fair price for their imported oil.

OPEC's power in setting the price of oil in the world market became very apparent during the 1970s. The member countries took control of their domestic petroleum industries and acquired a major say in the pricing of crude oil on world markets. During the decade oil prices increased precipitously on two occasions, once in conjunction with the Arab Oil Embargo in 1973 and the second during the outbreak of the Iranian Revolution in 1979. As the preceding graphic shows, the first instance in the 1970s when the world price for oil increased dramatically was during the second half of 1973 and early 1974. During this very short time period, the recorded price per barrel of West Texas Intermediate crude oil (WTI) rose from $3.56 to $4.31 from July to August in 1973, and then from $4.31 to $10.11 in January 1974. A new, almost order of magnitude higher floor level price of oil was established virtually overnight.

The circumstance that precipitated the dramatic increase in oil prices was the proclamation in October of 1973 of the Arab Oil Embargo in retaliation for the U.S. support of Israel in the Yom Kippur War. The embargo entailed a 25% output cut by the Arab members nations in OPEC, which was joined additionally by Egypt, Syria and Tunisia. The War ended on January 18, 1974 when Israel signed a withdrawal agreement to pull back to the east side of the Suez Canal. However, the end of the embargo was not announced until March 17, 1974. No official reference in history can be found showing an acceptance of higher oil prices by the western world or the U.S. in the settlement. However, the mechanical maintenance of the extreme run-up in prices post the conflict is an "inconvenient truth." The ensuing stock market decline of almost 50% reflected the carnage of the changing price level of crude oil. The S&P 500 closed at month end December 1972 at 118. By the end of September 1974 it traded at 64 points. A drop in stock market value of this magnitude was not recorded again until the financial crisis in 2008 – which incidentally also had a significant 100% run-up in oil prices prior to the market decline. If the run-up in 2008 is measured over a slightly longer period, October 2006 to July 2008, the price change in crude oil from $58 per barrel to $140 was very close in magnitude to the end of 1973 price shock.

Research concerning the cause of the 2008 financial crisis focused heavily on the liquidity crisis caused by poor underwriting standards and over-leverage in the U.S. mortgage market. However, the on-going Iraq War and the corresponding steady march higher in oil prices much more likely was the incipient cause, and the debacle in the mortgage industry a resulting effect. After all, oil based energy is an input into the national GDP, and higher price levels had a natural depressing effect on available income to pay off mortgage loans – *the reverse idea that higher mortgage lending led to lower income that led to higher oil prices is not logical.* Investors should always treat with a fair amount of skepticism politically expedient explanations focusing on only one very visible result of an economic downturn when trying to understand why financial markets move.

Oil's Shockingly High Correlation to GDP

What is it about energy, and in particular oil based energy that makes it such a driving force in financial markets? When looking at this problem, many investors may naturally visualize the price sign at the gas station and the hike in gas prices that inevitably accompanies a price spike in crude oil. The thought process is that oil spikes are inflationary.

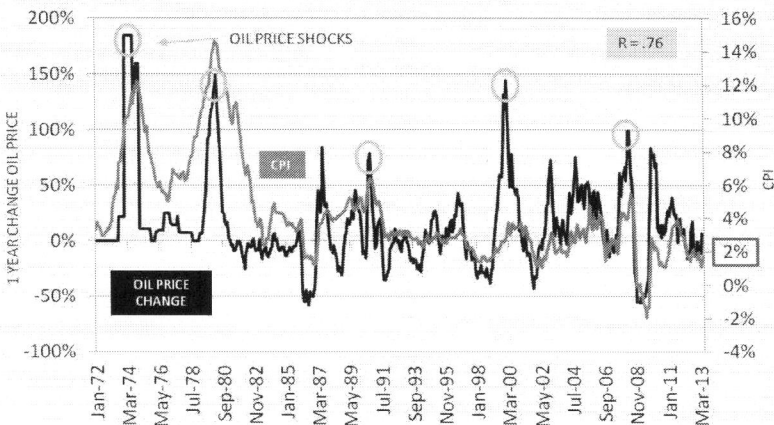

The data corresponding to the inflation impact of oil price spikes indeed does show a compelling relationship since the early 1970s. The correlation between the price of oil and the CPI index over the time period is .76. But as laid out in a prior chapter of this book, inflation is a monetary phenomenon. Oil may be referred to as black gold, but oil is not the basis for the U.S. currency. Since oil is a significant input into the economic output of the country, any movement in the price level significantly impacts the nominal value of GDP. In the short-run price spikes may appear as cost-push inflation. But for the run-up in oil price to be sustained, something else in the relative mathematical financial equation must change – either real GDP suffers or the monetary base expands.

This relationship of real GDP expansion versus monetary expansion is exhibited in the data showing the oil spike of 1979. The oil spike started during the Iranian revolution. As a result of the conflict, the Shah of Iran fled the country and Ayatollah Khomeini became the new leader. Domestic protests severely disrupted the Iranian oil sector, with production being greatly curtailed and exports suspended. Panic in the world energy market was widespread and pressure for oil prices to rise quickly took hold. The price level of WTI crude oil rose from $15.85 per barrel in April of 1979, to $39.50 in April of 1980, a 149% or 2.5 times increase in a very short time frame. The source of the price rise was twofold. The first was President Jimmy Carter's ordered cessation in Iranian oil imports, restricting supply into the U.S. market. The second, and probably more significant action, was a phased deregulation of oil prices which began on April 5, 1979. The deregulation action made economic large oil fields in the U.S. such as Prudhoe Bay, and in the ensuing years allowed domestic supply to fill the gap in volatile supply from the Middle East.

The details about the inflation ridden 1970s was covered extensively in previous chapters in this book. Actions taken to coordinate fiscal and monetary policy led to a perpetual rise in money supply during the time period, which flowed into the economy and supported price level increases in the oil market. The oil price shocks took hold and stuck without any price reversion exhibited from demand elasticity. The spike in 1979 and the subsequent market action were different. Prices reached a peak of $39.50 and then began to recede. The most significant aspect of the price hike was that it was disproportion in relation to the real U.S. economy. In addition, the Federal Reserve shifted its policy in the 1980s in a manner that slowed the money creation carousel such that the oil price increase could not just be pushed through in the U.S. economy. The real economy had to reflect the pain in the measured output of GDP, and a painful, 15 month recession occurred in the first year of the Reagan presidency, lasting from August of 1981 to October of 1982. Even after the recession ended, growth was slow to resume and it was not until the election neared for President Reagan's 2nd term that GDP finally begin to show signs of picking up with real growth of 7-8% in 1984.

The significant influence of oil on nominal GDP is captured in the following table. From April 1969 until July 2013 the correlation of the price of oil to nominal GDP was a very high .81, while inflation, a component of GDP showed a correlation of only .76. The S&P

R-VALUE OIL TO:	FROM / TO Jul-13		
	Apr-69	Dec-73	Jan-74
GDP	0.81	0.78	0.78
S&P500 INDEX	0.70	0.66	0.65
CPI-INFLATION	0.76	0.72	0.72

500, which is very highly correlated to GDP, only showed a .70 R-value relationship.

These relationships have significant meanings for investors. The first is that oil should first be viewed relative to its expected impact on the real economy. Inflation driven impacts of oil spikes are dependent upon the accommodation level of the Federal Reserve. In the case of the 1970s Fed policy essentially attempted to suppress the relative real impact of higher energy prices by allowing all other price levels in the economy to rise in unison.

Crude oil's impact on the real economy over the 40 year time period from 1973 to 2013 can be visibly traced in the following graph. Each of the areas circled in red on the graph represent times of significant price change in oil. The green line which is measured on the right side of the graph is the U.S. constant dollar GDP. When oil prices spike upward, a slight dip in the GDP line is observable reflecting the subsequent recession. But an equally interesting review of the long-term effect of oil price changes on the U.S. GDP shows that oil price moves can have positive and negative impacts. In the case of oil shocks, a short-term drain on real GDP always resulted, only recovered when the price of oil fell after the spike. On the other hand, upward growth momentum was exhibited when price levels moved down relative to GDP as they did beginning post 1980. This momentum increased beginning in 1986. During the time when oil prices declined and real economic growth in the U.S flourished, the Mideast was very stable. Only the War of Kuwait in 1990-1991 interrupted the tranquil time period. Timely action by OPEC, and in particular Saudi Arabia, to keep supply levels stable kept the '91 crisis short lived.

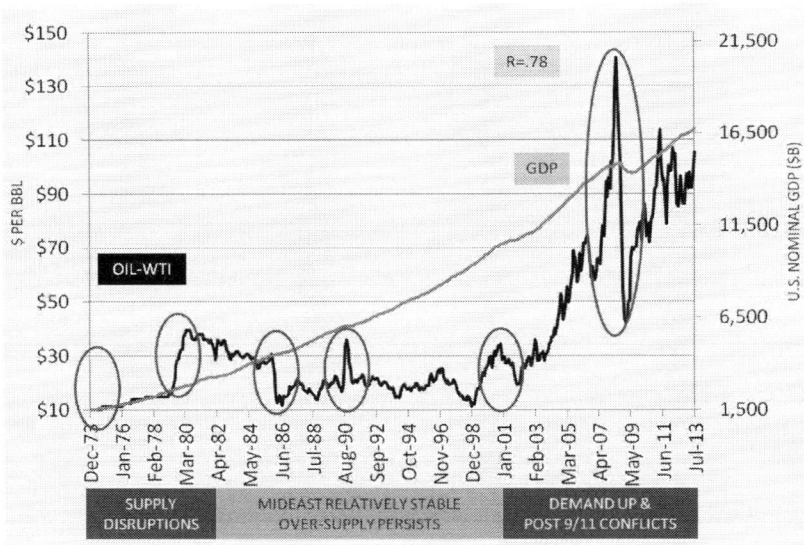

The data show a very interesting dynamic change beginning with the advent of Reaganomics in 1980. First, the higher price level encouraged greater domestic supply in the U.S. that by the mid-1980s led to a dissipation of OPEC pricing power. However, it does not tell the complete story. The human motivating forces that led to the Arab Oil Embargo in the early 1970s were veiled in a belief by many OPEC nations that the West was stealing their oil and not paying a fair price. As can be seen in the graph, the price level for oil set by OPEC from 1973 thru 1979 rose almost in lock step with U.S. nominal GDP that at the time was increasing primarily due to inflation. This was a time in which the U.S. oil price was heavily regulated – meaning that the government was setting a price, and that price was being controlled by OPEC. There was a détente in place allowing OPEC to raise price levels in line with the eroding effects of the U.S. monetary policy at the time. When the market was deregulated in 1979, OPEC took advantage of the Iran-Iraq conflict and greedily pushed prices even higher on a relative basis in 1980.

The price shock in 1973 and 1979 created large current account deficits in oil-importing economies like the U.S., and an equally large problem for oil export nations in terms of what currency in which to denominate the sale of their oil. This problem for Saudi Arabia was addressed by a Treaty in 1973 brokered by Secretary of State Henry Kissinger in which the United States agreed to provide military protection for Saudi Arabia's oil fields, and in return the

Saudi's agreed to price their oil sales in United States dollars only. The situation spawned a large petrodollar recycling industry in the capital markets as excess dollar accumulated by oil exporting countries were used to finance the growing current account deficit in the United States. In 1980, these petrodollars help Ronald Regan finance tax-cuts that eventually led to a revitalized economy after monetary policy was tightened to break the inflation cycle. U.S. fiscal policy shifted from "tax and spend" to "borrow and spend." Not all OPEC members supported the move to the U.S. dollar, preferring to maintain a high percentage of reserves in gold. Iran was the most vocal non-supporter.

Was it economic consequences, or was it an intra-government deal that broke the oil price cycle? The inter-dealings of OPEC and the U.S. government cannot go unnoticed. During the early 1980 time period, the U.S. current account deficit spending was financed at very high 12% to 14% interest rates. OPEC countries, and in particular Saudi Arabia, were able to create a financial annuity with their current account surpluses that was more lucrative than the selling of the actual oil itself. Iran and Iraq, however, did not save surpluses as aggressively. Not surprisingly they would end up being the source of instability in future years. Some historical accounts of the 1976 DOHA meeting of OPEC as written in "Showdown at Doha: The Secret Oil Deal That Helped Sink the Shah of Iran" by Andrew Scott Cooper of The Middle East Institute, suggests that the Kissinger deal with the Saudi Arabia intentionally excluded Iran, which contributed to the country's continual financial downfalls and the eventual ousting of the Shah of Iran.

Oil prices soared to all-time highs of over $35 per barrel in 1980, making prophetic a quote from the Shah of Iran in 1973 in a New York Times article that the West should pay "*10 times more for their oil*." At the time in 1973 the price for oil was $3.56 per barrel. The high price of oil gave all OPEC countries a chance to build very large current account surpluses. Some did so in U.S. based investments, like Saudi Arabia, and others in gold. The price of gold in dollar terms raced upward in direct correlation with oil in the time period. The price of oil was so constraining on U.S. and other industrialized country economies that eventually new supply sources became economically justified and demand, although highly inelastic, did decline. These trends are what economists attributed to the resulting over-supply and the subsequent price collapse in the mid 1980s.

The economic explanation focused wholly on an oil glut in the early 1980s, however, is lacking. It doesn't account for what pacified the region for almost 15 years thereafter, given its propensity for conflict to drive up oil prices against the "imperialist" forces in the West. One very evident appeasement was the high interest rates that the U.S. taxpayer was paying to Saudi Arabia and certain other OPEC nations on petrodollar reserves in order to promote and maintain Mid-East stability. At the time, very high interest rate Treasury bonds with 10 to 30 years maturity dates with interest rates of 12% to 14% were issued by the U.S. and much of the supply was purchased by countries like Saudi Arabia. The petrodollar re-cycling process created a co-dependency between a faction within OPEC and the United States. It was a comfortable situation from the mid 1980s until the year 2000 as interest rates remained sufficiently high, and U.S. GDP growth was strong. As rates began to decline, Saudi Arabian dollar based trade surpluses were deployed in additional ways – including major stakes in U.S. based companies like Apple, News Corp, Motorola and AOL. Perhaps the most significant investment by Saudi Arabian royalty family member Prince Al Waleed, was a stake taken in Citigroup purchased when the bank was in trouble in the 1990s. Although never amassing a controlling stake, the ownership provided a direct link for Saudi Arabia into the U.S. financial system.

The Saudi-U.S. relationship kept the Middle East in check for an extended time frame. However, as the end of the 1990s approached, interest rates on U.S. government debt were not nearly as high as in the early 1980s, and many Treasury issues from the 1970 and early 1980 time period were coming due for re-financing. Additionally the stock market was at all-time highs and showing signs of "exuberance", irrational was how Alan Greenspan described it. Cash flow of dollars into the Middle East was in the process of slowing. In addition, by the late 1990s the price level of oil was severely depressed in relative terms to the late 1970s. In absolute dollars, a barrel of oil in July 1979 was $21.75; in July 1999 it was priced at $20.07. The leverage of OPEC was seemingly very weak. But a push-back should not have come as a surprise.

A fundamental shift in the oil market began in the year 2000. Price levels approached the 1980 level peak of $39 per barrel in November 2000 before receding during the subsequent recession and stock market decline. Many analysts began to attribute the revised strength in the price of oil to Asian market growth in consumption, in particular China, which began growing at a compound annual rate of 7% beginning in 1990. This growth very likely did close the gap in world supply and demand. Drilling for new production, after the price per barrel had been maintained at $20 for such a long period, was uneconomical in most oil fields. The Saudi's, however, were the key to why the oil price moved higher so rapidly, whereas it had not done so for many years. The oil spike that lasted through the end of 2000 showed that the worldwide price of oil in dollars was no longer going to be controlled by OPEC below, in <u>relative</u> terms, the pre-Arab Oil Embargo level as it had been since 1986.

Oil Market Changed Post 9/11

The U.S. recovery from the 2001 recession became known as one of the slowest recoveries in economic history. "Jobless recovery" was a term used extensively in media references. Many explanations were posed. One was that productivity gains from technological advances led to firms being able to produce more with fewer workers. Another focused on Chinese trade policy and the idea that they were manipulating their currency to gain an unfair trade advantage. Both seem plausible, and were contributing factors. One very puzzling fact remains. If these factors were primary causes, rather than symptoms of a more significant cause, the actual decline in the economy in this time period should have been led by signs of these factors, and been purged by the recession. Rather, these factors became the new normal after the recession.

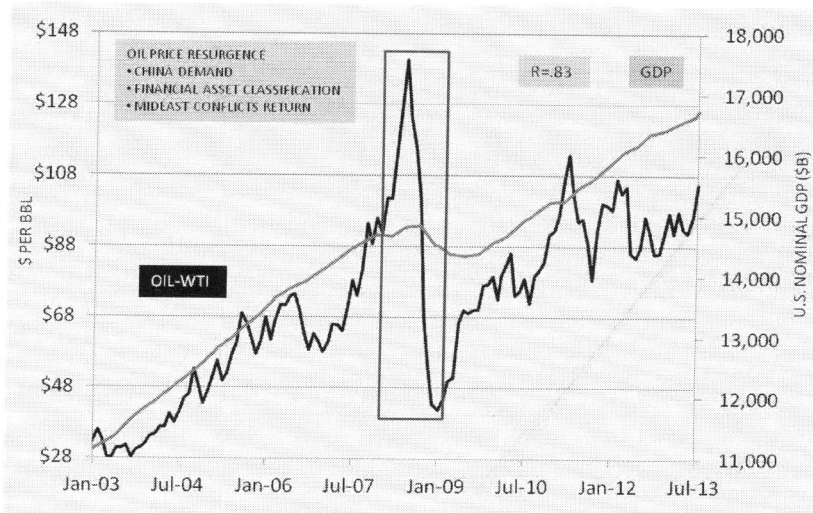

A review of the economic data, more specifically the price of oil, holds some insight into what was happening in the economy. The recovery post 9/11 was accompanied by the resurgence in the price level of oil. From 2003 through the interim peak in July 2008, oil rose in price from $28 to over $140 per barrel. The price change in oil became even more correlated with economic growth, and showed an R-value of .83 from 2003 through 2013.

The time period leading up to the oil spike in 2007-08 has many similarities with the late 1960s to 1973 time period. In both instances the Middle East exhibited a high level of conflict. In October 1973 there was the military action in Israel surrounding the Yom Kippur War; the larger conflict was an economic one with OPEC. Post 9 / 11 the U.S. found itself in two military conflicts. The two Wars the United States was fighting involved an odd set of foes in the Middle East. One was the War on Terror against Al Qaeda, and was being fought primarily in Afghanistan. Al Qaeda allies in the region were not always clear. Close allies tended to be associated with Palestine, Iran and Pakistan indirectly – not Iraq. In contrast, the Iraq War to oust Saddam Hussein over the possibility of weapons of mass created an entirely separate conflict, but with a foe that historically was a counter-balancing force against Iran. Just as in 1979, Iran and Iraq seemed to be the drivers behind an unsettled Middle East, only this time the U.S. was directly involved militarily, not just economically.

Combine the Middle East conflicts with continued growth in energy demand from China, which Iran was aligning much of its oil output to satisfy, and the price of oil climbed steadily on the world market from 2003 to 2006. U.S. fiscal policy and monetary policy, unlike the 70s however, were decoupled beginning in 2004 as Alan Greenspan began to tighten reserves in the U.S. banking system by raising the target Fed Funds rate. Government expenditures continued to grow to finance the war. Ben Bernanke raised the target Fed Funds rate three additional times to a peak of 5.25% as he took the Fed Chairman position beginning in 2006, putting the financial markets into a position of low relative liquidity. In spite of the tightening financial conditions, dollar assets from U.S. trade deficits continued to flow at high rates into Middle East country coffers.

The rapid increase in oil prices in 2007 through mid 2008, in spite of Fed tightening, is historically intriguing. In October 2006, the price of a barrel of oil was $58 per barrel. By July 2008 it was $140 per barrel. The escalation in price defies economic rationality. Research has been done by James D. Hamilton on the possibility that speculation in the oil futures market was a contributing factor[5]. OPEC openly states in the Brief History section of its web-site (www.opec.org) that the resurgence in oil price levels in the 2000s was based on a growing segment of the financial market treating oil as an asset class rather than just a traded commodity. In order for this to be possible, a substantial pool of investable U.S. dollars had to be dedicated to taking long positions in near-term futures contracts and the derivative contracts needed to be continually rolled over. As long as the price of oil was rising, this strategy was economically lucrative. The market data reflect almost a quarter trillion dollars worth of excess open futures contracts in the market during this period. The spike higher in oil prices, and the subsequent fall in prices back to below $40 per barrel shortly after the September 2008 collapse of Lehman Brothers lends credence to the possibility that the high volume of futures contracts relative to actual market demand for oil created the large price swing.

For this futures strategy to be effective in pushing oil prices higher, the trades needed to be executed by a group(s) with credibility and financial resources to assume the risk of actually delivering the oil to the market. This fact means that the "speculators" most likely would have been groups tied to the parties with the ability to deliver the oil in the market, such as OPEC members. However, my research found no public information available that could definitively show who the actual owners of the futures contracts belonged to, or whose interest they may have served. One thing is certain, however. The holders of any futures contracts which were purchased at the time the market peaked at $140 per barrel in July of 2008 took severe losses in subsequent months if they were not hedged. Within 6 months, the spot price of crude oil was trading around $40. In the previous 48 year period since OPEC was formed the market had not dropped by as much in such a short a period. Even the collapse in the first half of 1986 when the oil market fell from $30 to $12 was not as steep a drop in percentage terms.

What is the Fair Market Price of Oil?

An underlying premise of the Theory of Financial Relativity is that the trading pattern of market assets viewed in total isolation appears random. Without any market relative guidepost, trades become based on momentum, with the best predictor for the next trade being the projected path based on the last value. However, in the financial universe assets tend to correlate in traded

---

[5] "*Causes and Consequences of the Oil Shock of 2007–08*", James D. Hamilton, Brookings Papers on Economic Activity, Spring 2009

value to major market forces.

In the case of oil, the relative value takes on special significance in the financial market. Oil is both a major input into the U.S. real economy, and also a vital commodity that is not entirely under the control of the owners of the U.S. financial system in which it derives a significant part of its traded value. This dependency relationship between the price of oil and the growth in the U.S. economy has been linked to conflict through time as Middle East countries have constantly sought what they believe is a "fair" price for their natural resources. For investors, determining the relative value of oil must be done within the context of the on-going geo-political struggle. The importance of viewing the price of oil in this context is made particularly poignant given the fact that a majority of the U.S. stock market corrections post WWII have been preceded by a spike in oil prices or an oil shortage.

As this book was being written in the summer of 2013, oil rose to over $108 per barrel even as the economy struggled to show greater than 3% nominal GDP growth per year for the 4 years after the 2008 crisis. Tension in the Middle East was escalating. Syrian forces under the command of President Assad in August of 2013 were found to have used chemical weapons in an attack reported on August 21, 2013, killing over 1300 innocent men, women and children in Damascus. President Obama in the beginning of September 2013 sought approval of Congress to take military action against Syria. The oil market was on edge and traded above $100 per barrel for the first time since 2011 when tensions rose during the Egyptian revolution. No military action was taken by the United States in Syria and the oil market subsequently receded back below $100 per barrel in October.

Conflict in the Middle East, while there may be a legitimate dispute involved, almost always has a motivation to push the price of oil higher. In the case of 2013, why would there be a drive for higher prices? The market was at a seemingly healthy price level at around $100 per barrel. Was there a case for economic motivation that could possibly be linked to the inhumane actions in Syria?

In order to take a close look at this question, the data surrounding the Arab Oil Embargo in 1973 was gathered and compared on a relative basis to the economic data in the summer of 2013. The data in the table below was assembled for the month just prior to, and during the major jump in the price of oil between December 1973 and January 1974. What stands out in the data is the general relationship of the price of oil and U.S. GDP in January 1974 and July 2013. The price level of oil relative to GDP, after all of its volatility and seemingly random trading pattern during the time period, was almost identical – a nearly 1:1 proportional change. A coincidence you ask? Some might argue that it is. However, when viewed in the context of the economic circumstances surrounding the pricing of oil between the two time periods, the relative valuation begins to make more sense.

Oil is uniquely valued in the marketplace as both a commodity and a currency for the oil-rich nations in the Middle East. The commodity like features and its value as a highly necessary input into developed world economies make it very correlated to real U.S. GDP growth. As a currency, however, it responds to the ability of Middle Eastern countries as a cartel to control the relative price level of the oil to obtain and maintain a

OIL RELATIVE TO:		Dec-73	Jul-13	INCREASE
GDP ($B)		1,479	16,729	1131%
S&P 500 INDEX		97	1,686	1738%
CPI-INFLATION		46	233	504%
OIL-WTI	$	4.31 $	105.50	2448%
GAS / GAL	$	0.39 $	3.60	923%

OIL RELATIVE TO:		Jan-74	Jul-13	INCREASE
GDP ($B)		1,484	16,729	1127%
S&P 500 INDEX		97	1,686	1738%
CPI-INFLATION		47	233	499%
OIL-WTI	$	10.11 $	105.50	1044%
GAS / GAL	$	0.53 $	3.60	679%

standard of living relative to other nations. Since oil is traded in U.S. dollars, the movements in the price of oil, therefore, must be looked at relative to U.S. monetary and fiscal policy to get a true sense of why its price is gravitating to a particular point. During the 1960s and 70s, U.S. monetary policy was aggressively accommodative. This was particularly the case in the Nixon administration when the Fed became supportive of utilizing money supply growth to reduce the unemployment rate. This set of circumstances is very similar to policies being used in 2013.

The other aspect of the data shows that the stock market as measured by the S&P 500 grew at a much faster pace than oil in the 40 year time period from 1974 through 2013. Over time, GDP and the S&P are also highly correlated. What this information tells and investor is that oil and GDP may have returned to a point of balance within the context of the Theory of Financial Relativity, but that stocks in 2013 were more at risk of moving down if oil continued to rise at a faster pace than real GDP growth.

In 1974, the stock market dropped dramatically in response to the oil shock which sent prices above the $10 level from $3.50 per barrel. The stock market did retrace a portion of its losses between 1975 and 1976, but as the graph below shows, a continued rise in the price of oil kept a damper on stock prices until 1979 when Jimmy Carter deregulated the price of oil in the United States market.

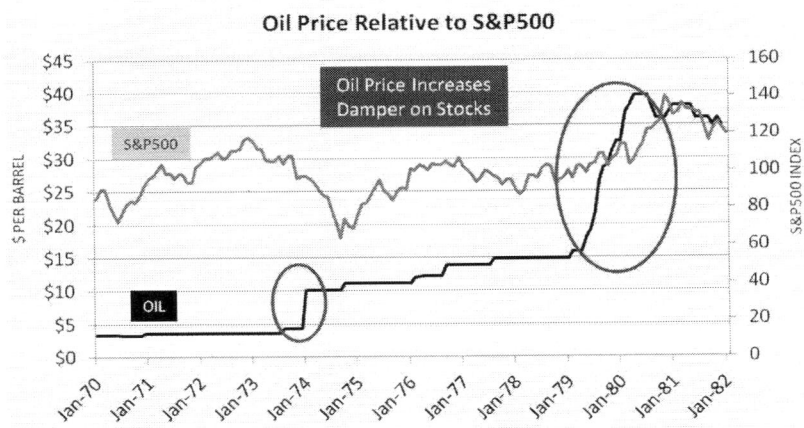

Oil Price Relative to S&P500

Investing in stocks between 1976 and 1979 was dead money in the stock market. The price of oil rose in virtual lock step with nominal GDP and real GDP growth was close to zero - stagflation. During the period GDP grew from $1.48T to $2.55T or 1.72 times. The price of oil increased from $10.11 to $15.85, 1.57 times. It was as if the U.S. government and OPEC were in a stalemate with oil price increases sapping real growth from the U.S. economy, leaving only inflation which resulted from excessive monetization of government spending.

From 2009 to 2013, the adjustment process to higher oil prices was gradual, and the actual shock which is most comparable to 1973 occurred in 2008. The monetary action that was taken from 2009 to 2013 by the U.S. Federal Reserve created the necessary market liquidity for the relative relationship between the Middle East oil currency and the U.S. dollar to support $100 a barrel for oil. The adjustment, however, was being made at the expense of real GDP growth. The adjustment produced a jobless recovery, just like the stagflation time period in the 1970s. Higher input costs forced businesses to use productivity gains as a means of dealing with higher energy costs.

The severe impact of rising oil prices in a wage constrained U.S economy can be seen in the table below which shows the change in oil prices relative to GDP from January 2003 to July 2013. Nominal GDP increased 150% from 2003 through July 2013, while the price of oil increased 320%. Stocks benefited relatively more over the time period, and measured inflation increased only 28% over the 10 year time period, far less than the 1970s when wages expanded much more freely under similar circumstances.

OIL RELATIVE TO:			
	Jan-03	Jul-13	INCREASE
GDP ($B)	11,147	16,729	150%
S&P500 INDEX	856	1,686	197%
CPI-INFLATION	183	233	128%
OIL-WTI	$ 32.94	$ 105.50	320%
GAS / GAL	$ 1.48	$ 3.60	243%

	JAN-03 TO JUL-13		
OIL RELATIVE TO:	GDP	S&P500	CPI
R-VALUE	0.83	0.61	0.83

Interestingly, the most visible indicator of inflation for consumers, the price of gas, increased at a slower pace than the increase in the raw crude oil that composes 67% of the price. Additionally, inflation increased only at a low rate. The reason the U.S. inflation index can suppress the pass-through of the oil based price increases takes a complex bureaucratic explanation. But in a nut-shell, the government takes the latitude to use substitution of one product for another, as well as increased quality as a means calculating its inflation measure. In the case of gasoline, if cars get better gas mileage, a portion of the gas price increase is deemed to be real growth. It doesn't matter that you might have to spend $30,000 on a new car to realize the improvement, you are deemed better off. Go figure.

Post the 2008 financial crisis, precipitated to a large degree by the oil shock, the stock market traded in a pattern very similar to the 1975 through 1979 time period. The big difference was that the U.S. government did not place controls on the price of oil. It did, however, institute a Federal Reserve monetary program which in conjunction with coordinated programs in Europe and Asia aggressively weakened the entire developed world of currencies in unison. The concerted action created the perception across markets that nothing was changing at a currency exchange level as the Western alliance printed new money at the same relative pace. The actions taken, however, required an unprecedented level of U.S. dollars to be pumped into the world wide financial system. During this time period the Fed balance sheet expanded from under $1T in assets before September 2008, to over $3.3T in mid 2013, and was targeted to reach $4T by 2014.

What did not increase as quickly in supply when all the other currencies rose so quickly? – Oil.

What happens when the value of the developed world currencies fall in value?
–Oil prices rise in response to the excessive liquidity.

And the price of oil did rise between the 2009 and 2013 time period as shown
in the graph below. The stock market also retraced it's loses from the 2008
decline. Whereas the price of oil was a damper on stocks in the late 70s, the
two markets moved more in correlation up to the $100 a barrel mark in 2011.
A move above $100 per barrel precipitated a drop in stocks in early 2011.
From that point to 2013 the stock market diverged in value as the price of oil
continually hit the $100 ceiling level and pulled back, even as Fed induced
market liquidity drove stocks higher in relative value.

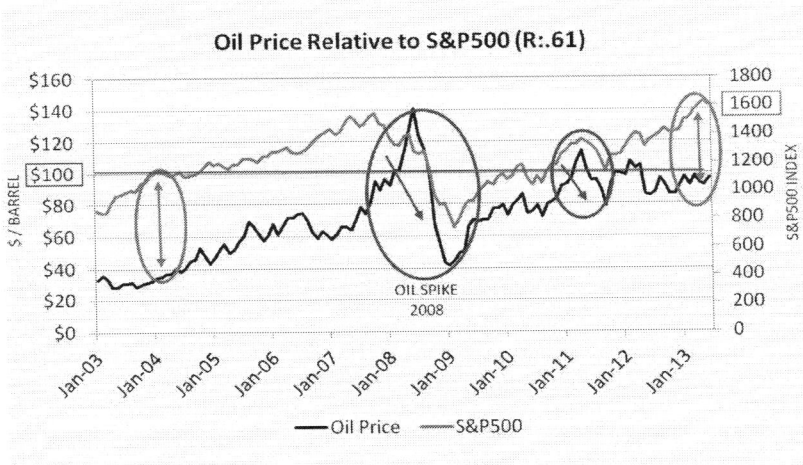

Oil Price Relative to S&P500 (R:.61)

As of the writing of this book, the Middle East tension level was on the rise.
Geo-political tension is the primary force over time that is resorted to when
the Middle East feels it needs to exert power to adjust the value of the oil
upward relative to the depreciated fiat currencies of the western developed
economies. U.S. energy policy, focused on development of shale oil & gas
energy supply domestically in fields such as the Bakken are a counter force in
the long-term against oil valuation demands of OPEC. However, oil pricing
in 2013 was still heavily under the control of OPEC and Saudi Arabia, and
investors should not expect that the region will idly accept lower or even
stable price levels as long as the U.S. Federal Reserve continues an ultra easy
monetary policy.

Lessons in Oil Price Relativity

Important lessons in financial relativity can be learned from the oil market. These lessons are critical because oil is a vital influencing factor in the U.S. economy. These lessons are summarized in 7 key points.

LESSONS ABOUT THE SHOCKING RELATIVITY OF OIL

- Oil is highly correlated with U.S. nominal GDP through time.
- Oil exhibits the characteristics of a currency for Middle-Eastern OPEC countries.
- Demand for oil is highly inelastic, and changes in oil prices impact the real U.S. economy much like taxes.
- Post 9/11, oil resurged to a relative price level to US GDP that was experienced in the early 1970s and the era of geo-political tension similar to that time period also returned.
- Continued geo-political conflicts and excess U.S. dollar liquidity may set the stage for re-valuation of oil to a much higher level in the intermediate term beyond 2013.
- Oil price spikes have preceded all six recorded recessions since the early 1970s.
- An oil price spike is experienced when prices rise to or above a previous all-time high, and the price rise doubles or even triples the price of oil in less than 12 months.

Distilling the essence of these lessons leads to the formulation of Guiding Principle #6 in the Theory of Financial Relativity. The Principle captures the highly correlated nature of energy based imports on the U.S. economy, and the corresponding force that is applied to maintain national income parity overtime between energy exporting countries and the United States.

6th PRINCIPLE OF FINANCIAL RELATIVITY

Oil price spikes are a foreign force "shockingly" correlated with stock market corrections.

From the 1960s through 2013, when dollar based depreciation severely eroded the relative purchasing power of oil exporting countries, an oil shock eventually transpired. Oil shocks are financial events that the Federal Reserve must respond to with equal and opposite force - monetary tightening. History shows that the Fed force always negatively impacts the stock market as interest rates are increased to restore currency purchasing power parity.

One aspect of the relative price of oil was not covered in the preceding chapter. The price of "black gold" is even more highly correlated with the value of pure gold than the U.S. economy. This fascinating relationship is explained in detail in the next chapter.

11 GOLD THE GLOBAL RELATIVITY REFLECTOR

"Nobody really understands gold prices and I don't pretend to understand them either," Ben Bernanke, Federal Reserve Chairman said during the Senate Banking Committee hearing on Thursday July 18th, 2013.

This statement seemed odd coming from a Federal Reserve Chairman of the United States of America. Odd because the use of gold as a standard medium for international exchange between the gold-bearing regions of Nubia and Egypt dates back to 1500 B.C. in recorded history. Odd because it was one of the first mediums of exchange used to preserve the purchasing power between sellers and buyers of goods or in repayment of debts. Odd because the characteristic of gold that allowed it to become a major medium of exchange through the ages, a very stable supply and universal acceptance, are what every central banker desires for their country's currency. These spoken words were indeed strange since they were spoken by the chairman of the United States Federal Reserve who is in charge of the largest and currently most universally accepted currency in the world - the U.S. dollar.

So why would Ben Bernanke publicly state that he doesn't understand gold prices? To his credit, he used the term prices, not value. The Theory of Financial Relativity assumes the price of any asset will appear random if viewed in isolation and not relative to other assets. Even the U.S. dollar is priced randomly if you look only at its trading pattern over time and do not correlate it to the myriad of forces at work that set its value as a medium of exchange. The statement made by Bernanke was born out of his duty as Fed Chairman to promote and protect the U.S. dollar as the supreme medium of exchange. Any indication that he knew why gold prices were reacting in some way in dollar terms would have been sacrosanct in 2013. From the Depression Era through 2013 the foreign currency market changed from being backed by gold, to being backed only by the full faith and credit of the government's issuing currency in which international trade was being settled. After 1971, gold was no longer an official part of the international foreign exchange system. However, gold continued after its abandonment as a means of exchange to provide a relevant financial function of reflecting the relative purchasing power parity between countries in the world.

What and Who Determines the Value of Gold

Ben Bernanke's comment does not mean that gold does not a have value that can be understood. Gold's value is most directly related to its use as a currency, not an asset. It is a reserve currency historically used by many Middle Eastern oil-rich nations and emerging market nations. When the western world abandoned the gold standard for international exchange, gold progressively became driven in value by the world-wide oil market and the nations which continued to utilize gold as a medium of exchange to settle oil trades or hedge oil transactions settled in U.S. dollars.

From 1968 through 2013 the dollar price of oil was highly correlated to the market value of gold. As the graph below shows, the R-value correlation between the dollar price per barrel of oil and the dollar price per troy ounce of gold was a very significant .885.

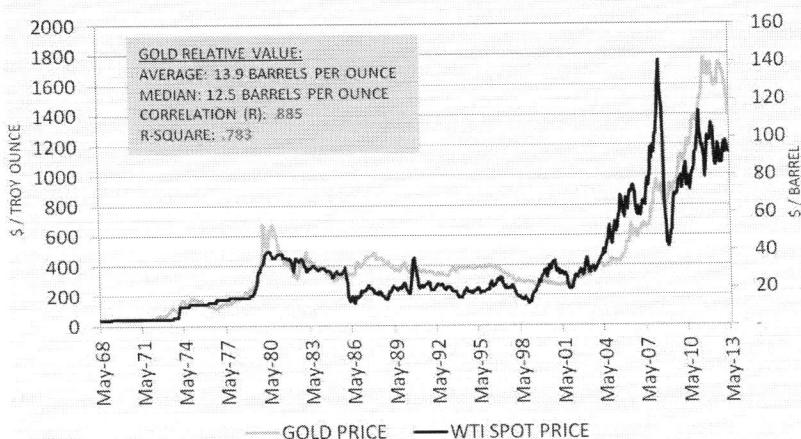

The divergence and then re-convergence in gold and oil price levels on a relative basis in 1986, 2001 (post 9/11), 2007-09, and then again from 2011 to

2013 are points on the above graph that investors need to pay close attention. The average number of barrels of oil that an ounce of gold bought from 1968 to 2013 was 13.9. The median price was 12.5 barrels per ounce. The correlation of oil and gold price levels was highest from the early 1970s thru 1985. This time period of very high correlation provides a clue about the dynamics underlying the relative relationship between oil and gold.

These points in history provide information that Ben Bernanke really did not want to delve into when he dodged the question about gold in his Senate testimony in July 2013. The forces driving the traded price of oil and other hard commodities are what gave gold its glittering value in 2013 relative to a world of fiat currencies. Gold increased almost 6 fold in value from the year 2000 to 2013. A U.S. dollar devaluation of this magnitude relative to gold was similarly experienced from 1973 to 1980.

Gold's Decline as a Legal Currency in the United States

In order for a country to maintain a stable government, certain systems are usually firmly under control – the country's military and its currency. This list also includes the communication system, particularly critical in under developed countries and more autocratically controlled nations. Some combination of these elements can be found underpinning the strongest nations throughout history. The control of the country's currency creates an interesting challenge. First, leaders are pre-inclined to dole out favors and spend money in order to satisfy the wants and needs of the country's population. But, at the same time, the currency level in the country must be "credible" in the sense that people believe it will hold its value in making transactions not only within the country, but also internationally. Therefore, a currency must maintain a consistent relative value through time. It cannot be eroded by governing leaders simply printing more currency and exchanging it for goods outside the country – unless the other countries are printing at the same relative pace. There must be a balance maintained.

For centuries, gold was used as a medium of exchange, including the United States. However, using gold as a basis for currency value can create problems for rulers in countries that have democratic elections. Adhering to a gold standard domestically means a country's money supply will be more influenced by outside forces affecting the supply of gold, which in a country with a growing population means scarcity unless the country can mine more gold, almost always a non-possibility. A constraint on a nation's money supply enforced by the gold standard severely limits the ability of charismatic leaders to execute grand visions once elected. The stable and consistent basis on which gold maintains relative value is usually at odds with the desire to re-distribution wealth within democracies.

The pressure to democratize the United States money supply, shifting away from the gold standard, really gained traction during the Depression years of the 1930s. During that time period, Keynesian based economic ideas were pushed on the economy by the government in an attempt to increase economic output and revive the depressed economy. The nation's currency prior to the Depression was exchangeable into gold at a set value. This constant exchange rate led to a contraction in the nation's money supply when people became more fearful, not just when the economy was over-heating. Gold became a lightening rod as one of the limiting factors in the effectiveness of democratic led government stimulus programs to encourage growth when the economy weakened.

The Gold Reserve Act of 1934 was a government action aimed at countering the contracting money supply effects during the Depression. The Act signed into law by FDR gave the government the permanent title to all monetary gold and halted the minting of gold coins. It also put the U.S. on a limited gold bullion standard by restricting dollar redemption into gold through the official banking system <u>except</u> to foreign central banks and licensed private users. The official U.S. exchange rate between foreign central banks and the U.S. was set at $35 per ounce.

In 1945, the Bretton Woods agreement was ratified by the U.S. Congress. The Bretton Woods system established fixed exchange rates between countries redeemable in gold by the U.S. Government at $35 per ounce, and required countries within the system to establish monetary policies which would preserve their currency at the fixed relative exchange ratio with the U.S. currency over time. The IMF and World Bank were created at that time as implementers and enforcement institutions. The one key aspect of this system was that the U.S. committed to backing every dollar overseas with gold. Other currencies were fixed to the dollar, and the dollar was pegged to gold. At the time it seemed to be a secure system. The U.S owned over 574 million ounces of gold, and there was substantial demand for U.S. produced goods as Europe and Japan re-built post WWII – keeping international demand high for U.S. goods and services in exchange for dollars.

However, the system began to show its fatal flaw in the early 1960s. In the

Bretton Woods system, if the supply of U.S. dollars was increased more quickly in relative proportion to the level of money in foreign economies, then the value of gold in dollar terms needed to rise in the exchange ratio to depreciate the dollar. If this did not happen and the exchange ratio was maintained, an arbitrage opportunity would result. The first signs of the uncontrollable nature of the Bretton Woods system were exhibited in Europe in 1961. Countries outside the U.S began to accumulate too many U.S. dollars in their reserve accounts as trade with the U.S. slowed on a relative basis. The U.S. no longer was running a current account surplus as it did immediately following WWII. To compensate for the growing imbalance, the central banks of Belgium, France, Italy, the Netherlands, Switzerland, West Germany, the United Kingdom and the United States formed the London Gold Pool and agreed to buy and sell at $35.0875 per ounce. This created an incentive for Americans to own gold abroad and exchange it into U.S. dollars at a higher exchange rate. The U.S. government tried to eliminate this loophole by outlawing the practice. However, it did nothing to solve the root cause of the growing system imbalance as money expansion within the United States raged higher, out of synch with the rest of the world.

In March 1968 the London Gold Market closed for two weeks due to a sudden surge in the demand for gold. When it re-opened, the official gold pool announced it would no longer buy and sell gold in the private market. There was a two-tier system which emerged as a result. The top tier was for official transactions between international monetary authorities at the unchanged price of $35 per troy ounce. The newly created tier was for all other transactions, where the value of gold began to be set based on a fluctuating free-market price.

Why was this happening? The fixed exchange ratio between the U.S. and other countries was being set by a regulated government rate, not relative to supply and demand based market forces. As more and more dollars flooded into the international system because of U.S. trade deficits driven by the Vietnam War and the Great Society program, gold became perceived by a growing number of nations and investors in the world as a more stable medium of exchange. In essence, the mighty U.S. dollar was being devalued. Government actions had little impact on the trend. During the late 1960s the U.S. Mint terminated its policy of buying and selling gold to parties licensed by the U.S. Treasury to hold gold. Gold as backing of Federal Reserve Notes was also eliminated. These actions were intended to lower the demand for gold. But, it was the excess supply of dollars in the market that was the problem.

By 1971, America's gold stock had fallen to a level in which foreign central banks held more dollars than the U.S. held gold. The U.S. was very vulnerable to a run on its remaining gold supply. Something had to be done. Direct devaluation of the dollar relative to the price of gold in order to maintain the Bretton Woods framework was not the chosen option.

What Changed in 1971?

On August 15, 1971, the United States unilaterally took the U.S. currency off of the gold exchange standard established by the Bretton Woods Accord for international exchange based transactions. At that point in time, the dollar exchange rate was allowed to float against all other currencies in the market – the determination of the exchange thereby being based more on market forces. Most other industrialized nations, such as the U.K with the pound sterling quickly followed. The abandonment of the gold standard opened the door for many industrialized nations to increase their currency reserves far more than ever before – and reinforced the failing Nixon policy at the time of increasing the U.S. money supply as a means of reducing the unemployment rate. As a result, there was a massive depreciation of the U.S. dollar exchange rate. Because oil was priced in dollars, this meant that oil producers began to receive relatively less real income for the same price. Prior to the U.S. moving off the gold standard, OPEC had a means of hedging the depreciating impact U.S. monetary policy was having on their county's ability to 'keep up" in real terms. They began to use the free market exchange price of gold as a basis for pricing oil and demanding that the U.S. dollar price of oil be adjusted upward relative to the change in the free market gold value.

When the U.S. abandoned the gold standard altogether and the U.S. exchange rate began falling dramatically over a short time period, pressure began to mount in the Middle East. From August 1971 to July 1973, the U.S. Dollar Index against major currencies in the world declined from 118.98 to 95.32, a 24.8% decline. Oil however, was held at a constant $3.56 USD per barrel during this time period. The purchasing power of the oil countries was considerably reduced in a very short period of time.

The pressure from OPEC to raise the price of oil during this time period was very high as witnessed in this quote from the Shah of Iran to the New York Times in 1973:

"Of course oil is going to rise... You western nations increased the price of wheat you sell us

by 300%, and the same for sugar and cement... You buy our crude oil and sell it back to us, refined as petrochemicals, at a hundred times the price you've paid to us...; It's only fair that, from now on, you should pay more for oil. Let's say ten times more."

The deteriorating situation driven by the de-valuation of the U.S. dollar post abandonment of the gold standard was the primary contributing factor leading up to the Arab Oil Embargo announced in October 1973.

In addition to the oil embargo, the OPEC cartel issued a joint communiqué stating that, from then on, they would <u>price a barrel of oil in gold terms</u>. Before the embargo, oil was priced relative to gold in the range of 24-30 barrels per ounce. As the embargo went into effect in January 1974 oil increased in price to over $10 per barrel. Relative to the price of gold, oil began to trade in 1974 at 12.8 barrels per ounce, which for the following 40 years was close to the median price. OPEC dramatically strengthened its economic position with the United States unilaterally, virtually overnight.

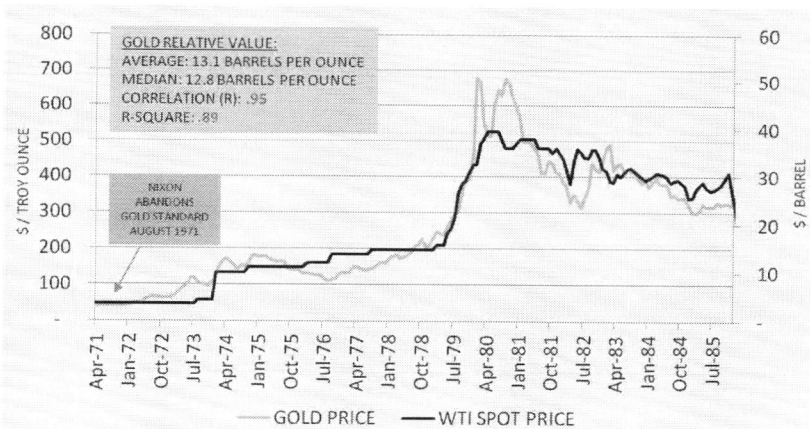

The price of oil in gold terms became an important signal point of relativity after the Arab Oil Embargo. From 1974 through 2013, when gold bought less than 12.8 barrels of oil per ounce, the world oil price in dollars was a constraint on industrialized economies. When gold bought more than 12.8 barrels per ounce oil policy was accommodative to growth in the industrial world.

The price of oil relative to gold from the Arab Embargo through the early 1980s traded in a tight range around the 12.8 barrel per ounce benchmark. The correlation R-value of .95 over this time period was very significant. In the graph, the oil price spike in 1974 is visible, and the corresponding gold price level change can also be seen. During this time period, oil prices became a constraint on real economic growth in the United States and globally.

With the advent of the floating foreign currency exchange system gold began to exhibit high volatility. From 1968 through 2013, gold exhibited a trading volatility as measured by its variance of .28, almost double the S&P 500 variance of .16. This reflects the higher risk in holding gold. But gold also showed a higher annual growth rate of 11.62% versus the S&P 500 growth rate of 10.5% over the same period. Some of the volatility in the late 1970s reflected outside investors taking momentum positions in the market. These investors were likely run out of the market when gold prices fell dramatically in 1981 and early 1982.

Principle #1 of the Theory of Financial Relativity states that U.S. GDP is highly correlated with U.S. stocks. Gold, on the other hand, is a better proxy for the rise and fall of the GDPs of countries that export raw materials such as oil. In the 1970s and early 1980s, the oil-rich nations were booming on a relative real GDP basis. Newton's Third Law of Motion states – *"every action has an equal and opposite reaction."* Maybe not because of a natural force, but more likely because of a man-made financial force, the good times did come to an end abruptly for some oil-rich countries at the end of 1985. What happened brings to mind the proverbial "pay-back is hell" analogy.

What changed in Early 1986?

During the hay days of the late 1970s and early 80s, oil producing countries economically flourished. Some, like Saudi Arabia, put aside assets for future needs. Others, like Iran, burned through resources much more quickly, in large part due to continuing conflicts with Iraq. This dichotomy led to a difference in perspectives as the world demand for oil slowed in growth relative to supply. Cheating on quota levels by member countries to maintain their own GDP growth at the expense of other members grew in frequency in the early 1980s. Usually Saudi Arabia was the OPEC member that stepped in and cut its own production level when quotas were not kept by others.

Saudi Arabia, however, had another growing problem. Its holdings of U.S. dollars grew as a consequence of the treaty with the U.S. which required them to trade oil in U.S. dollars in exchange for U.S. military protection of their oil fields. The excess dollars, which became known as petrodollars, were re-cycled into the United States at first through the purchase of U.S Treasuries which paid very high rates of interest at the time, as much as 12%-14% for maturities of 10 to 30 years. Suddenly the Saudi's found themselves in a position of co-dependency with the U.S. and other industrialized countries within the framework of probable economic outcomes. They faced the choice of either keeping the high price of oil strangle hold on the industrial world and risking a potential degradation in the value of their growing Treasury reserve positions, or they could take greater control of the situation and become more accommodative to economic growth in their developed nation alliance. The Saudi's were in a position to do the later, and that was the path chosen.

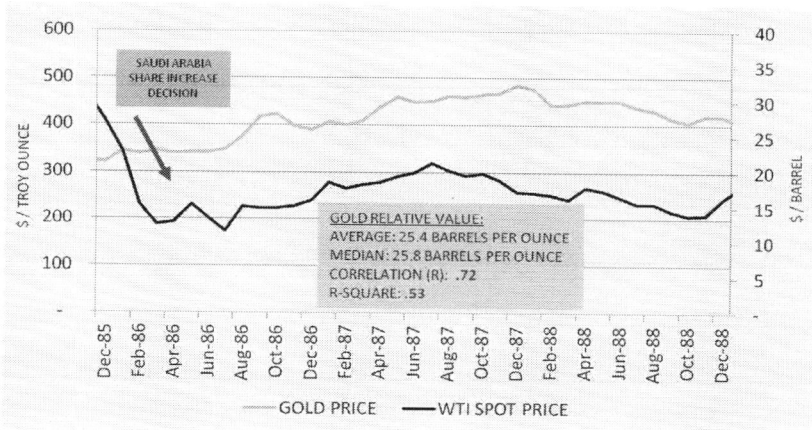

In late 1985, Saudi Arabia announced the unilateral decision to take a bigger portion of the world oil market. They increased production from 2 to 5 million barrels per day. As the graph above shows, the impact on the world price of crude oil was dramatic, dropping from $30 to $12 per barrel in 4 months. The move by Saudi Arabia in late 1985 changed the dynamics in setting oil prices, putting control completely in the hands of the Saudis. The United States and other industrial economies benefited greatly in terms of real economic growth as well as lower price inflation. The shift to a "borrow and spend" policy in the U.S. to finance increasing current account deficits was paying off in a somewhat perverse relative way.

The decline in oil prices on the world market in 1986 came at a time which greatly weakened Iran and most likely tilted the balance of power greatly in favor of the U.S. versus the Soviet Union. Several years after the oil price cut, Ronald Reagan made his famous speech beseeching Gorbachev to tear down the Berlin Wall.

The decline harkened in a time period that lasted for the next 14 years until the new millennium. During the time period the relative value of gold weakened considerably. The relative purchasing value of the currencies used by the allied powers aligned with the Soviet Union suffered, while the U.S. dollar and its attractive high interest rates became a growing safe-haven. The U.S. stock market blossomed, driven by higher GDP growth and declining interest rates.

The chart below shows the change in relative value of gold over the 1986 to 2000 time period. In 1986, the relative price level of gold in oil terms was 27 barrels of oil per ounce. This was the average price level that oil was trading just prior to the 1974 oil embargo. From 1986 through 2000 the correlation between gold and oil was inverted. The correlation during the 1990s was -.32, with an average of 17.7 barrels per ounce. There was only one major conflict and oil spike during the time period – the Kuwait War. In this time frame the Saudi's took quick action to bring price levels back to an accommodative level.

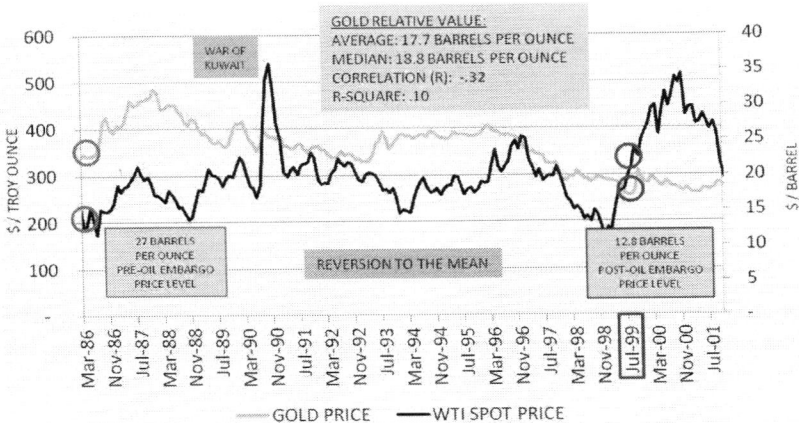

Eventually, the low relative price of oil began to become unsustainable in the market. The first reversion back to the post Arab Oil Embargo relative price level of 12.8 barrels per ounce of gold occurred in July 1999.

The spike in oil prices in the year 2000 to levels not seen on an absolute basis since the early 1980s, or on a relative basis since the Arab Oil Embargo triggered a recession beginning in April 2001. Although oil prices did pull back in the recession, the value of gold did not. The accommodation period led by Saudi Arabian from which the U.S. greatly benefited, was about to abruptly halt beginning with the terrorist attacks on 9/11 of 2001.

Post 9/11 Era Sees Surge Upward in Gold Value

After the 9/11 attacks and the recession in the U.S., the price of oil did not return to the relatively accommodative range observed in the 1990s. The balance of power in pricing oil shifted away from the Saudi Arabian alliance with the United States. The shift can be seen in the financial market as both the value of gold and the price of oil increased in lock step. The market reflected more countries performing transactions valued in gold. The market for oil grew more quickly in emerging countries like China and India – and that demand was being satisfied by OPEC members like Iran that used gold, not dollars as the relative medium of exchange.

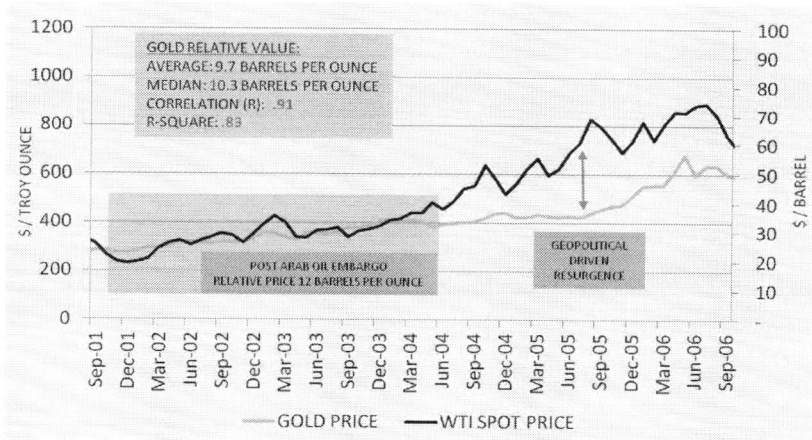

As indicated in the graph above, in September of 2001 the pricing level of gold in terms of oil was at levels experienced in the U.S. in 1974, and remained at the 12 barrel per ounce level through mid 2004. At that point, even as the Federal Reserve began to tighten interest rate policy, the gold price of oil became even less accommodative, falling below 10 barrels per ounce. The R-Value correlation of gold and oil during this period was very high at .91 reflecting the increase in dollar denominated oil sales being converted to gold reserves. Geo-political tensions in the Middle East were contributing influences on the rising market for both oil and gold during the time.

Gold and Oil during the 2008 Financial Crisis

A peculiar event happened in the gold market as the 2008 financial crisis raged in 2008. The price of oil screamed higher to $140 per barrel, but, gold on the other hand leveled off in dollar terms at $800 to $900 per ounce in late 2007.

The value of gold did not change substantially through the crisis. This curious occurrence is contrary to what many market experts expect as gold is assumed to be a safe-haven asset when market turmoil increases, and therefore it would be expected to go up as a crisis intensifies. This did not happen in 2008. The reason that it did not happen is likely because oil sales which typically would have been converted to gold reserves, were instead diverted. Why would this happen you ask?

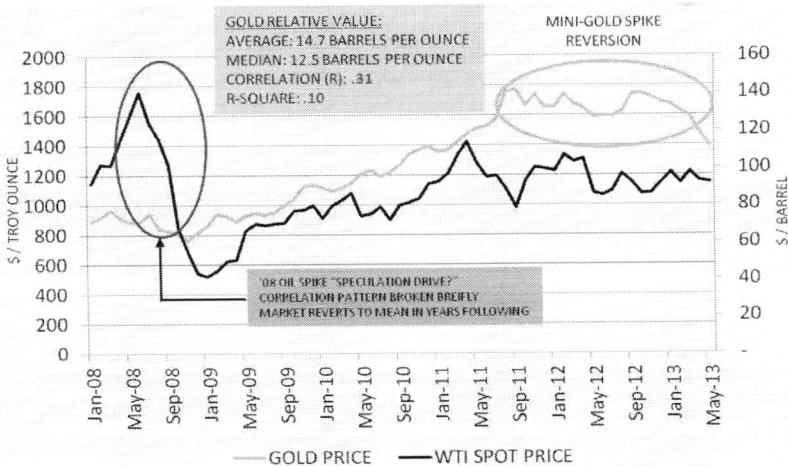

In the chart above, you can clearly see the divergence of the price of oil in USD relative to the gold value. At the peak oil price of $140 per barrel, gold was trading at 6.7 barrels per ounce. This price eclipsed the high relative levels observed during the mid 1970s. This pricing phenomenon does lend some credence to the research that speculation drove price levels higher in 2008. If actual oil demand was increasing and oil was actually being delivered by countries like Iran during this time period, the drive up in gold value would have continued. But the pricing action looks more like a trade which took excess dollars flowing into the Middle East, and continually bid the dollar price of oil up through the use of derivative contracts settled in dollars. The trade appears to have been hedged in gold at around $800 per ounce. As the circled area in the chart shows, the trade was reversed as oil declined to $40 per barrel, but gold remained above $800 per ounce.

If "cash was king" in 2008, gold was an equal partner, and possibly superior contender for the throne. Gold is typically stable in times of crisis, and its stability in 2008 may have been driven by the reduction in oil inventories and the storage of the liquidity in gold reserves by many OPEC member nations.

The metal was particularly strong through the '08 crisis and in the aftermath.

Gold's Relative Value from 2009 through 2013

The result of the oil spike and then collapse in 2008 found the price of a barrel of oil per ounce of gold back above the all important level of 12.8 barrels per ounce, an accommodative range for the U.S. economy.

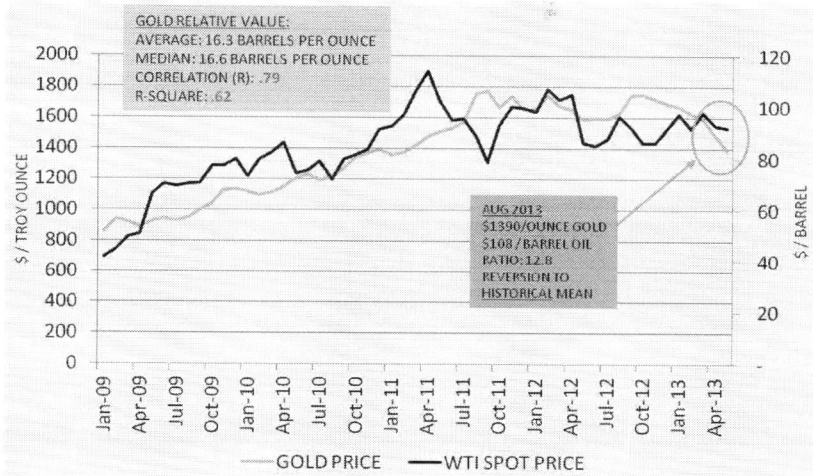

In fact, the range was a healthy 16.3 barrels per ounce on average from January 2009 through the beginning of 2013. The correlation R-value was .79 reflecting a market with a stable relationship between the price of oil and the price of gold. The time period between 2009 and 2013 was one of re-inflation after the 2008 financial crisis. The Federal Reserve of the United States was accommodative, increasing the liquidity level of in the market by flooding the market with U.S. dollars through open market operations. The quantitative easing operations during the time period increased the Fed balance sheet from $877B in January 2008 to $2T in January 2009 in order to arrest the financial decline. Most of the assets purchased were non-traditional, meaning that they consisted of mortgage backed securities, many distressed in nature, and banking system preferred stock. The non-traditional Fed program did not monetized government borrowing in the early part of the time period. This part of the Fed program provided focused liquidity to allow the financial markets to begin to recover from decline. As the non-traditional TARP loans were paid off by the banking system, the returned funds were re-deployed to purchase Mortgage Backed securities and Treasury securities. This drove interest rates lower, and was viewed as potentially inflationary by the market.

However, the Fed policy was not immediately inflationary, even though the Fed balance sheet continued to grow to over $3.3T as of July 2013, and on schedule to reach $4T by 2014. The lack of inflation left many investors scratching their heads as to why all of the "money printing" by the Fed and other Central Banks around the world was not showing up in the inflation statistics. As explained in the previous chapter, inflation was clearly evident in the market, but it was being exhibited as asset bubbles in the financial market, not consumer price inflation.

If the world was deflating after 2008, the gold market was not signaling any such direction. After catching its legs in early 2008, it began to climb from the $800 per ounce range up to a peak of around $1800 by September of 2011.

The 2013 Gold Market Correction

In early 2013, a gold market correction began to take hold, and gold fell in value from $1712 per ounce at the end of 2012, to $1192 per ounce at the end of June 2013. Hedge funds led by large investors that had participated in the run-up in gold value, pared their holdings. The billionaire investor John Paulson at the time was the largest investor in the SPDR Gold Trust. His share holding at the end of the 1st quarter of 2013 were 21.8M; when gold reached a low point in June 2013 his holdings were10.2M shares, a reduction of over 50%. The shaking out of the gold market after significant gains is not unusual. A similar and even larger decline in gold happened in the early 1980s as oil prices topped and the U.S. monetary and fiscal policy changed course. It was also a time period that Iran was in dire need of financial resources.

On a relative basis, it is worthwhile to analyze the wide swings in gold value in the early 1980s and 2013. Gold was at an all-time high in both instances, and made a significant correction downward in U.S. dollar terms. However, in the 1980 case, oil was at an all-time high level and was falling. The relative gold price of oil remained stable in the decline. At the time, the U.S. dollar was strengthening as both oil and gold declined while Fed policy held interest rates very high increasing the flow of funds into Treasury investments.

The 2013 scenario in the gold and oil market was very different than the early 1980s scenario.

1. The correction in gold value in 2013 was not joined by a decline in oil prices; on the contrary oil prices increased post the decline in gold.
2. Federal Reserve policy in 2013, although projected to slowly become tighter, was still very accommodative – the opposite of the early 1980s.

> In fact, the Fed policy in 2013 was much closer to the Nixon policy of the early 1970s, where money supply growth and reserve creation was being used as a policy to lower the unemployment rate.

After the correction in gold prices in 2013 the price of oil in gold terms was no longer accommodative; it had become economically constraining. The price reverted back to 12.8 barrels per ounce, the post Arab Oil Embargo price level. Historically this pricing pattern signals trouble ahead. Reversion to the mean of the gold price of oil, with the price of oil leading the charge higher signals Mid-East turmoil is very likely. This same relative set of circumstances

> "REVERSION TO THE MEAN AFTER THE GOLD PRICE OF OIL HAS BEEN AT PRE-EMBARGO LEVELS USUALLY MEANS TROUBLE AHEAD"

happened leading up to the Arab Oil Embargo and the conflicts that began post 9/11. Why would the oil price not fall as the gold price corrected? The biggest factor leads back to Iran and emerging market economies.

On July 1, 2013 the United States began to rigorously enforce a ban on gold sales with Iran. The purpose of the ban was to put pressure on Tehran over its nuclear program by under-mining the Iranian currency, the Rial. The ban affected sales to both the Iranian government and its citizens. Stopping gold sales to Iran was targeted at severely hampering the country's ability to sell oil reserves by using the gold market as the medium for exchange. This action, although its effectiveness was not yet known, very likely injected a potential element of supply constraint into the market, but more importantly if the economic pressure continued to build on Iran, an element of conflict as well. The Syrian Conflict which arose in August 2013 marked a potential starting point of a new wave of tension.

The value of gold settled into an intermediate trading of $1300 per ounce in the latter half of 2013. Economic War was being waged between the U.S. and countries which were heavily using gold as a medium of exchange, and the U.S. was intervening in the market in ways intended to suppress its drive upward in dollar terms. Such actions, however, did not hold bright prospects for success. Newton's 3rd Law of Motion remained in full force when it came to Middle–East oil and U.S. GDP growth. Without a major downward "relative" adjustment in the cost of oil in the U.S. as happened in the mid 1980s, the U.S. real economy was on a path to continue to suffer. There was hope that the U.S. might achieve relief from higher energy prices with the production increases driven by new domestic shale oil fields. However, the

U.S. was not in a position to sever its oil ties with Saudi Arabia, meaning that OPEC and the politics surrounding regional conflicts would drive the U.S. dollar price of oil for many years in the future. As in the late 1970s, potentially the only means of "pacifying" the situation was increasing interest rates on U.S. Treasuries to make the dollar relatively more attractive than gold.

Stock Market Performance and Gold

The value of the U.S. stock market and an ounce of gold since 1968 are not highly correlated as shown in the chart below. The correlation R-value is only .58 meaning that over the time period, there were other factors which more strongly influenced the relative change in the value of each asset. Based on the information presented in this chapter, as well as those leading up to this chapter, the lower correlation should not be a surprise.

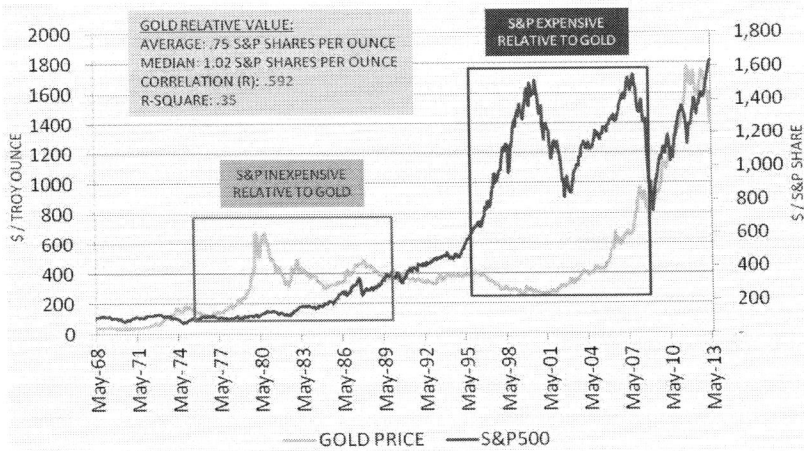

Observe, however, that through time the U.S. stock market if priced in gold exhibited a median value that held a 1 for 1 in relationship. This means that half the time from 1968 through 2013 if you exchanged a share of the S&P 500 priced in dollars, you got more than 1 oz of gold, and 50% of the time you got less than an ounce. The exchange rate varied widely, particularly in the late 1970s, when as the graph above shows the U.S. stock market was inexpensive in gold terms. The value of the U.S. stock market diverged in the other direction in the 1990s and in 2007 as stocks became very expensive if priced in gold terms.

The pattern in the two markets, although seemingly uncorrelated, are moving in very predictable fashion through time based on the relative price of oil, the resulting impact on U.S. GDP and the level of U.S. interest rates. The U.S. GDP is tightly correlated with the U.S. stock market. In the 1970s, the oil-rich nations through the power of OPEC gained a relative economic advantage. The U.S. real economy suffered as a consequence and U.S. stocks languished. To attract and keep currency reserves, the U.S. had to keep interest rates high, cutting deals with OPEC countries like Saudi Arabia to re-cycle petrodollars. Gold, however, became the more often chosen reserve by other OPEC members, and the value of gold traded higher in direct correlation with the price of oil.

The tide shifted in the mid 1980s when the Saudi's increased oil production and lowered the relative price for oil in the U.S. to levels witnessed before the Arab Oil Embargo. This change sparked economic growth to the advantage of U.S. GDP relative to the real economies in the Middle East. The value of holding U.S. Treasuries as reserves with a healthy interest rate kept oil profits re-cycling into dollars as opposed to gold. The early 1990s also witnessed trade with emerging market countries, including China and India, greatly expanding with the United States. This trade was performed in U.S. dollars, and required these countries to keep more reserves in U.S. Treasuries rather than gold. The growth in the percentage ownership of U.S. National Debt held by foreign countries in this time period expanded to record levels, along with the expansion of U.S. Debt in absolute terms. The U.S. GDP and the stock market exploded higher in the 1990s, while gold and the oil market languished.

The relative low pricing of oil came to an end as the year 2000 approached. In terms of gold, oil became priced at the same price it was after the Arab Oil Embargo. This run-up in oil prices contributed to a major break-down in the U.S. stock market after the year 2000. The 9/11 attacks signaled a return of a conflict driven Middle East, and oil prices began to march higher as did the value of gold. Gold became a proxy for the strengthening of OPEC oil rich countries beaten down by low price levels since the mid 1980s, as well as the growing relevance of the emerging market countries like India and China – whose increasing oil demand was being increasingly satisfied by countries like Iran.

The 2008 financial crisis realigned the value of the S&P 500. When priced in gold terms starting in January 2009 the stock market and gold were locked in a 1 for 1 value relationship for the better part of the next 4 years. This was the same point that the two markets traded after the Arab Oil Embargo.

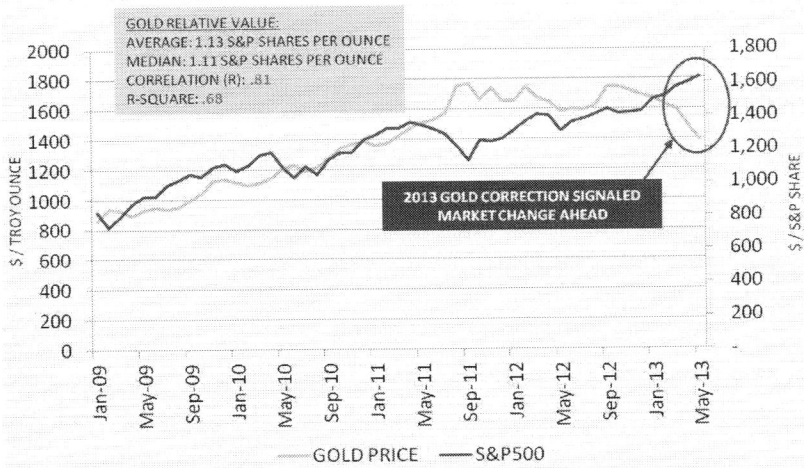

GOLD RELATIVE VALUE:
AVERAGE: 1.13 S&P SHARES PER OUNCE
MEDIAN: 1.11 S&P SHARES PER OUNCE
CORRELATION (R): .81
R-SQUARE: .68

2013 GOLD CORRECTION SIGNALED MARKET CHANGE AHEAD

GOLD PRICE   S&P500

From 2008 to 2013, the S&P 500 and the gold market traded in close parity with a correlation of .81. An ounce of gold bought slightly more than 1 share of the S&P, 1.13 to be exact, during the time period. The steep correction in gold prices in the first half of 2013 signaled a changing market dynamic. In the 1980s when this happened, oil eventually fell precipitously, owed largely to the Saudi Arabian move to expand oil market share. Stocks flourished.

In 2006 when the divergence between oil and gold happened, it was not due to a sharp drop in gold price, but rather a slowdown in the price rise in gold and a sharp spike upward in oil prices, eventually prompting a change in U.S. fiscal and monetary policy . In 2013 the odds were high that the gold correction down was signaling another move up in oil prices that would be accompanied by geo-political tension.

Lessons in Gold Relativity

Whereas the U.S. nominal GDP is the nucleus of financial relativity for the U.S. stock market, assets outside the U.S. usually derive relative value from the fiscal and monetary policies of governments which are not as highly correlated to the United States economy. When the gold standard for international exchange was abandoned in 1971, a void was created in how to account for the relative difference in cross country monetary policies. The use of floating exchange rates between countries was a partial solution that worked to the advantage of major developed world economies. However, there were relative losers in an exchange rate system where a floating U.S. dollar became the center of the financial universe. The biggest losers became export oriented countries, particularly natural resource based economies that priced raw materials for trade in U.S. dollars. The supply of natural resources rarely grows in synchronized fashion with U.S. monetary policy. Financial imbalances are inevitable in a dollar centric world market. Oil price shocks are a very good warning signal the financial market is out of balance, and a downturn is inescapable.

From the research presented in this chapter, 6 key points can be distilled about the gold market that will help make you a better investor.

LESSONS ON THE REFLECTIVE RELATIVITY OF GOLD

- The VALUE of gold is highly correlated with the spot market price of crude oil.
- Oil priced in gold has averaged 13.9 barrels per ounce since 1968.
- Before the 1974 Arab Oil Embargo, oil traded at 27 barrels per ounce of gold; after the Embargo, oil traded at 12.8 barrels per ounce of gold.
- The Arab Oil Embargo price level of 12.8 barrels per ounce of gold is an important threshold in the market. Price above 12.8 barrels per ounce, oil is economically accommodative; priced below 12.8 barrels per ounce oil is constraining.
- Saudi Arabia, through a Treaty with the U.S. to provide military protection for its oil fields, has agreed to always price and trade oil in U.S. dollars.
- Gold is not strongly correlated with the U.S. stock market; rather, it oscillates from being correlated to inversely correlated depending on whether an ounce of gold buys very few barrels of oil (negative for stocks), or many barrels of oil (pro-stocks).

Throughout history the best constant in the world financial market has been gold. Through time, the supply of gold has expanded in direct proportion to world population growth. This means that the value of gold in U.S. dollars is a global constant that moves up and down in non-correlated fashion to the U.S. stock market, the change reflecting only the comparative parity of the U.S. GDP to the GDP of its foreign trading partners that do not increase the supply of their currency at the same pace. If an imbalance of dollars is put into the world market relative to the GDP growth of the United States, the dollar price of gold changes in relative response. This reflective characteristic of the value of gold is the fundamental basis for the 7th Guiding Principle in the Theory of Financial Relativity.

7th PRINCIPLE OF FINANCIAL RELATIVITY

Gold valued in dollars is an absolute reflection of the magnitude of market force between the U.S. and its export trading partners.

All things being equal, the value of gold in dollar terms as shown in the last 45 years of data from 1968 to 2013 does not correlate to the U.S. stock market with any great significance; however, over time gold does tend to buy one share of the S&P 500 per ounce, oscillating from greater than 1 to less than 1 depending on U.S. government policy and economic growth. As long as the U.S. dollar remains the primary reserve currency in the world, this non-correlated pattern with a median value of 1 is expected to hold. Understanding where the financial market is relative to this oscillating pattern is a key to growing and protecting investment wealth over the long-term.

PART III
THEORY PRACTICE

12 ESSENCE OF FINANCIAL RELATIVITY

When the research regarding the U.S. financial market from WWII through 2013 is assimilated, a pattern emerges. The pattern involves market participant behavioral tendencies driven by four powerful entities at work in the financial system that exert force on a perpetual basis influencing economic outcomes. The entities include private market businesses and consumers, the U.S. government, the Federal Reserve and lastly, foreign entities with sufficient power to influence the U.S. economy. These entities exert force on the market, and the constant interaction results in an aggregate measurement of relative value tracked by economic GDP which is highly correlated with the DOW and S&P 500 stock indexes.

> "The Theory of Financial Relativity is a system of ideas explaining why investment markets move through time in a predictable rather than random pattern. The ideas are encapsulated in 8 Guiding Principles derived from the correlated effects that dominant forces have on the determination of relative value in the financial market. The principles provide a framework for developing signals that warn of impending losses and potential gains in investment value, extrapolating future market outcomes based on relative market scenarios and rebalancing investment portfolios in response to changes in market forces. The Theory has implications for understanding the persistent pattern of asset bubble creation and dissolution in the financial market."

The pattern when simplified is the basis for establishing relative value in the U.S. financial market, and ultimately the value of the U.S. dollar as the world reserve currency. Investment value of stocks and bonds within the financial system, although seemingly random if viewed in isolation, is determined in large part by an asset's correlation to these predominate major market forces.

Each individual asset also holds unique qualities which make it ostensibly more or less valuable. However, unique value is much more random, and the odds of uncovering exceptional unique value in a pile of stocks are akin to winning the lottery. Aggregate market value, though, is not random; and the value of each individual stock or bond in the system is driven to a large degree by its correlation to the overall market. In other words, if an asset is mispriced relative to the market, it creates unique opportunities for wealth creation that can be understood through good fundamental analysis. Value based investing is the essence of the formula used by great investors like Benjamin Graham and Warren Buffett.

If you hold a diversified portfolio of financial assets, the fluctuations in mispriced assets cancel out over time, leaving you with the average market return. Trying to trade into and out of mispriced assets is trading market noise. Money can be made in the market noise business, as traders and good fundamental stock-pickers will attest. But you have to be good at the process of assessing value, and at the core, you must have a firm understanding of the relative value of the stock market. Most stock investors would be better off if they simply bought the stock index.

8 Guiding Principles of Financial Market Relativity

As shown earlier in this book, if you manage to sell the aggregate market a signaled market peak, and then buy it back at the optimal market low point, you can double your realized return with far less volatility. How can this be the case? The answer lies in the non-random or systemic pattern of behavioral forces driving the market as explained by the Theory of Financial Relativity. The Theory is supported by 8 Guiding Principles derived from thorough analysis of financial data from 1941 through 2013.

To be a great investor, you must have a sense of where the market is at any given moment in time, not just what you believe the value to be based on the point in time you entered the market. The 8 Guiding Principles provide the foundation to assess the on-going relative value of the stock market. By examining the level of force being exerted from the predominant institutions within the financial system, and tracking the status of the market signals most highly correlated with a change in direction of relative value, true investment opportunities – not speculative opportunities – can be derived. Market signals provide the relevant information for investors to read the market and unlock the mysteries behind major market moves.

PRINCIPLES OF FINANCIAL RELATIVITY

#1 Nominal GDP is the Nucleus of Financial Relativity in the U.S. financial market.

#2 Interest rates are the yardstick by which Financial Relativity is measured.

#3 Higher levels of U.S. Debt relative to GDP depress real GDP and inflation.

#4 Inflation and asset bubbles are financial market imbalances always and everywhere linked to government fiscal policy excesses.

#5 The Fed is the Regulator of Financial Relativity with the power to create and extinguish market imbalances.

#6 Oil price spikes are a foreign force "shockingly" correlated with stock market corrections.

#7 Gold valued in dollars is an absolute reflection of the magnitude of market force between the U.S. and its export trading partners.

#8 Major stock market corrections are triggered by the Fed tightening monetary policy to remedy an inflation or asset bubble imbalance and restore global market relative balance and order.

Guiding Principle #8 - The Essence of Financial Relativity

Albert Einstein has a famous quote – *"I believe that whatever we do or live for has its causality; it is good however that we cannot see through to it"*

Einstein believed that a natural order to the universe exists independent of the human factor. The order leads to cause and effect reactions which always bring the natural system back into a state of equilibrium. In the financial market, a higher order also exists that is driving the overall system. Its existence beyond the human factor may stretch the philosophical limits of Einstein's beliefs, but as the empirical research presented in this book shows, it does exist.

The financial order in the U.S. financial system has a 4th dimension beyond private sector growth, government fiscal policy and Federal Reserve monetary policy. Foreign trading partners are a major element in determining financial order through time. From WWII through 2013, easy money and excessive fiscal spending continually drove the U.S. financial market until pressure built up in the system which had to be released through an adjustment in relative value. In every case when a market correction occurred, the fingerprints of a foreign conflict in the financial markets were left behind. Given the growing power that can be exerted by foreign forces on the U.S. market, investors need to make sure the international element is accounted for when assessing the relative value of the U.S. market..

Incorporating the foreign dimension to the Theory provided a perspective answering many of my questions when I began researching this book. Why was there so much money available to finance Caspian Networks in late 2000 when the technology market was so clearly overvalued? Additionally, why did a similar market event occur in the mortgage market from 2003 through 2008? Answer – asset bubbles linked to excessive monetization of foreign trade deficits.

I was involved in many road-show presentations to raise venture capital in the year 2000. Sovereign wealth funds from the Middle East and Asia Pacific were very actively looking for investments during the time period. Foreigners had ample dollars to put to work and, at the time, the issuance of new Treasury bonds was curtailed because the Federal budget was balanced thanks largely to stock market capital gains that increased tax revenues leading up to the year 2000. But the system was inherently unstable, and the withdrawal of the fickle capital flow from overseas shut-down the party. The excessive influx of funding into the tech market came to a grinding halt, and much of the capital that arrived at the end of the game went to "money heaven".

On 9 / 11, a different investment environment emerged. The relative value of the market changed dramatically as the technology asset bubble deflated and President Bush unleashed a set of tax-cuts which flowed straight into consumer pockets, and correspondingly overseas to buy consumption goods. Issuance of U.S. Treasury debt began again, owed largely to the resumption of deficit spending, and foreign held dollar liquidity resumed its upward trend. The asset bubble that had been focused on the technology market to consume excess foreign dollar holdings was shifted to the oil and housing market.

Interestingly, through this time period the U.S. GDP was hardly affected because spending drove economic growth, and government borrowing from foreign sources deferred inflation. But, the stock market re-set in order to adjust to the make-over in U.S. economic policy. National policy shifted away from butter and focused on guns, and monetary policy became aggressively accommodative from 2002 through 2004.

The oil market run-up from 2003 through 2008 is easy to explain in retrospect, and is even explained on the OPEC web-site. OPEC proclaims to the world that a main reason the price of oil increased after the year 2000 was that it shifted from being a commodity to an "asset class." Quick translation, dollar based trade surpluses in the Middle East were provided a new investment option by Wall Street allowing a perpetual roll-over of dollars in oil derivative contracts rather than just being re-cycled in U.S. Treasuries and stocks. The mortgage market meltdown was also an international affair. Money from overseas investors filled Wall Street investment banks, and was piped straight to the American consumer as low cost first and second mortgages on payment terms which could not be supported by income growth. Granted the banking system capital structure was far too weak at the time to support the risk and size of the business being undertaken, <u>but</u> *the root cause of the crisis was the source of the asset bubble, not the symptomatic result. And that source can be traced to government deficit spending financed by foreign trade surpluses.*

The last element in the causality puzzle was an accommodative Federal Reserve which monetized an ever increasing amount of the deficit spending in 2003 and 2004, as well as lax mortgage lending standards allowing a large money multiplier effect to pervade the financial system leading up to the 2007-08 crash. Eventually it was the Federal Reserve under command of Ben Bernanke which stepped in to puncture the bubble in 2008 by selling U.S. Treasury debt from its balance sheet in the midst of a liquidity crisis – a very odd and inopportune time to exert a high level of negative monetary force. The system deflated like a bad soufflé. The excessive capital in the mortgage market, like my experience in the tech industry in 2000, dried up very quickly once the liquidity was removed. The market deflation was exacerbated by the 2007-08 oil shock, which suspiciously appears to have been driven by the oil derivatives market – in other words, an asset bubble created by too many dollars chasing too few assets.

The research supporting the Theory is not limited to the 2001 and 2008 market crashes. The same common elements date back through time to the market corrections since WWII. In 1946, adjusting economically after WWII played a large role in the relative stock market correction. Then in 1957, the correction was strongly linked to the Suez Canal conflict. Oil shortages were evident in the corrections throughout the 1960s. The 1973-74 major market correction was strongly driven by the abandonment of the gold standard and the increasing conflict over the fair dollar price for Middle East oil. This conflict constrained the growth in the U.S. throughout the 1970s decade, and eventually led to a complete overhaul of the method used by the U.S. government to fund government spending. Beginning in 1980, when I entered college, little did I realize that the foundation was being laid for the government to perpetuate its propensity to overspend by borrowing dollars from foreign governments - dollars created to drive GDP growth through foreign trade that instead landed back in the U.S. as investments. Reciprocity in the trading process was not forthcoming. The result was a treadmill of higher and higher deficit spending, but to the delight of Washington politicians, spending without the detrimental impact of consumer inflation. Suddenly asset bubbles instead of consumer price inflation became the normal mode price increases were exhibited in the U.S. market.

In late 2013, the cycle of asset bubble formation was still on-going. No acceptable resolution to remedy the problem, like the way that consumer price inflation was curtailed in the early 1980s, was being put forward in the political process. The system was seemingly on auto-pilot to perpetuate the problem for as long as foreign governments were willing to fund U.S. consumption. The reason there is no remedy is most likely because the root cause of the problem is the opposite of the remedy for keeping consumer prices so low. Allowing foreign countries to become so embedded in the fabric of the sovereign financial system creates a steadily debilitating set of dynamics in the U.S. financial system, because there is little incentive for U.S. economic policy to take action, driven only to respond with force to suppress inflation, not asset bubbles, until a severe crisis point is reached. The actions taken in 2009 and progressively expanded by Fed purchases of assets in 2013 only perpetuated the growing problem.

The financial system at the end of 2013 was re-acting in a manner which the Theory of Financial Relativity guides that it will. The pent-up imbalances in the system, no matter how much the Federal Reserve tried to chase the foreign dollar based reserves out of the Treasury complex with QE in 2013, just showed up in the stock market and other hard assets like oil and gold instead of increasing trade and creating jobs. Economic growth still languished. Unless, the GDP growth part of the relative equation changed, like the current account surpluses run in the late 1940s that created the needed impetus to right the financial ship and reverse the U.S. dependency on foreign financed deficit spending, the system was headed for continued build-up of financial asset bubbles that would eventually have to be deflated. Eventual bubble deflation will parallel the circumstances that led to past market downfalls, even though the specific blame for why it happens might change in the media headlines. A comment by Albert Einstein in a discussion with Rabindranath Tagore in 1930 provides a useful analog:

"One tries to understand how the order is the higher plane. The order is there, where the big

elements combine and guide existence; but in the minute elements this order is not perceptible."[6]

When the market inevitably breaks down, the rational for why it happens will likely be linked to a "minute element" that provides an expedient way to promote political acceptance of a new path chosen. However, the root cause of the eventual market outcome will be linked to the essence of Financial Relativity, Guiding Principle #8.

> **8th PRINCIPLE OF FINANCIAL RELATIVITY**
>
> Major stock market corrections are triggered by the Fed tightening monetary policy to remedy an inflation or asset bubble imbalance and restore global market relative balance and order.

Testing the Theory through Practice

A critical test of a theory is whether its explanation of a particular behavior or recurring activity can be utilized to solve a problem or create improved results. In the case of the Theory of Financial Relativity, the proof is whether the Guiding Principles provide a better understanding of the financial markets, thereby giving knowledgeable investors the ability to make more advantageous choices in managing their own personal wealth. On this relative score, the Theory has three practical uses that investors can put into action to improve investment performance.

> **PRACTICAL USES OF THE THEORY OF FINANCIAL RELATIVITY**
>
> #1 Developing signals to identify financial system peaks and lows corresponding to market corrections instigated by major market forces.
>
> #2 Extrapolating probable future market outcomes based on the current relative alignment of major market forces.
>
> #3 Managing an investment portfolio that is systematically re-balanced over time based on the relative position of the major market forces.

The first practical use of the Theory is the development of market signals based on the study of market corrections from the 1950s through 2013. Since the Theory states that the market behaves in a systematic manner relative to definitive market forces, it stands to reason that major stock market downturns and the ensuing rebounds through time should exhibit similar relative characteristics each time a correction occurs. This indeed is what history showed during the time period studied, and the next two chapters

---

[6] Andrew Robinson and Dipankar Home, "The Mathematician and the Mystic." www.resurgence.org, http://www.resurgence.org/magazine/article3380-the-mathematician-and-the-mystic.html .

illuminate the details about this market phenomenon.

The second use involves identifying a point in history that exhibits similar relative circumstances with respect to the major market forces present in the market, and extrapolating the likely future market outcome. There need not be an impending market correction for this type of analysis to be constructive – although the wall of fear is ever present in the market. In fact, disciplined review using this relative perspective can help avoid trading out of good investments simply due to market noise. Additionally, this structured form of analysis can help identify inflection points in asset values other than just the stock market such as expected relative rates of change in interest rates, oil prices and the value of gold.

The last practical benefit of the Theory for investors is helping identify the optimal time to rebalance a portfolio and the appropriate asset class to trade into during a rebalancing action. Managing an investment portfolio requires a keen sense of the relative value of the market through time. Relative value is not the same for every investor, and therefore, not every portfolio should be structured with a bog standard formula like putting 60% of assets into stocks and 40% into bonds. Investors need to structure their portfolio in a manner that meets their own relative needs, not someone else's idea of what is best, while also accounting for the predictable systemic forces in the financial market. Within this context, a more robust portfolio management system is introduced in Chapter 16 that flows from the concepts underlying the Theory of Financial Relativity.

13 AVOIDING MARKET BONFIRES

The last section of the book is focused on how changes in major market forces are exhibited in financial market value, with particular emphasis on the U.S. stock market. The forces are private sector growth, government fiscal policy, Federal Reserve policy and foreign trade. By understanding how these forces create changes in the market you can better realize when relative value will be created and when it is about to disappear.

This book is about investing, not macro-economic theory. Although economic statistics provide figures, government data is generally not actionable information. If you attempt to invest by responding to the most recent government economic report, one you will probably be too late as the market already reflects the information; and two, you very likely are investing based on market noise used by the momentum trading community to swing from one hot idea to the next. Winners and losers are constantly created in the momentum trading aspect of the market. The biggest winners are the brokerage houses that take a cut of every transaction. Program traders with high powered, low latency computers, also benefit by taking a micro-penny over and over again in the churning of the massive stock market liquidity pool.

When something goes wrong with a computerized trading program "flash crashes" result like the one on May 6, 2010. I remember it well. On that day Procter & Gamble, one of the most conservative stocks in the U.S. market dropped from a traded price of $63 to under $40 in just a few minutes. The market quickly followed suit and the DOW Jones Industrials dropped over 900 points in 15 minutes. At that point trading was paused in an e-mini futures contract for 5 seconds and the problem cleared. When the dust settled, the market began to recover and ended the day down just over 300 points. But there were unfortunate investors who were sucked into the downdraft and traded in fear, losing money as a result. The victims had no real sense of relative value – just like the computers that went bonkers.

True investing, as opposed to speculating, is about managing and keeping wealth. Putting stop loss orders in place on a stock, or re-acting to panic driven news stories is not investing. Investing takes conviction, and the ability to put money to work and keep it working through thick and thin. It also takes one more critical element, knowing when the stock market is truly going to roll-over and go down – when it is relatively over-valued. Selling high and buying low is an investment move that can pay off when a market correction happens. As was shown in Chapter 4, the rate of return on investment in the U.S. stock market can be enhanced by almost 100% simply by avoiding or taking advantage of the 20% of the time when the market goes through these cathartic episodes.

Warren Buffet has said that trading the market is fool's gold. I agree, particularly if you actually own entire companies, or significant stakes in a publicly traded entity. If you hold a portfolio with large stakes in individual companies, you cannot liquidate when major market corrections are about to take place. In a word, Warren is the captain of the assets he owns and is stuck supporting the financial system patriotically to the end. But don't feel sorry for him – he benefits greatly from the lower than normal borrowing cost his portfolio size derives from the financial system; and, he is astute enough to keep cash on hand buy undervalued assets when "blood is on the streets."

Rebalancing a portfolio of assets in anticipation or in response to forces that cause markets to be out of relative balance is the essence of the Theory of Financial Relativity. You must be able to rise above the noise. Being able to spot good value within micro-markets is not demeaned in any way. However, you are unlikely to create and grow wealth by simply focusing on momentum trading. Most investors do far better by simply maintaining a diversified portfolio of 20 or more stocks.

In order to get ahead in the game, you must take advantage of situations when the market becomes grossly out-of-balance created when government fiscal policy, Federal Reserve policy and the relative value of the dollar is at odds with the international marketplace. These situations do not happen that often. In the graph below, the time periods are marked in red. The length in time it took for the U.S. stock market to make its "relative" adjustment can be read as the difference between the optimal time to exit the market and the optimal time to re-enter.

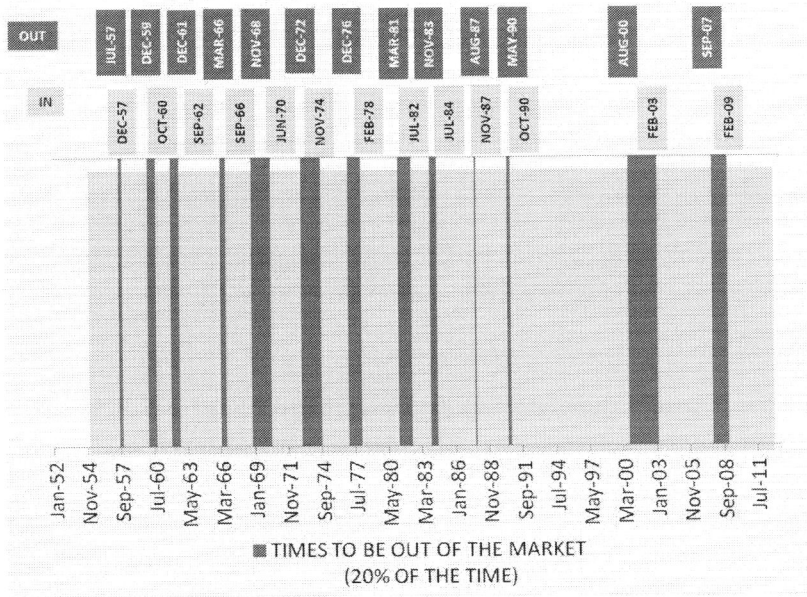

■ TIMES TO BE OUT OF THE MARKET
(20% OF THE TIME)

How do you make the assessment as an investor that the market is about to go down in value and continue to adjust downward for a significant period of time? It sounds on the surface like a task that requires a PhD. However, it does not. What is needed to perform well as an investor is simplification, not complexity. You simply must know what the market signals are for these events and how to read them – much like an experienced tracker can find wild game when no animals appear present in the environment. Paraphrasing Albert Einstein, *"Everything should be made as simple as possible, but no simpler"*.

You don't need to be a clairvoyant soothsayer that can predict the next U.S. GDP level – a task that Federal Reserve forecasting proves over and over, is rarely possible. You don't need to hit the number on the head for the amount of jobs created last month as reported on the first Friday of each month by the U.S. labor department and reported by CNBC on air at 8:30 sharp. You don't even need to predict the absolute level of interest rates, although knowing the directional movement in rates is important. You must get above the noise and interpret real market relevant information. This information is associated with changes in the flow of funds into and out of investments at critical moments in the market.

What you need to do as an investor is pay attention to the <u>rate of change</u> in specific and timely market variables that signal the advent of a major decline in stock market value.

Highest Correlating Factors Associated with Stock Market Crashes

As explained in detail earlier in this book, U.S. nominal GDP is the nucleus of Financial Relativity for U.S. stock investors. The value of the major stock market indexes correlate in virtual lock step through time. The level of interest rates provides the relative ballast that moves the traded market value up and down over time in relation to the absolute level of GDP. The changes in the functional variables most correlated with the change in stock market value are shown from the 1950s through 2013 in the graph below.

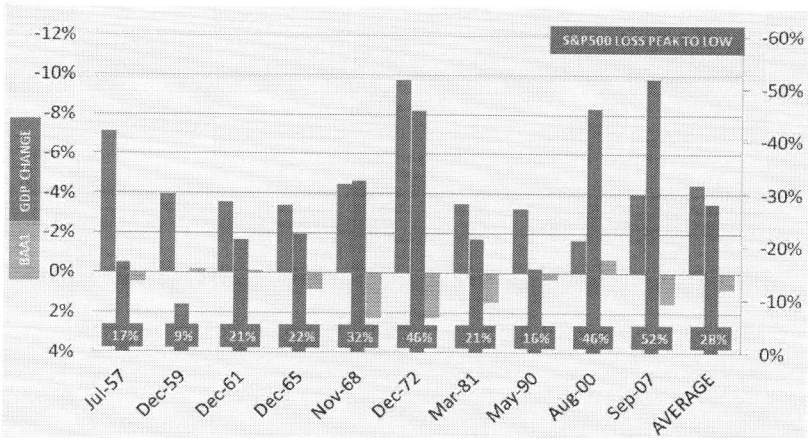

As the data reflect, the market corrections are, not surprisingly, highly correlated with impending declines in real GDP (blue bar associated with left axis). A 3-4% decline in real GDP is typical during each correction. Recessions were recorded during every time period shown in the graph.

Interest rate changes are also associated with the stock market decline. The change in the BAA1 long-term rate which correlates most closely with changes in stock market value is shown by the green bar and associated with the left axis in the chart. <u>Increases</u> in long-term risky bond rates decreased most during stock market declines in the late 60s through the early 1980s, and then again in 2008. Keep these time periods in mind, for as you recall they involved foreign policy events that surrounded major oil shocks. The deepest declines in the market post WWII were experienced in 1972-74, 2000-2002 and 2007-09.

Reading the DOW Signal

If you were able to perfectly predict the level of U.S. GDP into the future, as well as the level of BAA1 interest rate, with a fair degree of certainty you could forecast the likely level of the U.S. stock market. However, variables such as GDP are not known in a timely fashion. The best you can do is to understand the general trend, and whether the change is a function of real growth or inflationary price pressures. Timeliness is the biggest issue with using GDP as a metric in assessing relative stock market value. By the time the actual figure is released the market already reflects the information. You can much more likely accurately project the upcoming GDP figure by taking the year over year change in the stock market and adjusting it for interest rate changes. The stock market index value itself, therefore, becomes a critical information source for investors.

Forecasting the absolute level of interest rates is also a guessing game. The absolute level of rates does affect stock market value, but the act of forecasting rates does not provide actionable information. Even the futures market is a very poor information source for absolute rate targets. However, futures are generally good for directional, rate of change forecasting. Given the constraints on knowing the future in absolute terms, investors need to resort to the most useful information available. The way to derive actionable information from the term structure of interest rates is to track and analyze the relative interest rate spread between securities with different maturities and risk.

Based upon the historical research, the best signal that the U.S. GDP was under stress and was about to undergo a recession turned out to be the stock market itself – more precisely the DOW. Various market indexes exist, and the information sent from a change in one relative to another is sometimes useful. In the case of the DOW and S&P 500 index, the relationship in the short time period before a steep market decline is useful to understand, and very often actionable.

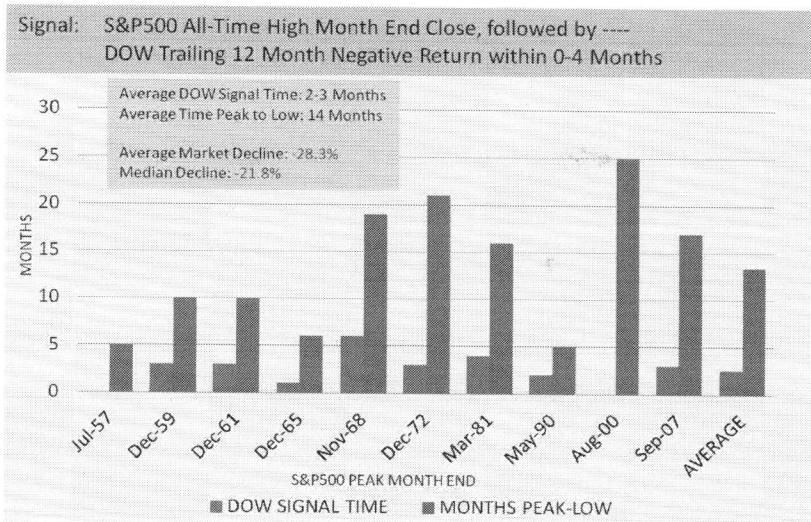

Signal: S&P500 All-Time High Month End Close, followed by ----
DOW Trailing 12 Month Negative Return within 0-4 Months

Average DOW Signal Time: 2-3 Months
Average Time Peak to Low: 14 Months

Average Market Decline: -28.3%
Median Decline: -21.8%

S&P500 PEAK MONTH END

■ DOW SIGNAL TIME   ■ MONTHS PEAK-LOW

The first ingredient in understanding that the market is about to roll-over is that it must be at an all-time high to begin with. The stock market declines regularly. If you looked at the DOW and S&P 500 trading patterns in isolation, they appear random. But the points in time when the market declined significantly since WWII all have an important characteristic in common – they all started after the index reached a new all-time high.

The second ingredient that preceded the steep decline was that the initial move down in stock market value happened in a manner such that within 3-4 months of the all-time high, sometimes sooner (see the blue bar in the graph), the DOW trailing twelve month return turned negative. It does not mean that the market had fallen significantly yet, just that year over year, the market was exhibiting signs of trouble. On the margin when the market is trading at an all-time high and suddenly year over year returns become negative, a significant and timely signal is sent t investors. It means that the rate of change either upward in the interest rate complex or downward in GDP growth is so significant a drag on the market that it can no longer sustain higher and higher valuations. Putting together these two tendencies exhibited by the market when it peaks results in a major indicator of impending market breakdown. The signal has been named the DOW Signal within the context of this historical research. If read properly, this signal is a warning sign that investors can use to rebalance their portfolio prior to major market moves down.

DOW Signal Summary:
- The DOW Signal occurs when the year over year returns on the DOW at month end close turn negative, usually within 3 months of setting a new all-time high.
- The Signal occurs on average one month ahead of the S&P500 exhibiting a similar recorded result.
- Since 1955, end of month year over year negative stock market returns are very rare outside of the 13 time periods researched.
  - 17 times, 2.4%
- A large majority of negative year over year returns posted from 1955 through 2013 happened during stock market corrections.
  - 200 times in total, 28%
  - 183 times during corrections, 26%

One key aspect of the DOW signal is that it typically occurs ahead of a similar S&P signal. The DOW decline based on month end closing index values typically beat the S&P in showing the market weakness by up to a month in the time series analyzed. The DOW shows the market weakness first. So, if you are an investor in the S&P index or riskier assets, the DOW as a bell-weather to pull-back resources has historically been effective.

How effective? From 1955 through mid 2013, year over year declines in the DOW index measured at month-end close occurred only 200 times. In the 13 major market corrections studied during the time period, 183 of the negative year over year returns in market value occurred in sequence after the DOW signaled the optimal trading exit point. The remaining 17 signals in the time series were associated with the late 1970s, and a few false positive readings slightly ahead of the optimal market exit point.

Using one indicator as a sell or buy signal is not advisable when managing investments for long-term wealth. Although the DOW signal is fairly reliable and is directly linked back to the nucleus of Financial Relativity, GDP, it becomes much more robust when combined with the rate of change in several key market metrics. These metrics are associated with interest rates – the yardstick of relativity, and energy prices as reflected in the change in the price of oil. By understanding these signals, the chance of trading out of good investments due to market noise becomes much less likely.

Fed Funds Rate Hike Signal – Indicative but not Timing Predictive

One constant reality in the U.S. financial market is that the Federal Reserve holds the power to set and change interest rates. The Fed manages the level of rates, particularly as they relate to the interest rate paid on government Treasuries, through open market purchase and sales activities. These actions taken by the Fed produce credit market accommodation and tightness based on the intention of the Federal Open Market Committee. In other words, the Fed, depending on the level of pressure it receives from the political process and secondarily from the financial market, uses interest rate policy to attempt to achieve an intentional U.S. economic outcome. The intentions, no matter your politics, are usually laudable. It would likely be far worse to have a Fed completely oblivious to the results of its actions. After all, the Fed is in charge of the country's money supply. "Don't fight the Fed" is an adage which signifies the immense power and influence of the Fed over the financial market. When the Fed makes a policy move, it usually is significant, particularly if it involves a change in direction in interest rate policy.

In managing your investments, taking the time to understand what transpired through history prior to stock market collapses from a Fed policy standpoint is time well spent. Since the Fed has the power to influence rates so strongly, in a perfect world you might think they would intervene and keep the market from dropping dramatically just by adeptly adjusting rate policy. The rate that Fed watchers follow most is the Fed Funds rate, the rate one banks pays another for funds held on reserve overnight. The Federal Reserve sets the target, and then manages reserves in the financial system in order to achieve the target rate experienced in market.

In a real case study of just how Fed interest rate policy matched the rise and fall of the stock market, the graph below shows Fed interest rate policy from 2004 through 2010.

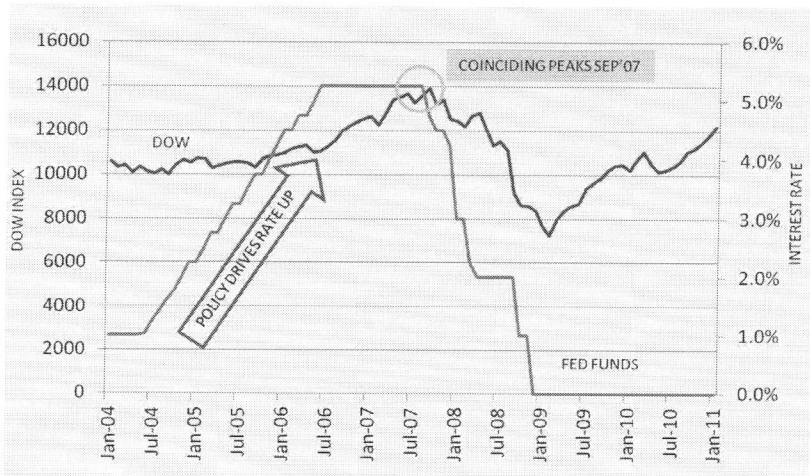

In this instance in financial history, the Fed hiked the Fed Funds rate substantially from a 1% level in June 2004, which at the time was considered very aggressive on the lower bound, all the way to 5.25% in June 2006. The last three rate hikes were executed when Ben Bernanke first took over as Fed chairman in 2006. The stock market did not show a year over year decline through the rate hike period. As the Fed Funds rate leveled off at 5.25%, stocks got a second wind and moved to a new all-time high in September 2007. In a move which is very telling in retrospect, but unusual historically, the Fed actually lowered rates in September of 2007 as the stock market was peaking, but also simultaneously tightened rather than eased monetary policy by selling U.S. Treasuries. In other words, the Fed began to withdrawing liquidity from the market and rates went down instead of up. The Fed Funds rate was reduced to 4.75%, but monetary conditions were tighter. The Fed move was initially interpreted falsely by the market as an easing move.

The DOW signal of year over year negative market returns did not occur until January 2008, four months later. Is it possible that "Don't fight the Fed" means when they lower rates after an intermediate rate hike period, it means get out of the market? The saying usually means when the Fed lowers rates, stay in the market. The answer to this question does not give a clear picture when major market declines over a long time period are reviewed:

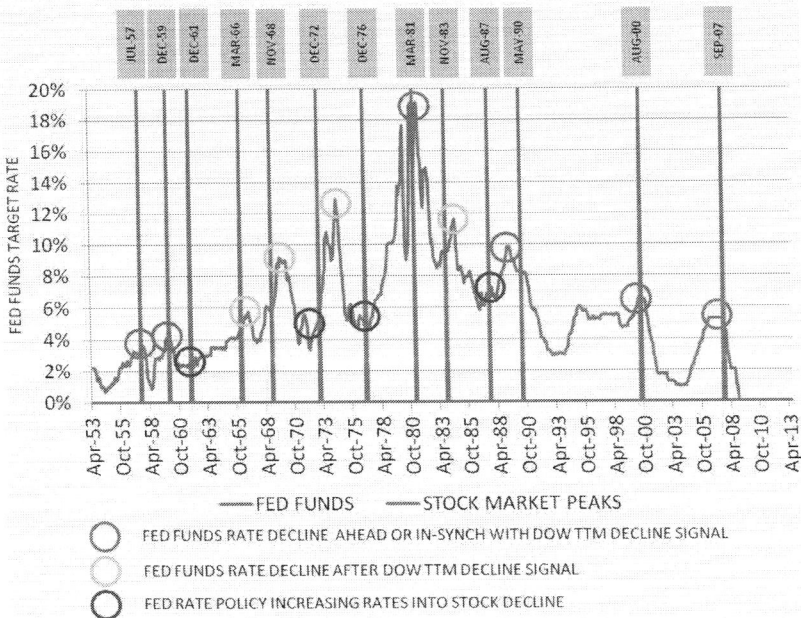

Typically, Fed Funds rate decreases are associated with an impending stock market decline when they occur after a period of rate increases. In the 13 market corrections since 1957, the Fed was almost always beginning to lower the Fed Funds target or holding it at an intermediate high level at the market peak. In 10 out of the 13 times when the DOW was already signaling a pull-back, the Fed Funds rate was also peaking. These points are shown circled in green and yellow in the graph above. In 4 cases, 1981, 1987, 1990 and 2007 the Fed actually intervened with lowering of the Fed funds target prior to the market decline, and slightly ahead of the DOW signal. In all four cases the rate lowering was accompanied by continued quantitative tightening, not easing. The Fed rate policy can also send erratic signals at times such as late 1995 when rate hikes stopped, and the stock market plowed ever higher rather than pulling back in usual response.

> "In 12 out of 13 Major Market Corrections since 1957 Fed Policy increased Interest Rates in the 12 month time period leading up to the decline"

From 1957 through 2013, there was one signal clearly indicative of an impending market decline. When the DOW signals that the market is rolling over, in a super-majority of the historical cases the Fed was increasing the Fed Funds rate and reserve policy was tight in the year prior to the decline.

Combining the DOW signal with the rate policy actions of the Fed leads to a much more robust predictor of market corrections. But, an additional indicator provided by the term structure of interest rates usually provides an even better signal of a looming market breakdown.

Canary in the Coal Mine Indicator: Negative 10 - 2 Spread

Waiting on the FOMC to raise rates is not the most reliable market correction signal available. To be sure when the Fed tightens credit conditions and the stock market is at an all-time high, investors should be wary. Another way to read the interest rate market involves tracking the difference between interest rates of one maturity against another. The "spread" between rates on the Treasury Yield Curve historically signals the market turning point more precisely than simple "Fed watching".

The best "Canary in the Coal Mine" signal of a stock market top occurs when short term interest rates are greater than long term rates. This trading phenomenon produces a negative differential or spread between short and long maturities on the yield curve. During the time period from 1953 through 2013, the 10 year minus 2 year Treasury spread was a leading economic indicator, and for good reason.

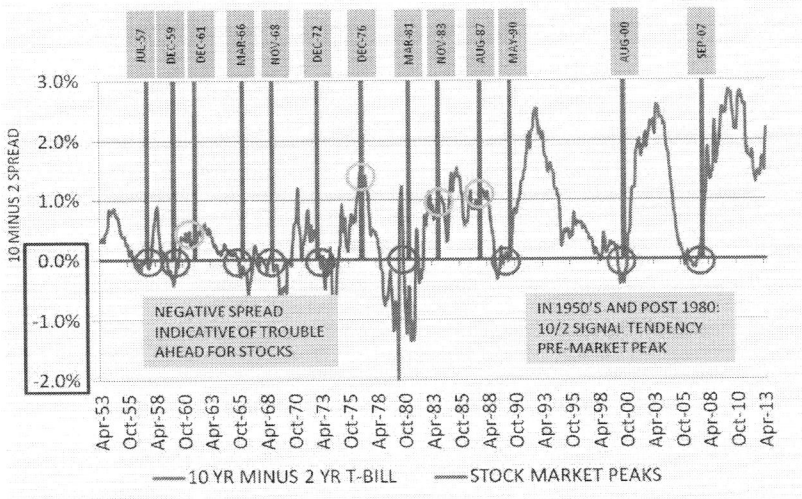

Every time during the period the 10 - 2 spread turned negative, a recession resulted within 6 to 9 months later. As the graph below shows, when the spread was negative, it also accurately signaled the stock market peak in 9 (green circle) out of 13 of the stock market corrections in the period. The 1976 correction was not an all-time high for the stock market and the Fed was not working to remove reserves from the system at the time. It was the beginning of President Carter's administration. The 1987 crash is a unique outlier that produced a major stock market decline, but happened so quickly, and reversed almost as quickly, that it qualifies almost as a freak event in relativity. The 1961 and 1984 events were minor corrections at times when the market was trending higher. In 1961 the Fed was not moving the Funds target higher; in 1984 the Fed was increasing rates prior to the market decline, but backed off the policy rate hikes before the 10 - 2 spread turned negative, and likewise the stock market correction was minor.

The table below captures the spread and stock return data in 11 of the stock corrections since 1957. The information conveyed by a negative differential yield spread is compelling. When the 10 - 2 spread was negative leading up to an all-time high in the stock market, the likelihood of a market correction of greater than 20% increased. In the year after the market peaked and the 10 - 2 yield spread returned to more typical levels, the diametric opposite happened

164

to stock market returns. As a reference, negative S&P 500 year over year returns occurred 28% of the time during the analysis period, with negative 9% or less returns happening only 15% of the time. In most every case shown in the table, stock market losses 1 year into the correction were more than 8%.

One additional observation about the 10 - 2 yield spread is that when the stock market is undergoing a correction <u>the directional change in the spread reverses course</u>. After the market peak, the spread typically expands to a more accommodative (upward sloping) yield curve

STOCK MARKET PEAK	MIN TTM 10 / 2 SPREAD	TTM S&P500 RETURN	1YR FWD 10 / 2 SPREAD	1YR FWD S&P500 RETURN
Jul-57	-0.17%	11.47%	0.78%	-5.22%
Dec-59	-0.43%	10.41%	0.42%	-3.83%
Dec-61	0.25%	26.30%	0.49%	-12.18%
Mar-66	-0.29%	15.12%	0.07%	-9.09%
Nov-68	-0.24%	14.89%	-0.51%	-12.96%
Dec-72	0.31%	15.69%	-0.07%	-17.80%
Dec-76	0.57%	18.89%	0.51%	-7.84%
Mar-81	-2.13%	32.04%	-0.33%	-17.65%
May-90	-0.16%	12.46%	1.29%	8.03%
Aug-00	-0.41%	15.00%	1.21%	-25.30%
Sep-07	-0.14%	14.30%	1.61%	-23.77%

level, usually in a very short time span. The evidence of this statement can be seen in the table to the right. One year after the market peak, the spread was positive in all but three cases, and 25 to 150 basis points wider in 10 out of 11 cases. Astute investors know that when they see the sign in the bond market of a quickly reversing negative 10 - 2 spread it means the stock market is in the process of contracting.

Why does a negative 10 - 2 spread occur prior to a correction and then return to a positive spread during a correction? In simple terms, the pattern is a function of the way the Fed works. Leading up to the market correction, the Fed <u>sells</u> Treasury securities from its balance sheet in order to remove lending reserves from the system. It removes reserves to tighten credit in response to a FOMC decision that rates need to be increased due to inflation pressures or some other driving force. When the Fed is put into a position that it must act, market participants not only respond to the action being taken, they also game the Fed as a participant in the market. This causes over reactions in market rates in both directions. The first reaction is the run-up in stocks as banking reserves are being removed. The market increase is an irrational investor behavior if looked at over the long term since the Fed action is intended to slow the financial system down. However, the opposite usually takes place in the short run. Then, as the stock market begins to sell-off, the Fed enters the market and <u>buys</u> Treasury securities to calm the panic to provide system reserves and liquidity as the financial system contracts. The securities purchased are usually short maturity, and therefore the two year Treasury goes down in yield much more quickly than the ten year.

High Inflation 1970s: 10 - 2 Spread Indicator Short Circuited

The 10 - 2 spread metric when back tested works well over time and tightening of spreads are witnessed prior to almost all of the major market corrections post WWII. The typical sequence is that the market begins to heat up, inflation begins to be exhibited, and the Fed administers a dose of reserve contraction medicine and then cleans up after the mess. Maybe a little cynical in the illusion, but it captures the typical order of events.

The data from the 1960s and 1970s, however, does not show a Fed willing to administer the typical financial discipline. As documented in previous chapters, it was a time period in which inflation became "acceptable" as a "theoretical" tradeoff to lower the unemployment rate. The Phillips Curve as it is known in academic literature, turned out to be a load of nonsense. So the typical contraction of the 10 - 2 spread in 1968 and 1972 into negative territory began happening after the stock market peaked. The Fed throughout this period was adding reserves to the system to support government bond auctions, creating economic "sugar highs," but was not withdrawing the reserves to keep inflation in check. This process began with the even-keel policy in the early 1960s, and resulted in the Fed responding to inflation with rate increases rather than real economic growth driven expansions. Their policy timing, therefore, was out of synch with the business cycle, and they were adding reserves when they would normally be withdrawn, and vice-versa. This can be seen in the 10 - 2 spread becoming tighter one year after the stock market peaks in 1968, 1972 and 1976.

The 1970s exhibited how the U.S. monetary system can get off track at the behest of fiscal policy, weakening the U.S. dollar and making the country vulnerable to foreign financial attacks like oil shocks. The major oil spike in 1973 precipitated by the Arab Oil Embargo and the subsequent steady increase in oil price levels through the remainder of the decade, were very much a response by the Arab world to the lack of financial discipline by the U.S. Federal Reserve. Relative balance in the management of the U.S. financial system when it comes to inflation returned after 1980, and the more typical pattern of the 10 - 2 spread also returned.

Oil Spikes also Indicative, not Timing Predictive

Multiple examples from the 1950s through 2013 exist in which oil shocks dealt heavy blows to the U.S. economy and as a result the U.S stock market declined. The proof of this fact is that all of the 5 recorded recessions from 1973 through 2009 period were all associated in some way with a major spike upward in the price of oil. Even going back to the 1950s, supply shortages in the oil market can be found leading up to a U.S. recession. In each instance, higher oil prices or energy shortages eroded real economic growth and also drove up inflation forcing the Federal Reserve to respond by tightening monetary policy, exacerbating the economic decline.

Five major oil spikes since 1972 are shown in the graph below. The price of oil in every instance was moving "shockingly" higher at the point in time it was optimal to exit the stock market. *The definition of an oil price "shock" is a 75-150% increase in price levels within a 12 month timeframe, usually taking prices above a previous all-time high.* The 1987 price spike was significant, but it did not take prices back to the 1980 high levels of $39 per barrel. Prices only reached $21 per barrel, but were launched upward from lows a year earlier in the $12 range. The market trepidation of a return to the price spikes of the 1970s, may have contributed to the triggered fall in the stock market in the fall of '87. However, the 1987 Crash was short-lived, and the steady decline in oil prices post the stock market fall contributed to a quick market recovery.

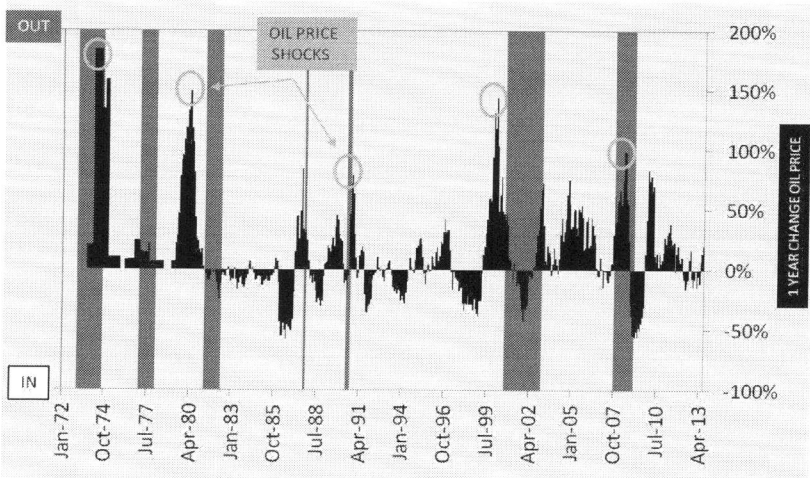

The oil price shocks, much like the Fed Funds rate policy leading up to the stock market correction, are <u>indicative</u> of an impending market correction, but not precisely timing predictive. No simultaneous timing trigger associated with a price peak in oil and a decline in stocks was found in the historical data. For instance, the stock market already signaled a top at the end of 1972, but the oil shock occurred with the Arab Oil Embargo in late 1973 and early 1974.

To be sure, if you were <u>not</u> out of the market at the optimal time point, by the time the oil shock hit, the exit sign was flashing red. By September of 1974 the market hit a low of 64, fully 48% below its high of 118 at the close in December 1972. In 1990 in order to be in the best investment position you needed to exit the market prior to the oil price peak precipitated by the Kuwait War. And in 2008 when oil price levels remained suspiciously high even as the U.S. financial system was in the midst of "cardiac arrest", the optimal exit point had already passed. In both cases the DOW signal was already triggered.

Juxtapose these shocks with the late 1970s spike when President Carter deregulated prices and the Iranian revolution constricted supply pushing prices to interim all-time highs of $39, over 10 times the price level prior to the Arab Oil Embargo in 1973. In that instance, the point in time to exit the market actually occurred post the 1980 election of Ronald Reagan. This same pattern occurred in the year 2000 as oil prices spiked and held at the $35 level (coincidentally close in dollar terms to the 1980 peak) early in the year 2000 and held into the November 2000 elections. The major run-up in oil prices happened before the optimal withdrawal time point for stocks in August of year 2000.

What should be getting clearer from the explanation of the data is that a unique oil price spike is not the precise timing trigger for stock market re-valuation. From the early 1970s through 2008, it was a necessary condition – a major contributing factor, particularly as it relates to the size and length of time that it takes the market to form a new bottom. However, the Fed policy response to the oil shock, and in some cases the Saudi Arabian calming of the market as happened in 1987 and 1990, are what really precipitated the stock market reaction. Reading the interest rate market and Fed policy in conjunction with the oil spikes brings the picture into full view. The Fed is not just responding to domestic economic variables when it responds to an oil shock. The monetary actions have to be viewed in the context of the dollar relative to the real income levels and growth of countries whose raw materials or goods are traded in dollars. Oil shocks, therefore, become a very important signal because they reflect conflicting intra-government relationships driven by the ability of the dollar as a reserve currency to hold its value relative to scarce resources such as energy. Oil shocks, as a result, become the primary external counter-correlating factor in a dollar reserve centric world.

Government Spending Policy and Market Peaks

In researching this book, very little direct correlating evidence was found which attributed a fall in government spending either in absolute or slowing in pace to a major decline in stock market value. This fact is most likely due to several factors. One, government expenditures rarely decreased in rate of growth in the time period from the end of WWII until 2013 - spending perpetually pushed higher. In fact, between June 1954 and June 2011, current government expenditures grew from a yearly spending rate of $63.5B to $4T. During that entire period, only once did the yearly rate of change in government spending actually go down. That was in the 12 month time span between September 1955 and 1956. The compounded average annual growth rate in fiscal spending during the 57 years was 7.65%. Any influence on the stock market from the growth in government spending which perpetually moved higher was in the form of how the Federal Reserve policy complimented the spending. In the case of the 1960s, higher spending rates were monetized by the Fed leading to higher rates of inflation. Therefore, based only on historical correlations, market peaks are more precisely associated with changes in the level of interest rates driven by Federal Reserve policy, not changes in government spending.

From mid 2011 through 2013, government expenditures slowed in growth and even showed slight year over year declines, owing to military cut-backs and Sequestration in 2013. This increased the possibility of a new relative element triggering a stock market correction that was evident in the stock market in the 1940s. Post WWII, President Truman introduced and implemented balanced budgets which severely curtailed the wartime budget in effect during the FDR administration. Then, as in 2013, U.S. Debt to GDP was over 100%. The effect on the stock market from the fiscal policy change is covered in detail at the end of Chapter 7 about the National Debt. In 1946, the Truman Budget cut government spending so extensively that inflation fell dramatically, and real economic growth may also have been impacted. However, the real economy in the U.S. at the time blossomed, supported by a strong trade surplus generated by the export of goods to countries overseas that needed to rebuild after the War. The 1946 time period is one of the few in the post WWII era where the rate of change in government spending can be most directly associated with a stock market correction after an all-time peak. In 1946 the DOW peaked in May at 207. By September of 1946 it closed the month at 169. It was not until the beginning of 1950 that the stock market recovered to a new all-time high.

Putting the Signals Together –Year 2000 Market Correction

In order for readers to see the timing and relationship of the market correction signals in a direct sequence of events, the year 2000 and year 2008 downturns have been put into easy to review graphic format.

Beginning with the year 2000 sequence, in December of 1999 the DOW hit an all-time month end closing high of 11,281. It was during a time period of rising oil prices. Oil was approaching the all-time high water marks set in 1980, but had not yet reached those levels. In dollar inflation adjusted terms, the price level was still much lower. However, priced in gold terms, oil broke the Arab Oil Embargo threshold of 12.8 barrels per ounce. Four months into the year 2000, the DOW posted a year over year decline at month end close. It was the first time this had happened since December 1990.

The S&P 500 did not exhibit the year over year signal in April 2000. In fact the S&P 500 powered to an all-time closing peak of 1518 in August of 2000. It was not until November 2000 that it confirmed the DOW signal, posting a year over year decline of -5.3%. This corresponded with the interim peak in oil prices of $34.40 at month end. By January of 2001, Fed policy changed, and the Fed Funds target rate was reduced from 6.5% to 6.0%. This change was reflective of movements in the Treasury yield curve that had already taken place.

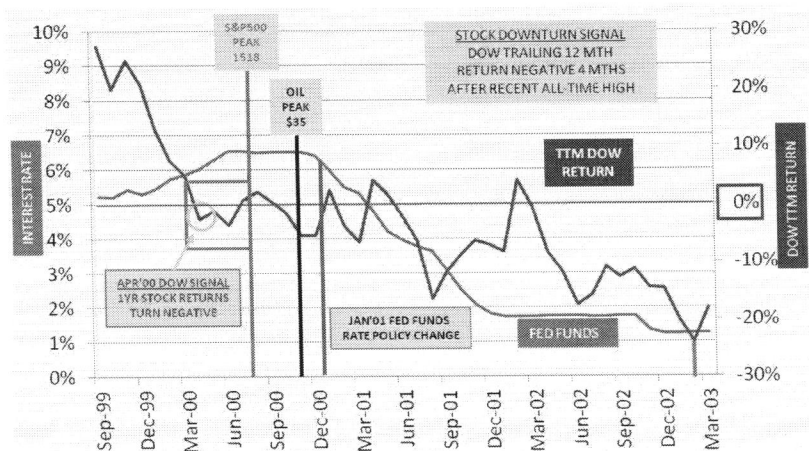

The most visible interest rate signal in the year 2000 that the stock market was about to turn over came from the reversal of the 10 - 2 Treasury yield spread.

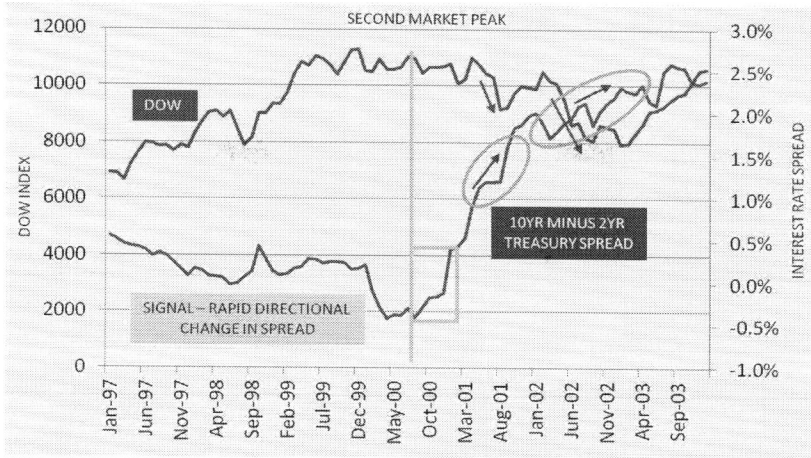

During the early months of the year 2000 stock market correction, the 10 - 2 spread began to rapidly expand from a negative -0.41% in April when the DOW gave its first signal, to a positive +0.4% in January 2001 when the Fed cut the Fed Funds target. The expansion of the spread continued aggressively through 2001 and on into 2002. The interim stock market bottom as measured by the S&P 500 was not established until February 2003 at 841 (month end close data, not intra-month). By 2003 the yield curve was steeply sloped with a 10 - 2 spread approaching 250 basis points.

2008 Crisis – Relativity Signals Work Again

In the 2007-08 market correction sequence, the DOW hit an all-time month end closing high of 13,901 in September of 2007; the S&P 500 followed in October at 1549. Just like the year 2000, oil prices were rising, only this time the price levels were well above the all-time high water marks set in 1980. As the FOMC lowered the Federal Funds target from 5.25% to 4.75% in September 2007, oil prices were at $75 per barrel. From that point forward, the oil market moved dramatically higher, reaching an all-time high in June 2008 of $140 per barrel. By that point in time the stock market was in virtual free fall with both the DOW and the S&P showing losses in excess of 20% from their highs in 2007. The wrath of the Middle East was truly being applied to the U.S. stock market. The $140 high mark in oil prices at month end June 2008 was 10 times higher than the $14 mark oil 10 years earlier in 1998. This price jump upward in history was equaled only in the 1970s.

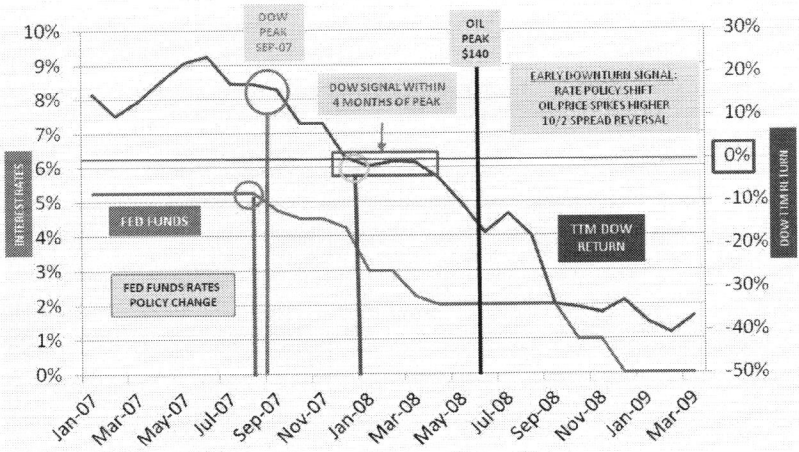

The DOW signal and S&P signal coincided during this downturn, occurring in January 2008, 3 and 4 month respectively after the all-time interim highs set in September and October 2007. It was the early move by the Fed which produced a counter-acting violent move upward in oil prices that really signaled the 2008 stock market crisis.

In the 2008 crisis, followers of the 10 - 2 spread really had a front row indication of major troubles looming ahead. Starting well ahead of signals from the stock market and ahead of the Fed Funds policy shift by the Federal Reserve, the 10 - 2 spread was rocketing upward to a much wider level ahead of the other indicators.

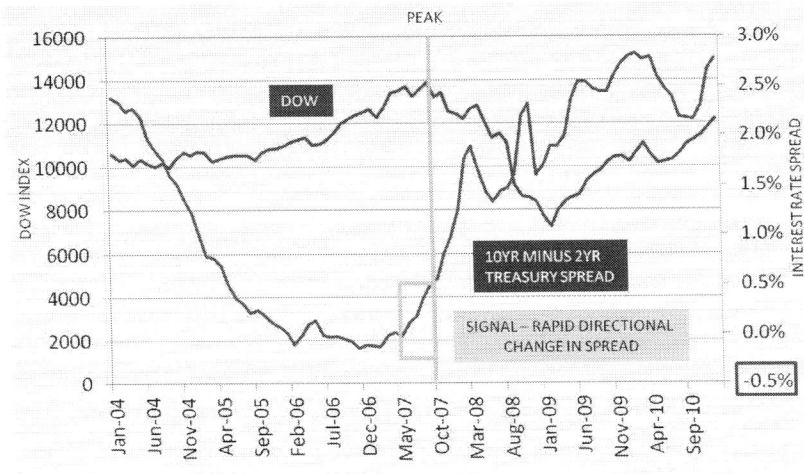

Trouble was definitely in the works, as history reflected from the failure and fire sale to J.P. Morgan of Bear Sterns in March 2008 and the bankruptcy and liquidation of Lehman Brothers in September of 2008. It should not go without notice, however, that these failures all transpired during an oil shock which doubled prices in less than 12 months. In May 2007 the 10 - 2 spread was -.02%, and had been slowly trending toward positive territory since the beginning of the year. By October as the stock market was peaking, the spread had expanded to +.51%. Similar to 2001, the expansion of the yield spread continued aggressively throughout the stock market correction. The interim stock market bottom measured by the S&P 500 was not established until February 2009 at 735 (month end close data, not intra-month which showed a low of 666). By 2009 the yield curve was steeply sloped with a 10 - 2 spread approaching 300 basis points

Fed Zero-Rate Policy Distorts Interest Rate Signals

In order for the Theory of Financial Relativity market signals to be effective, there must be a free market setting of Treasury interest rates to get a clear indication of impending stock corrections. The short end of the Treasury yield curve under the Obama administration for the time period up to the publication of this book was being pegged to the zero-boundary in order to repress rates and lower government financing costs. Under these circumstances modified yield curve indicators must be utilized in order to understand if the financial system is unstable and the stock market is going to correct. The modified indicator most likely to be effective is the spread between maturities further out on the yield curve such as the 10-5. A flattening of the long end of the yield curve when short rates are being price controlled provides similar information to a negative 10-2 spread.

During a zero bound rate policy, investors need to beware of market characteristic exhibited in the 1970s. Maintaining a zero-bound policy, by definition, means that the Fed keeps reserve levels in the banking system high in order to keep rates low. As long as the U.S. banking system co-operates, as was the case in the late 1940s, rates can be pegged and government financing costs held in check. In 2013 there were ample reserves in the system to ignite inflation. The reserves were not increasing inflation at the time because the strict underwriting regulations controlling lending and a government spending policy that was unusually contracting – a spending pattern that possibly would change in 2014 as the Affordable Care Act subsidies were scheduled to go into effect.

As the market entered the spring of 2013, the market winds changed and rates on the long end of the Treasury curve moved higher despite high volumes of Treasury purchases by the Fed of $85B per month. Net sellers of debt in this time period were foreign governments, which should come as no surprise. Unlike the 1940s when U.S. citizens and institutions held 93% of the U.S. National Debt, in 2013 almost 50% of publicly traded debt was in the hands of foreign governments. The inter-play between the relative value of the dollar and the maintenance of the purchasing power of U.S. Treasuries held by foreign governments was dictating the future government policy direction and expected outcome for the U.S. stock market in 2013.

The biggest risk in 2013 was a potential run on the U.S. Debt from foreign governments. In 1970 the risk was a run on the U.S. gold reserve. The two monetary illnesses require the same cure – higher U.S. interest rates. The primary difference in the two timeframes was that government spending was considered in check as the end of 2013 approached, allowing the Fed leeway in remaining accommodative and not raise interest rates. However, government policy was returning to the Phillips Curve model of accepting inflation as a trade-off to lower unemployment, and entitlement spending was scheduled to continue to increase. The future was not certain, but the probability was rising that Fed policy was slowly digressing to produce a re-run of the 1970s, with a dramatic run upward in interest rates being triggered by actions of foreign governments in response to U.S. domestic policies. As of the writing of this book, the government shut-down in October 2013 was a battle indicative of how aggressive the defense of the domestic spending and continued borrowing policy was going to be. During the shutdown, the market correction triggers were not yet pushed to alert status. The long-term interest rates, which rose going into the shut-down, stabilized awaiting the outcome of the negotiation. Inevitably the market was marching to a point, yet again, when the seemingly irrational highs in the market would break-down only when the artificial subsidizing government forces could no longer be sustained and market imbalances must be addressed – as stated in Guiding Principle #8 of the Theory of Financial Relativity.

Stock Market Correction Signal Summary

The information in this chapter can be summarized into a concise set of signals investors can use as bell weathers of impending market corrections.

FINANCIAL RELATIVITY MARKET CRASH SIGNALS

1. The DOW Index records a negative year over year change, typically 2-3 months after establishing an all-time high - ALWAYS.

2. Leading up to the DOW signal, there are signs that the FED Funds rate policy will begin reversing previous rate hikes - ALMOST ALWAYS, EXCEPTION WHEN FED RATE IS BEING HELD AT THE ZERO BOUND OR BELOW INFLATION AS IN THE 1970S.

3. At the DOW signal point, the 10 - 2 Treasury spread is near or below zero and a reversal to a more positive spread is underway – USUALLY, 9 of 13 CORRECTIONS SINCE 1957.

4. Oil price shocks always result in a market decline; if a shock occurs when stocks are at an all-time high, deep and prolonged market corrections occur - USUALLY, 5 of 7 CORRECTIONS SINCE 1972.

5. ZERO BOUND OR INFLATION DRIVEN EXTREME CASE SIGNAL – Long-term rate rise triggered by foreign reaction to Fed AND / OR Fiscal policy direction.

FED AND FISCAL POLICY ACTIONS RELATIVE TO FOREIGN MARKETS TRIGGER CORRECTONS

The first signal listed, the DOW signal, must always happen – but does not always happen first. More often, the bond market, the wise old man in the financial market, makes the call first. Indications will be exhibited in the rate pattern between long and short maturity risk-free and riskier securities. You cannot usually wait on the Fed to make the first move to signal trouble ahead. Once the Fed starts lowering rates, the writing is probably on the wall. And, if a foreign country is applying economic pressure on the market, such as an OPEC oil shock or sale of U.S. Treasuries by foreign governments, a deep and lasting market downturn is inevitable.

14 COAST IS CLEAR SIGNALS

In 1975 Jack Bogle, founder of the mutual fund giant Vanguard, provided a great service for investors, particularly those who do not have the time or expertise to pick stocks on their own. With the introduction of the first stock index mutual fund, Vanguard created a means for investors to purchase a slice of the aggregate stock market with one simple order. No hassles from a broker, no research required. Simply trust that the investment in the market index, a diversified collection of U.S. company stocks, will provide an optimal risk reward return that is better than you could otherwise achieve. Many investors, particularly small investors that have retirement IRA and 401-K accounts, utilize this path for investing extensively.

Advice to diversify your investment portfolio by purchasing the aggregate market index fund which tracks the S&P 500 is very sound. Since the S&P 500 is highly correlated to the U.S. GDP, buying the S&P 500 index is essentially purchasing a slice of the U.S. GDP and taking a position in the success or failure of the U.S. economy. You can do better than the average index, but only if you can pick winners in the market. Once burned by a big failure investing this way, however, most investors quickly realize they need more than a couple of stocks in their portfolio in order to sleep well at night. It turns out that owning about 17-20 stocks across a broad swath of the economy will achieve the level of diversification that simulates the same variability you get from an aggregate market index fund. In other words, no stock should be more than 5% of a portfolio, a suitable rule if the stocks are large cap companies. The smaller the company, the more diversification required. For small cap companies the allocation should not exceed 1% to 2%.

So, diversification is good. End of the lesson repeated over and over throughout this book.

Where I sway from the party line coming forth from the investment fund industry, however, is in the advice to "buy right and hold tight" or "stay the course" once you have chosen an asset allocation. These are 2 of the 10 lessons in what Jack Bogle puts forth in his book "The Clash of the Cultures: Investment vs. Speculation", as ways an investor can lessen their chances of not losing their hard earned money in a market that increasingly appears to be driven by speculation rather than investing. As pointed out earlier in this book, chasing the latest momentum driven stock, particularly with a leveraged position, is speculating. Simply staying the course in your own portfolio will not change this activity, or the outcome of this activity in the market one iota.

Changing your portfolio composition when signals are clear that what you own is over-price or under-priced is not speculation. If you own an aggregate stock index, or a portfolio of stocks which is highly correlated to the index, you have to make an assessment through time if that investment is doing the job of preserving the purchasing power of your hard earned savings or wealth – and take steps to protect your assets in situations when purchasing power may be lost. The first step in this process is being able to identify when the stock market is over-valued and will be re-priced through a market "correction." The last chapter of this book laid out a framework for identifying a market peak. The signals of a market downturn are very visible when the time is ripe for it to happen.

When a stock market correction happens, it may be small 10-15%, or large, up to 50% in the case of 1974 and 2008. The stock market collapse in 1929 was a whopping 83% drop. The magnitude of the drop is a function of the strength of the forces that precipitated the drop. Mutual fund industry leader Jack Bogle advises that investors should never take advice which leads to trying to "to time or trade the market", because the ones telling you to get out can never tell you when to get back in. This statement is very accurate, as far as my research has been able to conclude, when the market is in a typical upwardly bias trading pattern. However, if the market is in the throes of a certified correction the signal at the bottom, although slightly different, is just as clear as the market top.

Important Reason to Rebalance – Staying Power

When working in Silicon Valley in 2001, I had the opportunity to experience a part of the capital industry in the world that most investors rarely get to see from the inside. At Caspian Networks, founded in the late 1990s by Dr. Larry Roberts as a company known as Packetcom, I was part of a recruited management team from Nortel Networks to execute a plan to build the router that would take over the networking industry. It would be the Cisco killer. Oddly enough, the largest investors in the company, U.S. Venture Partners and New Enterprise Associates, placed lead partners on the Caspian Board that made substantial money from investments in Cisco and Juniper Networks. Capital re-cycling in the venture world is a major part of the game.

Another critical aspect of the Venture Capital industry is making sure your portfolio companies are sufficiently funded. Gathering funding in support of new ideas and inventions is a continual process. In the year 2000 most of the ideas were driven by internet technology. At Caspian Networks, a large amount of capital was raised and invested in research, facilities and human capital in a very short period of time. From the Series A round closed in 1999 for $15M, subsequent rounds took the company funding level by 2001 to $124M in funding which had been burned through entirely. Round C, closed in early 2001, double the funding again, taking the total investment in the company to over a quarter billion dollars.

As the round was in the process of being put together, the discussions with the Board surrounded a very interesting issue which stuck in my mind. It did not involve, as you might expect, whether the company was going to have enough capital to get its product through customer trials and became cash-flow positive. The discussion concerned whether the company was going to have enough capital to make it through the next economic downturn. Capital, rather than energy, is the lifeblood of Venture Capital industry. And the wealth of experience of the individuals on the Caspian Networks Board had a sense that the market was going to go into an extended downturn. And, several years later, after I had already moved on even though the start-up was flush with cash, it turned out that they did not have enough resources to survive.

At the time, I did not have the luxury of all the data assembled in putting together this book, but it was clear in 2001 that the market for capital was getting ready to close. In fact, the shut-down signal was given by the DOW in April 2000; it was just slow to be acknowledged by the S&P 500, which turned negative in year over year returns in November 2000. But the capital markets at the time were clearly unstable. Capital flowed excessively into the technology market in the late 1990s and valuations could not justify the new influx of dollars. Looking back at the signals from the time period including the 10 - 2 interest rate spread, the DOW Signal, the run-up in oil price and the tight Fed policy, the situation was definitely flashing red in the year 2000.

What no one could answer in the management discussion involving Caspian funding needs was how long the downturn would last. It was an important question because if the company was not sufficiently funded to survive the period when investment capital was sure to become scarce, it faced the prospect of being shut-down or sold at a fire sale price. For the Venture Capital industry the 2001 market downturn turned out to be a very long drought for technology investments. The entire downturn re-vectored capital flows from technology into a war based economy and a steady escalation of the price of energy.

Historical market data provides guidance on how long a market downturn will usually last. The average length of market corrections in the stock market was 13.4 months in the 13 corrections between 1957 and 2008. The correction which began in the year 2000 took 25 months for the stock market to bottom. The corrections which involved major conflicts with the Middle East tended to take longer adjustment time periods.

In other words, the answer to the question "how long will a downturn last?" is – until the capital market says the coast is clear. The question cannot be answered at the outset of the downturn. You can try to take precautions as the VCs in the case of Caspian were doing by trying to make sure funds were sufficient to weather the storm. For VCs storing cash to weather the storm is usually the only option for companies which are incubating. At a market top they sell the good investments through an IPO or merger with a public company. Making sure the most promising companies in the portfolio are flush with cash going into a downturn becomes a matter of ensuring survival.

DOW Reversal Signal

Having the staying power to survive a market correction is a fundamental rule in the Venture Capital industry. Robustness is a good quality in any investment portfolio. The strategy to achieve robustness involves taking precautions against the forces that instigate a market correction by increasing the liquidity on hand at certain points in time. Notice, however, that the VC industry does not do a wholesale sell-out prior to a market correction. The VCs raise cash levels in their best companies by selling shares, at high price levels, with the intention of riding out the storm.

When selling stocks at a market peak and setting aside funds for surviving the downturn, the keys to success become knowing when to re-enter the market. One important signal is always given by the king of the capital markets – the DOW index. Just as the DOW signaled the peak by a change of 12 month returns from positive to negative, the DOW signals the revival of the capital market by the slowing in the rate of decline year over year. This happens when the 12 month rate of change in the DOW, measured at month end close, hits a low point, and then shows a lower 12 month negative return the following month. Visually on a chart the slowing rate of decline looks like a trading bounce. However, the trick is that it must be a bounce that holds.

The graph below shows the trailing 12 month return of the DOW from 1953 thru 2013 plotted against the most optimal time points to re-enter the stock market during the 13 recorded corrections.

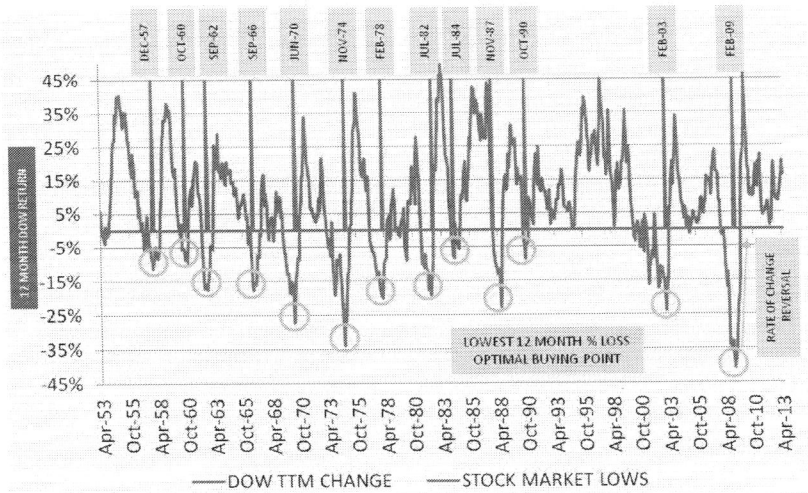

The graph shows that the "buy low" re-entry points mathematically coincided with the instance that the 12 month return in the market hit the absolute bottom, and then the following month reversed. In February 2009 the year over year loss was almost 45%.

How does an investor recognize when the bottom is formed? In certain cases, especially in the 2001 decline, false positive signals appeared before the bottom was actually reached. False indications given by the DOW rate of return signal can be overcome by waiting for confirmation that a bottom is in place. With respect to the DOW signal, <u>confirmation is virtually assured if the DOW trades at progressively lower year over year losses for three months in a row</u>. Once this pattern occurred in the corrections from 1958 through 2009, the DOW quickly re-established its typical trading pattern and very rarely posted a year over year decline until the next market top was formed. The first year after a correction bottom is a point in time that investors want to be invested in the market. Historically some of the highest capital gains in the stock market are experienced during that year. For instance, from Feb 2009 to Feb 2010, the DOW gained 47.6%. The year after the Feb 2003 low the S&P 500 was up 36.1%, and in November of 1975 the DOW posted a year over year gain of 41%.

Three months of progressively lower DOW losses year over year is a very fail-safe signal for market re-entry during a market correction. However, not being in the market for those three months in most every case was wasting an opportunity to earn valuable returns. Understanding the Theory of Financial Relativity becomes valuable in identifying the market reentry point sooner. The DOW signal is correlated to behavioral actions in other parts of the market. These actions are transmitted through the measuring yardstick of Financial Relativity, interest rates.

This means that the best way, and usually quickest confirmation that a true market bottom is in place comes from the bond market.

Long term Bonds Signal Stock Market Low Reversal

In Chapter 6 of this book, the relationship of the BAA1 seasoned long-term interest rate was shown to have a fundamental inverse correlation with the value of the U.S. stock market. This relationship empirically held through good times and bad from the mid 1950s thru 2013. When stocks were declining heading into a correction during this time period, the absolute level of the BAA1 rate usually increased. Similarly, as the market began to improve, the rate typically began to decline. But, which came first, the relaxing of the rate, or the stock market improvement? When money trades into stocks and other riskier investments after an extended period of fear generated by a market downturn, it must flow from some other asset class. The most likely trade after a market falls dramatically is from less risky assets into more risky assets. Market participants consistently and predictably use similar sources of funds to trade into BAA1 long-term bonds and the stock market when a market correction is coming to an end. This behavior makes the BAA1 rate relative to less risky assets a good confirming signal of a stock market reversal.

In the graph below, the BAA1 rate spread over the risk free proxy for a similar maturity bond, the 30 Year Treasury, is plotted. The timeline for the graph stretches from 1953 through mid 2013. The difference between these two interest rates provides a very good measure of the "fear" level within the market for longer term capital over the timeframe - the wider the spread, the greater the fear, and as a result the higher the cost of capital for businesses on a relative basis during market downturns.

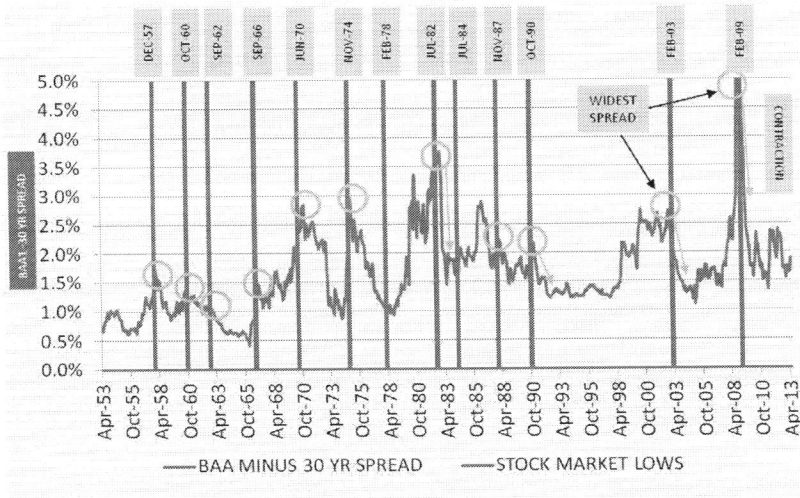

As the graph shows, at times when the stock market was under-going a correction, the BAA1 / 30 YR spread widened, in most cases significantly. The more the spread widened the deeper and faster the drop in stock value as witnessed in 1974 and 2008. In the benign stock corrections of 1983-84 and early 1963 the spread did not change dramatically, indicating that the downturn was not going to be severe.

In virtually every instance, it was the reversal of the spread that signaled the revival of the market for risky assets. During 11 of 13 market corrections from 1957 through 2008, the spread tightened as the stock market began to reverse and trade higher. This tightening provided the confirming signal that the market for risk assets, including stocks, was again open for business.

Typically, as one might rationally expect, the first risky assets class to reflect improving financial market conditions is investment grade corporate bonds.

These bonds are higher in the capital structure than common stock and considered lower in risk than the aggregate stock market indexes. In the table to below, the BAA1 / 30 YR spread is analyzed during the four months leading up to and then the year after multiple stock market correction low points. As stocks formed a correction bottom during these times in history, the BAA1 / 30 YR spread in 6 of the 11 cases was already contracting before stock lows were reached. The lower spread reflected a flow of funds into riskier assets in the bond market prior to the point it was considered safe to return to stocks. But more importantly, in the month after the stock market began to turn upward, the spread contracted in most every case, providing the double confirmation needed that re-entry into stocks was safe.

S&P500 MARKET LOWS	BAA1-30YR SPREAD	MAX T4MTH BAA1-30YR SPREAD	TTM S&P500 RETURN	1YR FWD BAA1-30YR SPREAD	1YR FWD S&P500 RETURN
Dec-57	1.73%	1.73%	-11.32%	1.05%	32.63%
Oct-60	1.20%	1.36%	-5.74%	1.15%	26.56%
Sep-62	1.03%	1.08%	-16.74%	0.75%	28.57%
Sep-66	1.15%	1.15%	-14.44%	1.24%	25.97%
Jun-70	1.91%	2.11%	-25.51%	2.37%	35.62%
Nov-74	2.62%	2.62%	-27.08%	2.28%	30.00%
Jul-82	3.25%	3.41%	-18.32%	1.99%	51.40%
Nov-87	2.28%	2.28%	2.07%	1.64%	12.55%
Oct-90	1.88%	1.88%	-10.59%	1.56%	28.95%
Feb-03	2.19%	2.73%	-24.03%	1.33%	36.15%
Feb-09	4.37%	5.76%	-44.78%	1.78%	50.20%

SPREAD BEGINS TO NARROW APPROACHING MARKET LOW
WITHIN 1 YEAR, SPREAD LOWER, STOCKS HIGHER

As shown in the table, the BAA1 / 30 YR Treasury spread was significantly lower in 9 of 11 market scenarios the year after the stock market reached a correction low. In all 11 cases, stock returns over the following 12 months were exceptionally high, usually in excess of 25%. The late 1960s and early 1970s showed up as outliers in the contraction of the spread, and can be traced back to the inflationary monetary policies during the time period which distorted interest rate signals. This factor is important in understanding stock market corrections when inflation is a major problem in the U.S. capital markets.

Investors can also gauge market fear by computing the absolute level of the BAA1 / 30 Year spread, and comparing it to other points in time. The higher the spread, the more likely fear is present in market. The table to below provides statistics on the typical spread level at different times in history.

From 1982 thru 2013, the time period after the Monetary Control Act of 1980 deregulated interest rates, the median BAA1 / 30 YR spread was 1.76%. In 33% of the times the spread exceeded 2.0%. In a mere 14% of the times the spread was greater than 2.5%. Based on this data, the 200 - 250 basis point spread threshold becomes an important level that investors need to remain aware over time.

MARKET STATSTICS 1953-2013	
MEDIAN BAA1-30YR SPREAD	1.53%
% TIME SPREAD > 1.76%	37.1%
% OF TIME SPREAD > 2.00%	27.5%

MARKET STATISTICS 1982-2013	
MEDIAN BAA1-30YR SPREAD	1.76%
% OF TIME SPREAD > 2.00%	33.9%
% OF TIME SPREAD > 2.50%	14.0%

Signals were Clear in the 2003 Reversal

Back-testing is a useful method to review the effectiveness of market downturn signals. For instance, examine the market reversal in 2003 in the following graph.

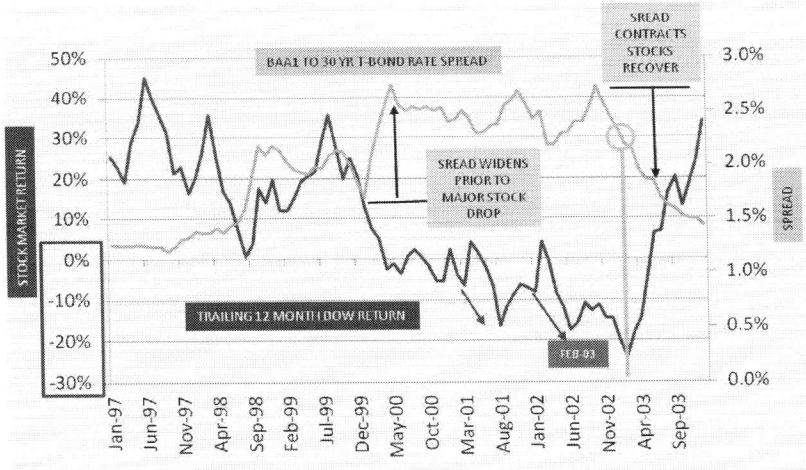

The DOW Signal is shown in the red line (left axis) on the graph above, and the change in the BAA1 / 30 YR spread is shown in green (right axis). A severe widening of the interest rate spread can be seen in the graph as the market deteriorated beginning in the middle of 2000. The DOW signal was confirmed by the 10 - 2 spread reversal from negative to positive as shown in the last chapter of this book. Leading up to the correction, money was flowing from risky assets into Treasuries which were at relatively high yields and low price if viewed from a risk perspective. Eventually the stock market rolled over and began to post negative returns, with the DOW posting its first year over year negative return for this time period in April 2000.

Signals of the stock market breakdown began in April 2000, but the data reflect a market that was not sure whether to go down or bounce back up. A key market top indication was that any increase in the DOW after April 2004 was countered by a move up in the BAA1 / 30 YR spread. The interest rate market and the stock market were not in synch at the time. In addition, the spread level remained at elevated levels well above 200 basis points. Recover signals from the DOW were not confirmed by a sustained reduction in the BAA1 / 30 YR spread until early 2003. In the timeframe leading up to the Feb 2003 stock market low, the BAA1 / 30 YR spread finally began to contract, providing the double confirmation that a true market bottom was formed and stocks propelled higher in retrospect.

Market Reversal Signals Worked Again in 2009

A similar, but more dramatic exhibition of the market signals at a market top, correction and subsequent reversal can be seen in the 2008 financial crisis data.

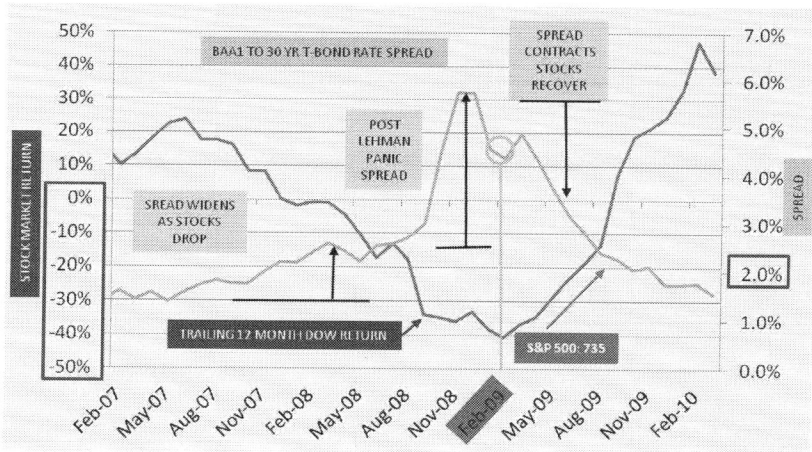

Leading up to the 2008 crisis, year over year negative DOW returns in late 2007 were accompanied by a movement of the BAA1 / 30 Year spread into the above 250 basis point "hot-zone." Early spring 2008 witnessed moves down in stocks, prompted by the collapse of Bear Sterns. It was not until the Lehman Brothers liquidation bankruptcy in September 2008 that the interest rate market catapulted into the "panic-zone" as measured by the spread. Stocks declined in inverse correlation to the rapid rise in riskier interest rates and the increased fear in the market.

Then in late 2008, just like 2003, prior to the true bottoming of the stock market the BAA1 / 30 YR spread began to reverse. The fear in the market, as measured by the spread, showed a substantial reduction from over 575 basis points to fewer than 500 basis points leading up to the S&P 500 low posted in February 2009 of 735. The actual intra-month low point for the S&P 500 was on March 9, 2009 at 676, but the month end close was higher by the end of March than February, reflective of the changing attitude toward risk assets at that point in time. The combination of DOW Signal information and the BAA1 / 30 YR interest rate spread confirmed that a solid market bottom was in place.

15 EXTRAPOLATING MARKET OUTCOMES

The robustness of the Financial Relativity Theory lies in its practical application. This chapter is dedicated to reviewing the financial market as it churned progressively to new highs in 2013. The purpose of the assessment is to provide a clear example of how to extrapolate a probable future market outcome by matching similar market conditions from prior points in history to the present market situation. Using the Theory in this fashion validates its overall soundness. Validity is enhanced each time the market resets in relative value at some future seemingly unknown, but not unexpected and clearly signaled, point in time – not unexpected because the order created by the actions of the predominate forces within the financial system inevitably will produce another incident in history in which pent up market pressures must be unleashed in the fashion predicted by the Theory of Financial Relativity.

U.S. GDP Force Feeble after 2008 Financial Crisis

During the 2008 financial crisis the U.S. economy underwent a severe contraction. The constant dollar GDP in August 2008 was measured at $14.8T dollars. Two year later in 2010, GDP was at virtually the same level - $14.9T. The change in economic output through the period was due only to inflation. Real output in the economy from the third quarter of 2008 through the first quarter of 2010 as shown in the graph below was negative.

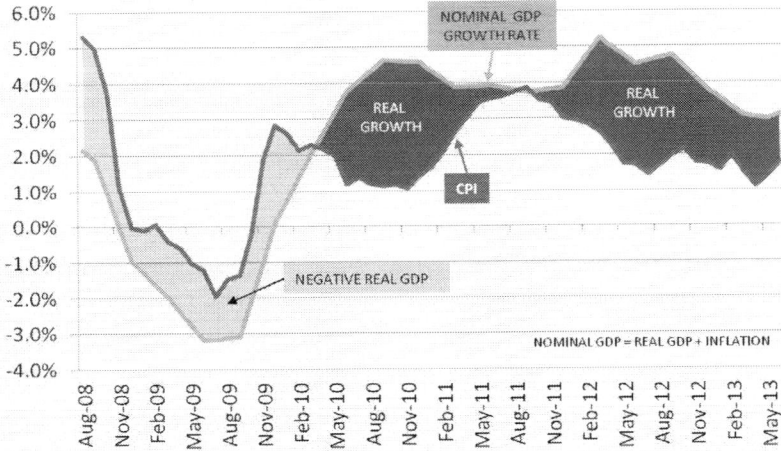

The tourniquets applied to the U.S. economy by non-traditional Federal Reserve programs and expanded U.S. fiscal policy during the crisis took time to return the system to positive real growth. Growth finally returned in 2010. Real growth, however, was very weak, less than 2% per annum from 2010 through mid-2013. If inflation, which averaged close to 2% is included, nominal GDP struggled to get above 4%. After such a deep recession, and the expansive fiscal and monetary programs, it was expected that growth would be much stronger. In order to evaluate the relative value of the stock market in mid-2013 and to assess where the market was likely headed, a more detail review of the time period from 2009 through 2013 was required.

2009 Fiscal Policy a Historical Re-Run

When President Obama took office in 2009, his first major piece of legislation was an $800B increase in government fiscal spending. It was not a one-time increase. The spending increases were programmed into government programs, and the yearly government spending rate increased from $3.2T when the financial crisis peaked in September 2008 to over $3.9T two years later, and eventually over $4T. The jolt in spending was advertised as a means of "creating or saving" hundreds of thousand s of jobs. A review of history does not provide a clear understanding of where all the money went, or why it was spent in the way that it was. The democratically controlled Senate during this time period refused to provide a budget to reconcile the spending barrage. But one fact is historically certain; the fiscal policy did not produce a lot of taxable income in the process. As seen in the graph below, the government had to borrow well above normal levels to finance the expenditure increases, driving the debt to GDP level over 100% in 2012. This was the first time since the 1940s the ratio was at such an extreme level. It remained above the 100% mark into 2013 where the ratio showed signs of a slight decline owed to lower wartime spending at the end of 2012, higher tax collections from tax increases put in effect at the beginning of 2013, and direct payments of profits from Fannie Mae and Freddie Mac.

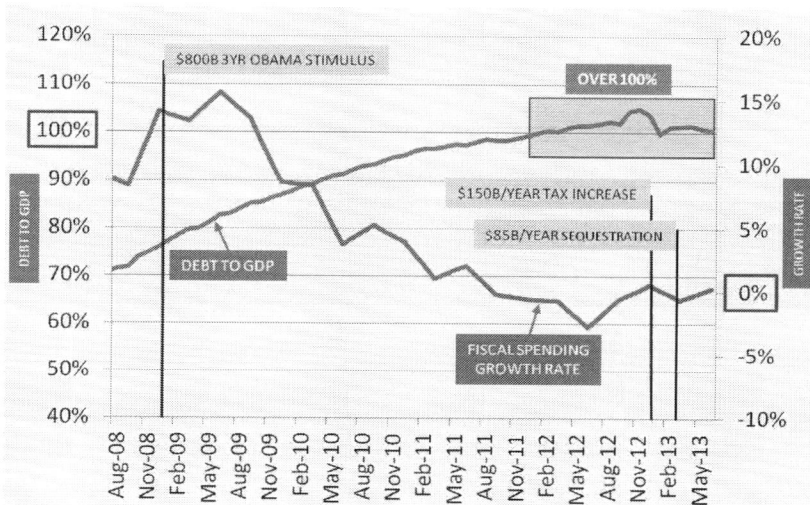

The government spending level went up in 2009 and flattened, not going back down after the crisis ended. The spending levels beginning in late 2011 through 2013 reflect the leveling off of the expenditure level. The real driving force putting a lid on government expenditure growth at the time came from the relative size of the U.S. National Debt. Reaching the 100% debt to GDP mark left the Obama led government in a tenuous position with respect to the full-faith and credit of the U.S. currency, just like in 1946. FDR ran enormous government deficits during WWII, and after the War the U.S. balance sheet was weak. President Truman entered the situation in 1946 and dramatically slashed the spending rate – not just leaving the wartime spending programs to run in place. The result was a post war recession, but also a successful transition from a wartime economy to a peacetime industrial economy. The peacetime economy ran high current account surpluses with international trading partners in rebuilding war ravaged economies throughout the world.

Both the 1940 scenario and the Obama government fiscal path are born from Keynesian economic theory. A central tenet of Keynesian theory is the belief that government spending should be used to increase aggregate demand during poor economic times. Likewise, the Theory holds that government spending should be withdrawn when the economy recovers and government surpluses should be run. However, the idea of actually scaling government spending was lost after the 1940s. From the 1950s through 2013 the more common implementation, whether the government was run by Democrats or Republicans, was to increase spending without bothering with the reductions afterward. That is what happened in the 2011 to 2013 time period. It was laudable that the government was able to cap expenditure rates during these several years, albeit at very high levels juiced up in the 2009 timeframe.

The real test for fiscal spending and the National Debt would happen post 2013, particularly if economic growth continued to exhibit poor results. The slowdown in debt growth owed to the slowing pace in growth in fiscal expenditures was a very big reason that the Federal Reserve could insert massive reserve levels in the system during 2010 through 2013 without a blow-up in consumer price inflation. The inflationary control was also owed to the very strict lending restrictions in place which kept the banking system reserves from being deployed in consumer and small business loans; rather, the reserves were mostly backing the financing of the government debt increase. However, this set of circumstances was very subject to change moving into 2014. The biggest government spending wildcard in the works was the Affordable Care Act. The subsidies associated with the act made government spending and borrowing needs very unpredictable, and President Obama was making a continual public argument that the law was in place; therefore, the government was on the hook to spend the money to pay the bill. With the system already primed with a massive level of reserves put in place by Federal Reserve quantitative easing programs, the domestic economy fiscal forces were building to unleash inflationary pressures not seen since the 1960s if government spending were to move up.

Nixon and Keynes Live in the 2013 Federal Reserve

The Federal Reserve thrust itself into an "activist" economic policy role virtually "overnight" with the unprecedented purchase of $1.2T in non-conventional assets when Lehman Brothers went bankrupt in September 2008. Prior to that point in time the Fed, dating back to its inception, had never actively entered the financial markets and taken large positions in privately held businesses. In the case of 2008, the positions taken were in the U.S. banking system. The capital to support the purchase of preferred stock in the banks was created out of "thin air." At the beginning of September 2008, the Fed had $800B in assets on its balance sheet, composed mostly of U.S. Treasuries and government backed mortgage securities. Within several weeks and a magical credit and debit entry on its balance sheet, the Fed had over $2.1T in assets, $1.6T of which was ownership in the banking system.

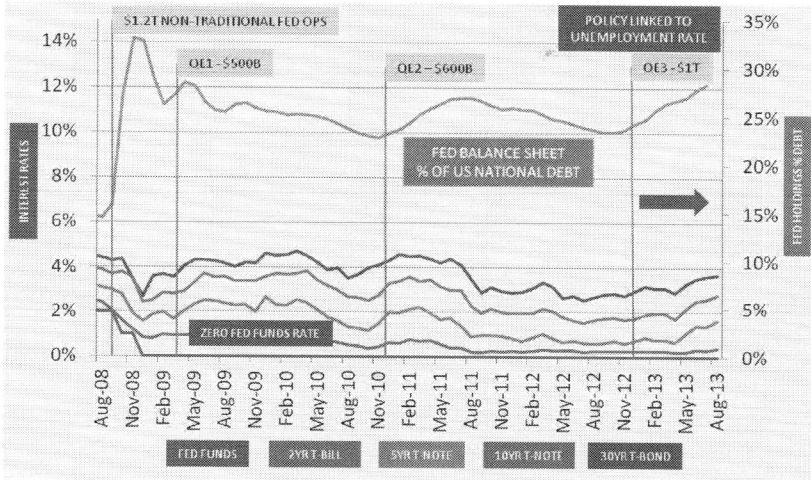

This point in history could have been a major turning point in which the U.S. banking system was nationalized, furthering the advancement of the U.S. economy toward a socialist system. However, the decision was not made to go down that path, although it was heavily feared in early 2009 as Obama took office. Going down the path might have dealt a serious blow to capital formation in the United States, the prevailing argument at the time. In the spring of 2009, the banks began raising capital to buy-out the Federal Reserve position, and a great burdening force was lifted on the market.

But the banking system recapitalization program, known as TARP, was not the last of the Federal Reserve actions implemented during the crisis. The force of the newly empowered "activist" Federal Reserve was pushed upon the financial market in increasing fashion after the crisis, even as fiscal spending growth leveled off. The programs being pursued by the Fed are chronicled in the preceding graph. One of the most immediate actions taken by the Fed was to take the Fed Funds rate to the zero bound at the end of 2008. The policy remained in place through mid-2013, and no formal date was in sight for ending the extended period of low rates. The zero rate policy was also born out of Keynesian economics, and was used in the 1940s as a means of lowering the cost of government borrowing, not as many assume, to lower the cost of consumer borrowing. This was evident in the 2013 timeframe as consumer lending rates remained at historical high rates, while savings rates plummeted to near zero. The only low borrowing rates in the market were mortgage rates, which through government subsidies and controlled lending were brought down to the benefit of a select subset of American people.

The next major program initiated by the Fed involved quantitative easing. Beginning in the 2nd quarter of 2009 the Fed began a purchase program to buy Treasury securities on the open market, thereby sending an influx of cash reserves into the system. The purchase level was $500B in 2009, and the program kept the Fed balance sheet at a level it hit after the Lehman crisis, about $2.1T, as many of the banks sold common stock to recapitalize. If the money trail is examined closely, the Fed was buying Treasuries from many investors who were converting the Treasuries into bank stock. Once the capital was in the bank, it was locked up by capital requirements – so the inflationary impact was minimal so long as the lending standards remained strict and government Treasuries were given preferential standing like a fat upward sloping yield curve for the banks to derive profits by holding the issuance.

Monetary policy accommodation during this time period, although high, was actually decelerating on a relative basis from 2008 through the end of 2010. This can be seen by looking at the size of the Fed balance sheet as a % of the publicly traded U.S. National Debt (green line) in the graph on the previous page. The percentage fell from its peak of 33.1% at the end of 2008 to 22.8% by the end of 2010. Interest rates through the time period were at historically low levels, but were beginning to show signs of rising late in 2010. It was at that point that the Fed announced a new round of quantitative easing (QE2), $600B in Treasury purchases in 2011. QE2 was followed by a portfolio rebalancing, known as the Twist, where the Fed concentrated its purchases on long-term Treasuries and sold short-term maturities to attempt to drive down interest rates on the long-end of the yield curve.

In 2011, QE2 was successful in lowering the term structure of interest rates across all maturities to historical low levels. The weak growth in the economy and continued lack of recorded consumer price inflation contributed to the downward momentum. Interestingly, oil prices during this time period bounced above $100 a barrel, only to dip back below the mark once the crisis in Egypt was calmed. As QE2 and the Fed Twist program ended late in 2012 the Fed balance sheet was $2.9T in size consisting of $1.7T in Treasury securities, $1T in government MBS, and about $200B in non-traditional holdings still outstanding, down significantly from the $1.2T taken on in late 2008.

By historical standards, the Fed was seemingly stretched at this point well beyond its mandated market function. The banking system at the end of 2012 was flush with reserves. The Fed balance sheet as a percentage of the National Debt was at a high historical water mark of 24.3%. By comparison after WWII the Fed typically held 10% of the publicly traded U.S. Treasury debt on its balance sheet. In the inflation plagued 60s and 70s this percentage grew to a peak of 24% in 1974 before steadily declining through the years back to the 10% by the mid 1980s as inflation subsided. Why wasn't the aggressive Fed bond buying policy producing inflation similar to other points in history?

The answer to the question "where was the inflation?" lies in fact that the massive Fed program was producing inflation, just not consumer price inflation. The stock market churned higher, even as the country's GDP growth continued to show weak results. One of the behavioral tendencies of domestic government institutions is to resist negative forces through their actions– in the case of the Fed easy money is the natural tendency when GDP growth is low as long as there are no signs of inflation. Since the inflation meter was no running hot in late 2012, political rancor began to grow in Washington that the Fed was not doing enough. In historical context this policy position is odd – an extreme position with little basis for validity. However, the public argument put forward was that the Fed needed to continue monetary easing until unemployment reached 6.5%. Even though the historical evidence is quite the contrary – that monetary actions are very poorly correlated with employment as Nixon found out in the early 1970s - the Fed choose in 2013 to launch QE3, an even bigger quantitative easing program of $1T in asset purchases.

By 2014, the Federal Reserve was on track to have a balance sheet $4T in size. As QE3 began implementation, however, it did not produce a decline in interest rates like the QE2 program. In fact, interest rates on longer dated Treasuries spiked up beginning in May 2013 and continued to increase almost 150 basis points across the yield spectrum from 5 to 30 years. A couple of possibilities exist as to why long-term rates went up in spite of the Fed QE program. First, the new round of purchases was beginning to push the level of out-right Fed ownership of Treasury securities into a zone much more closely correlated with inflation. Prior QE rounds focused more heavily on MBS securities which were not as tightly linked to lending reserves in the financial system, and therefore the pass-through effect on the money multiplier was not as strong. The purchase of MBS securities was a government program to encourage the housing market to recover by suppressing long-term mortgage rates. A re-inflation of housing prices did occur in the time period. In 2013, the Fed began to focus more on Treasury security purchases.

During the first half of the year Fed ownership of Treasuries increased to 16.3% of the outstanding publicly traded issuance, a threshold that compared to the mid-1960s and other points in more recent history when inflation started to increase such as 2007 and 2008. Crossing this relative threshold in 2013 likely triggered holders of Treasuries priced at very low interest rates to begin to sell. Both foreign and U.S. investors began to sell holdings in of Treasury bonds.

OWNERS OF U.S. PUBLIC DEBT JUNE 2013*

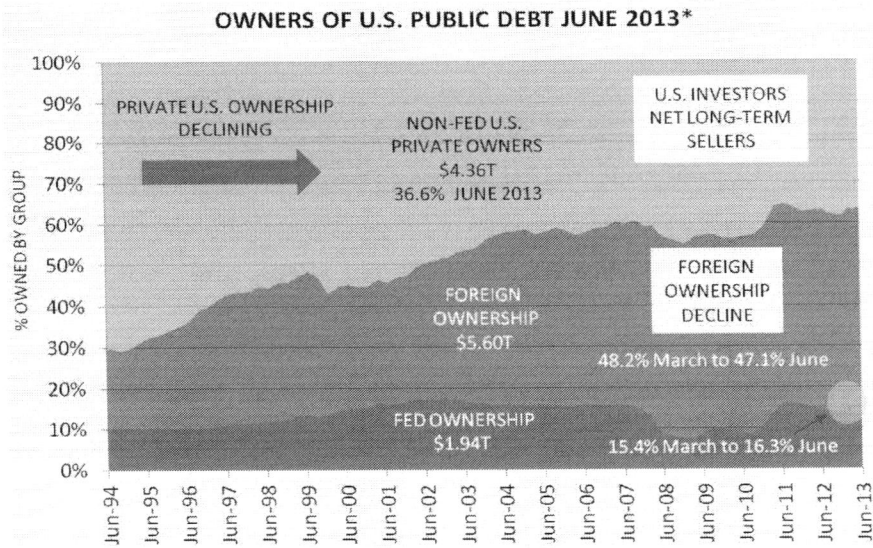

* Total Public plus Intra-Government U.S. Debt March 2013 - $16.8T, June 2013 - $16.7T

The market selling action was predictable based on the Financial Relativity Principle #8 which states that *"Major stock market declines are triggered when U.S. monetary and fiscal policies are driven by outside forces to remedy a financial market imbalance."* Although there was no major stock market re-action yet, the loaded gun pointed at the U.S. economy was a potential run on U.S.

Treasuries by foreign holders of the U.S. National Debt. In mid-2013 there was only a slow leak in the system. It coincided with a massive increase in monetary and fiscal expansion programs by Japan announced in April 2013, labeled in by the news media as "Abenomics." Additionally, European austerity policies were reversed in the time period. As a result, the time period witnessed an orchestrated move of industrialized nations to weaken their currencies. The fall-out from this money printing blitzkrieg could be seen in nations that sold goods in dollars but were not simultaneously able to adjust their currencies in relative fashion – in other words they were in-directly getting a price cut, unless they were able to off-set the massive monetary devaluation with price increases. The oil market price action above $100 a barrel was a predicable reaction.

Another Financial Relativity Principle demonstrated in the first half of 2013 was that the interest rate market is where relativity changes are most readily observed. Although the Fed was in the process of buying massive quantities of U.S. Treasuries in an attempt to keep rates low, the opposite was happening on the long end of the yield curve. The more the Fed purchased, the more foreign governments off-set the purchases with sales of their reserves. Rates in the process increased. The rate structure in the U.S. is not nearly as controlled by Fed policy as it was in the 1940s when almost 100% of the debt was owned by U.S institutions and private citizens. In those days the pegging of interest rates through controlled Treasury financing placements in the U.S. banks and insurance companies was not difficult. The U.S. banking system was mandated through regulation to co-operate. However, after the disintegration of the gold standard under Nixon in 1971 foreign countries began to accumulate U.S. currency reserves in order to complete trade transactions with the United States. The reserve currency status of the U.S. dollar leads to a financial predicament whereby in order for the U.S. to maintain expansionary domestic policies, the international community holding large U.S. Treasuries balances is given veto power which is voiced through the U.S. interest rate complex. In cases when the U.S. Federal Reserve resists allowing rates to adjust upward, secondary shocks are sent through other markets, particularly evident in the oil market.

The most important information forthcoming from the mid-2013 review of Fed policy was that the easy money policy was encountering growing resistance, and it was not logically correlated with better economic growth; moreover, it was most directly linked to selling of Treasuries pressure both domestic and foreign based.

Oil Market Reflects Foreign Force Pressure on the Rise

As detailed in an earlier chapter of this book, the real price of oil needs to be reviewed in terms of the relative number of barrels and ounce of gold will buy, not just the absolute U.S. dollar traded price. If an ounce of gold buys more than 13 barrels, oil is considered inexpensive in relative dollar terms. Likewise, if an ounce of gold buys less than 13 barrels, oil is expensive. The ratio serves as a constant proxy for the relative relationship of U.S. fiscal and monetary policy to the real income generating capacity of oil exporting country economies. World supply of gold has historically grown at a rate equal to population growth; whereas fiat currencies are prone to grow at a much different pace – this differential is the source of on-going trade conflicts through-out history, with oil being a "shocking" pressure point.

GOLD PRICE ——WTI SPOT PRICE

After the 2008 financial crisis the relative price of oil in gold terms began to trade at a price level that was inexpensive historically. In the time period both gold and oil increased in dollar terms, but on a relative basis an ounce of gold was consistently purchasing from 16 to 18 barrels of oil. The fact that gold was increasing in dollar terms most likely kept non-U.S. allies satisfied with the pricing arrangement. However, in late 2012 and early 2013, gold prices came under severe pressure. The sell-off drove the price level of gold from over $1700 per ounce to below $1200, a drop of over 40%. The rational for the sell-off was never fully clear in the gold market. But the sell-off was odd because it coincided with the start of the $1T Fed QE3 program, not a particularly logical point for investors to suddenly rush to dollar denominated assets for the long-term. In reviewing the selling data, it appears, but will never be absolutely confirmed, that the synchronized increase in currency reserves by industrial world central banks was caused by the sale of gold ETF funds directed by major hedge funds at the behest of the U.S. government to suppress the traded price of gold <u>and</u> the simultaneous sale of physical gold reserves by central banks to keep the price of gold suppressed. It was a magical means of promoting the relative value of fiat government backed currencies, even though there was a massive influx of new money entering the market, while depressing the currency level of the unofficial competitor –gold. The move to depress the price of gold was also linked to U.S. National Security actions to depress Iran's economy in an effort to force cessation of its nuclear program.

The losers in early 2013 from the orchestrated Japan, U.S. and European monetary actions and the dramatic drop in the value of gold were emerging markets and natural resource based economies. For instance, if an ounce of gold bought on average 16 barrels of oil as it did prior to the gold price drop, oil would have to be priced at $75 per barrel to maintain the ratio. Likewise, if a country held gold as a reserve and needed to convert it to dollars to buy wheat, the price of food just got more expensive. Many emerging market countries do not have the pricing power to change the price of their exports in order to keep up with the deteriorating purchasing power of their reserves. However, oil is different. Pricing of oil was showing signs of relative strength through August 2013, which is the expected relative response.

The eerie part of the reshuffle of relative prices was that the new price level in August of 2013 converged on 12.8 barrels per ounce of gold, right at the level marked by the 1973 Arab Oil Embargo. This relative price level made oil expensive in dollar terms for western economies. Oil price strength in the 3rd quarter of 2013 was being caused by the loss of purchasing power due to a drop in gold prices. The price action in the oil market was a reaction by foreign governments and OPEC countries to maintain reserve currency parity with the aggressive United States monetary policy. When the Arab Embargo threshold is approached from a position where oil prices are increasing in order for OPEC countries to maintain real income parity, conflict usually increases. These conflicts may be linked to secular battles that have been on-going for many centuries, but they always seem to provide a convenient excuse to raise the price of oil since 1973.

Stock Market Rides Favorable Fed Forces to New Highs

In a letter to his son in 1930, Albert Einstein wrote "*Life is like riding a bicycle.*

To keep your balance, you must keep moving." The quote struck me as a fitting description of the stock market index progressive climb upward to all-time highs in the summer of 2013. Even though the U.S economy showed little growth momentum, U.S. fiscal policy was doing very little to encourage GDP growth, regulatory restrictions in the banking sector were curtailing loan growth, oil based energy was becoming relatively more expensive, and long term interest rates were beginning to rise – the stock market just kept pedaling to new all-time highs.

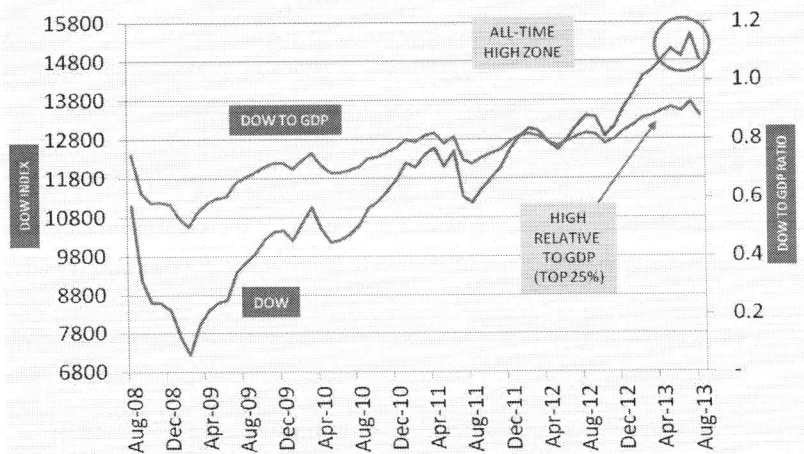

As shown in the above graph, new all-time closing month highs were reached in July, and prospects for even higher levels to be reached were evident as time marched on toward the fall of 2013. The market was becoming relatively expensive. Relative to GDP the DOW was being priced at close to .97 times GDP which placed the pricing in the top quartile historically. However, in the time period investment dollars had few relatively good options and, therefore, continued to be attracted to the momentum trade in the stock market. Reserves in the financial sector were high, and although lending may have been suppressed for many loan types, margin lending on stocks was not one of those areas. Margin debt on NYSE investments in July 2013 reached $382B, up from $234B in January of 2010. The margin ratio was fairly consistent through the time period, but the absolute increase reflected the increasing flow of reserves into the financial system.

Increasingly the stock market was the most attractive alternative in the financial market. Prospects of higher interest rates driven by relative currency devaluation across the world were driving money out of Treasuries and other interest bearing assets. A move up in the stock market in the early stages of a rate reversal period is not unusual. However, historically for the stock market move up to be sustained in the face of higher interest rate it must be accompanied by real GDP expansion.

Fed Hesitant to Remove Accommodation in 2013

In mid 2013 President Obama announced his intention of appointing a replacement for Fed chairman Ben Bernanke in January of 2014. The process of selecting a replacement was well underway in the summer of 2013, with two candidates Janet Yellen and Lawrence Summers being the front-runners. Larry Summers was seen as slightly more "hawkish" in his tendencies toward dealing with the expansionary policies being undertaken by the Federal Reserve in 2013. No one will ever know how Mr. Summers would have approached Fed policy, because he withdrew his name from consideration before even being selected. As of the writing of this book, Janet Yellen was the apparent heir to the throne. But regardless of the ultimate choice, the issue of managing the Federal Reserve policy going forward was of supreme importance to the market. The immediate stock market response to the idea of a candidate like Janet Yellen being Ben Bernanke's successor was to trade the market to even higher highs.

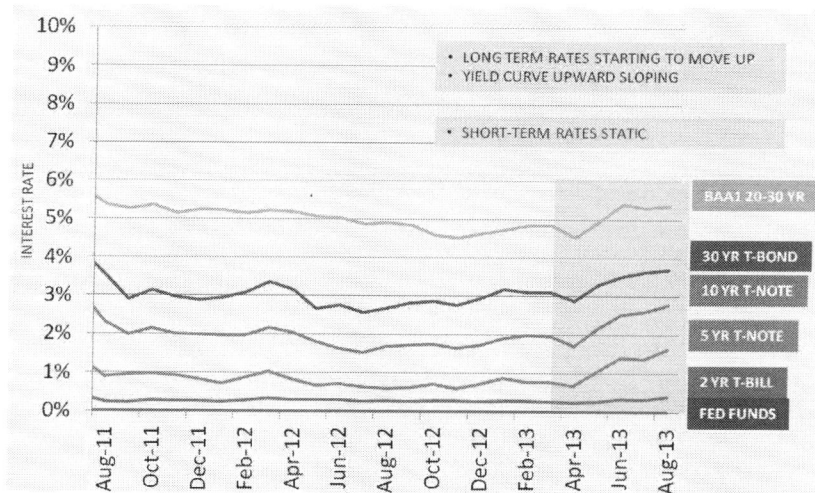

The Obama choice and the market reaction was a predictable response based on the Principles of Financial Relativity. Domestic institutions will not exert negative force on the market unless an external force such as an oil spike or CPI-based inflation is clearly evident. Larry Summers represented a potential negative force. On the other hand, the Yellen candidacy represented a belief that easy money would continue at the behest of the White House for a much longer period. The knee jerk reaction by the stock market to trade higher in reaction to the Larry Summers withdrawal from consideration was very telling about the financial markets at the time. As the chart above shows, interest rates on the long end of the curve were just beginning to increase back to levels previously witnessed in 2011. The very short term rates, however, were not impacted by the rise. The movement in long rates was being determined to a much greater extent by free market forces, whereas the short-term rates were being price controlled for the benefit of the U.S. government. The monetary accommodation level in the system was very high, and prospects that it would remain so for an even more extended time period caused a continued surge in funds out of Treasuries and into stocks.

The challenge for the Fed at the time was managing its growing balance sheet and the dependency of the U.S. stock market on its actions in the context of likely reverberations from foreign trading partners and even non-partners in the case of many non-U.S. allies. The Fed requirements for removal of its accommodative polices were stated at the time in terms of domestic thresholds and growth.

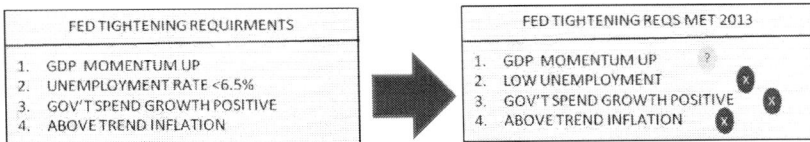

FED TIGHTENING REQUIRMENTS	FED TIGHTENING REQS MET 2013
1. GDP MOMENTUM UP 2. UNEMPLOYMENT RATE <6.5% 3. GOV'T SPEND GROWTH POSITIVE 4. ABOVE TREND INFLATION	1. GDP MOMENTUM UP ? 2. LOW UNEMPLOYMENT ✗ 3. GOV'T SPEND GROWTH POSITIVE ✗ 4. ABOVE TREND INFLATION ✗

As seen in the graphic, little of the signs the Fed generally looks for in the economy before they withdraw accommodation were present in 2013, meaning that a policy withdrawal was not imminent unless there was an outside force big enough to cause a removal. Other than slight movement in rates upward accompanied by the sale of Treasuries by some foreign governments, the outside shock or inflation pressures were not yet evident. However, the asset bubble pressure building in the financial system from the extreme policy actions was growing, and would eventually need to be released.

Signals Reveal the Market Relative Value

Stock investors are a naturally worrisome bunch. Most investors constantly worry about whether their investments are safe. The definition of safe usually means their stocks are increasing in value, not just maintaining value, and definitely not losing value. No one can know in absolute terms what the fair value of the stock market will be tomorrow, but current value is indicated by the market indexes during every trading session. Uncertainty best describes the world that investors live in, and great investors react to information in order to make sound judgments about whether to buy, sell or hold.

Market data can be very complex if not put into a consistent framework. Even having every market data point does not mean that the fair value of the market can be determined by even the most powerful computer. In the fast pace traded financial marketplace, the fair value at any point in time is the last traded price. Once the next trade is placed, the market is given a new value. The absolute price levels of the stock market or GDP have little analytical significance in determining relative value. Investors need to follow the change in the stock market relative to relevant market forces. The best way to measure the rate of relative change in the forces being applied to the market is by developing indicators of impending change known as market signals. Several well correlated forward indicators were detailed in previous chapters of this book. These metrics are utilized to assess the relative value of the U.S. stock market at the end of the 3rd quarter in 2013 in the section below.

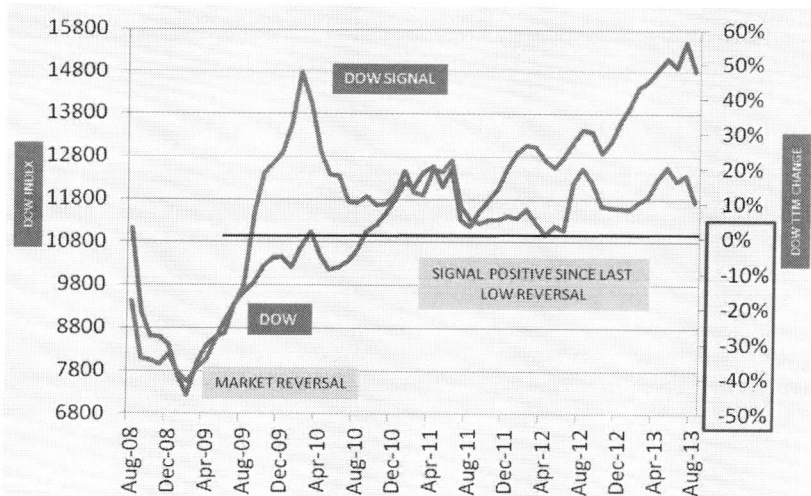

In the summer of 2013 the stock market traded to new all-time high levels in July. Since the market was at an all-time high after completing a reversal off lows in February 2009, the warning signals of a market correction was the best way to begin assessing the on-going relative value of the stock market. The primary indicator, the DOW Signal, was in positive territory, meaning no imminent problem was expected in the stock market. Since the low reversal in 2009, the DOW maintained positive year over year momentum. As of

August 2013, the typical trading pattern had not been broken. This pattern is driven by the upward bias in underlying GDP growth. Even though GDP growth was weak throughout the period since 2009, it was still a net positive; and, other forces were in place to maintain stock price increase momentum.

In 2012 and 2013 stock returns were very strong, well in excess of returns possible in the Treasury or Corporate bond market. The one time in June 2012 when the DOW signal almost triggered, the market indexes bounced hard as stocks rallied for the rest of the year. The signal was close to red, but it was not confirmed by any other indicator at the time.

At the end of August 2013, the primary signals of an imminent correction were still benign. The biggest warning light was the DOW reaching an all-time high. All major corrections post WWII, and 12 of the 13 examined in this book all happened when the stock market was at an all-time high. However, none of the other indicators were hot. The DOW continued to show year over year positive returns.

The Fed interest rate policy continued to maintain a steeply upward sloping yield curve. Therefore, the 10 - 2 spread was wide, 240 basis points in August 2013. There also was no looming signal that the Fed would reverse its zero rate policy. In fact, Ben Bernanke as Fed chairman spoke on several occasions that the Fed Funds rate would likely be a poor reflection of tightening credit markets when the Fed actually planned to raise rates from the zero-bound. When the 10 - 2 signal is distorted, the spread between Treasuries further out on the maturity spectrum should be reviewed. The 10 - 5 spread is the best likely substitute.

SIGNAL AND STATUS AS OF AUGUST 2013		NOTE
DOW AT AN ALL-TIME HIGH?	YES	DRIVEN PRIMARILY BY FE
DOW SIGNAL NEGATIVE?	NO	+12 MTH CHG TREND IN-TACT
10 / 2 SPREAD LOW OR NEGATIVE?	NO	USE 10 / 5, STILL POSITIVE
FED FUNDS PEAK, REVERSAL IMMINENT?	NO	SIGNAL LIKELY TO BE LATE
OIL SPIKE IN PROGRESS?	MAYBE	LIKELY TO BE THE LEAD SIGNAL
FISCAL+FED POLICY INFLATIONARY?	MAYBE	FOREIGN CREDITORS SELLING

As of August 2013 the 10 - 5 spread was 110 basis points, a level it consistently traded at during the prior several years. Collapsing of this spread and a flattening of the yield curve was not evident as of August 2013, and was not an apparent threat to continued support of high stock market relative value at the time. The Bernanke "put" was working wonderfully.

Oil price movement was the one signal that trouble was potentially brewing for the stock market. In spite of, or more likely because of the gold market break-down, oil prices showed strength in mid 2013. Oil spikes since 1972 accompanied all major stock market corrections, usually because they forced the Federal Reserve to reverse lenient monetary policies. The rumblings in the Middle East became louder in mid-2013, and the gold price decline in the first half of 2013 was a severe, likely intentional, blow to Iran. Although the indicator was not showing an oil spike in progress, the relative strength in price levels and the factors associated with the pricing made it the likely leading indicator in the next correction cycle for stocks.

Extrapolating Probable Relative Market Value in 2013

As of the publication of this book, the stock market continued to rise, but with escalating risk of a downward correction. Bonds, on the other hand, were likely to see much more near-term upward pressure on rates for the foreseeable future.

The biggest wildcard in determining the relative value of the U.S. stock market in the fall of 2013 was government fiscal policy. In October of 2013 a Washington budget battle led to a partial government shut-down, or "slim-down" as it was called, creating greater uncertainty with respect to the direction of government spending. Government spending and regulation was a constraint on GDP growth during the time period. However, no matter how the budget negotiations turned out, the forces in the market were in the process of shifting. If the budget became more constraining, which was unlikely, the best relative scenario to judge the market would be 1946. It was unlikely because the GDP growth prospects of the mid 1940s, driven by current account surpluses, did not exist in 2013. If the budget negotiation ended in a usual "I will not own this decision" Washington political stalemate, then entitlement spending was on track to rise aggressively in coming years. This would bring the 1960s and 1970s into focus as the probable relative comparable scenario.

Based on the position of the relative forces driving the market in 2013, it was possible to utilize the time periods of 1946 and the 1970s to extrapolate a likely relative market value path.

This extrapolation scenario generated based on available data in the fall of 2013 graphically looked as follows.

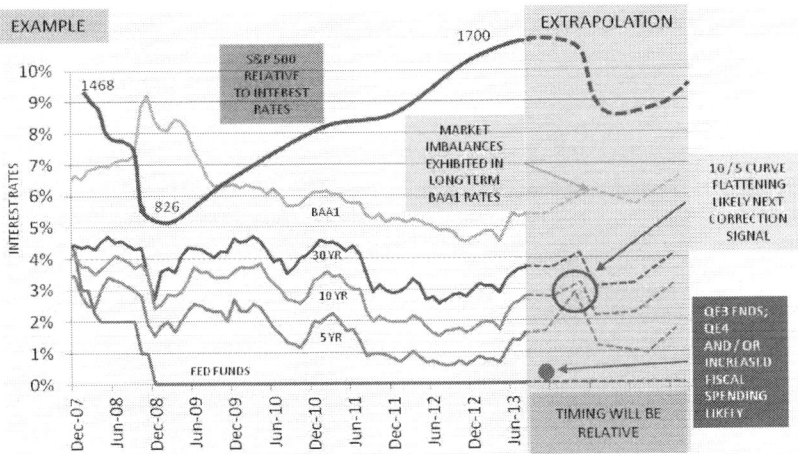

The 2014 and beyond extrapolated path was derived from the following assumptions: 1) a price controlled Treasury yield curve, most constrained on the short end as in the late 1940s; 2) a Fed policy that continued to purchase Treasuries well into 2014 based on slow employment growth; 3) a government spending and regulation policy that constrained lending driven economic growth but drove upward spending levels on entitlements with the implementation of the Affordable Care Act, and, 4) oil price pressures on the economy which escalated upward through time in lock step with monetary easing as happened in the early 1970s. The combination of forces were expected to drive long-term U.S. interest rates up in response to foreign owners shifting reserves away from Treasuries and into oil, gold and other hard assets.

The exact circumstances faced in mid 2013 had no exact parallel in post WWII history. However, the outcome under very similar circumstances in 1946 was known. The similar circumstances in the 1940s included government fiscal policy tightening, interest rates pegging on the zero bound, and a stock market valued relative to GDP on a 1:1 relative basis. In the 1946 instance stocks fell 20% in a major market correction. The outcome from using policies similar to 1971 was also known. In 1971 the U.S. became ultra easy with monetary policy relative to foreign markets by abandoning the gold standard and targeting the unemployment rate in the rational for monetary accommodation. Government fiscal spending also increased at a high rate. The policies led to the Arab Oil Embargo oil shock, as well as rapidly rising interest rates on the long end of the curve. Stocks eventually fell by almost 50% in 1974.

In mid 2013, the economic set-up, unfortunately, reflected the worst characteristics of both points in history. The only saving grace for the stock market continued to be the fear of rising long term rates chasing investment into stocks. The Theory of Financial Relativity did not show confirming triggers at the alert status in August of 2013. However, the financial extrapolation was warning that the financial system at the time was moving progressively closer to a point in which the financial asset bubble inflation was eventually going to be popped.

Parting Note about Extrapolation

The Theory of Financial Relativity is *not* a framework for predicting precisely when major market events will occur – just as predicting the exact timing and precise point of landfall of the next major hurricane to hit the U.S. mainland is not possible. The Theory focuses on explaining why the major market moves occur so that probable market movements can be extrapolated once the exact trajectory of market impacting forces becomes known. With this important information, proper actions to protect, and even create wealth, can be taken. However, unlike natural events like hurricanes, which cannot be stopped by human action, financial market crashes are a human phenomenon. Although human behavior is as much a part of the physical universe as the blowing wind, human actions can be influenced. This leaves hope that better understanding of the cause and effects of the human behaviors which create stock market calamities can be utilized to mitigate the severity of these events in the future.

16 RELATIVE PORTFOLIO MANAGEMENT

The majority of this book focuses on the stock market and how to read the market in order to provide insight into why the market moves, and when major market moves can be expected to happen. A more practical issue faced by investors needs to be addressed as I bring this book to a close. The issue involves the management of your hard earned savings and wealth. Creating wealth and maintaining the purchasing power of your savings is not an easy task. "Cookie cutter" recipes or "one shoe fits all" answers do not exist. Good financial planning requires a comprehensive approach to your individual and family needs. Good portfolio planning is a relative mix of both art and science.

When asked to examine someone's portfolio I usually start by evaluating several key concerns. The first is the age and life needs of the individual. A big red flag usually waves at this point in the evaluation. It is triggered by the mismatch between when the investor expects to need to use money from his or her investments, and the actual capability of the portfolio to provide predictable cash flow when needed. Risk tolerance of the investor is also considered. Most people I know are inherently risk averse, and when it comes to stocks are even more so. This instinct is healthy, and allocations of savings into paper investments that could quickly disappear need to be well understood before jumping in. I do not know anyone who is invested 100% in stocks. But I do know more than a few individuals who have almost 100% of their wealth locked up in a single business. Dealing with this situation is far different from the professor who is setting aside money for a home down payment, kid's college or eventual retirement. Both individuals probably have the same goals for their savings, but getting there will require a much different path.

But the mantra in the asset management firm commercials is to set up a financial portfolio, set an asset allocation, usually 60/40 stocks to bonds, possibly with some gold and leave it alone. The recommended strategy is: "Just add to your portfolio over time and take from it when you need to. The managers of the funds will take care of your money." If you were just using a very narrow definition of savings to mean "retirement" and the individual was 25-40 years old, this formula might be good advice for some. The "leaving it alone" advice as shown in this book is naïve, but for many an average return may be the best option over 30 years. However, parking money in a 401K stock index fund and hoping for a return is not portfolio management.

What about all of the other savings that you hopefully have or will accumulate over a lifetime? That is the issue you really need to address when reviewing your financial portfolio. Most people I have met do not invest heavily in the stock market, even when forced to do so in their 401K- based savings account. Outside of retirement savings, I commonly see 80%+ in cash equivalent investments and a smattering of stocks or bonds, usually concentrated in one or two companies. Because the behavior is so common, I assume good reasons exist – not that it is irrational. My conclusion is that people naturally manage their personal resources to meet their own relative needs. The first and foremost need is having cash and potentially income on hand in the situation that their job or business suddenly is not producing. Seems like very rational behavior, particularly in the current progressively jobless era and slow to no growth economy.

Duration Mismatch – Big Problem for Most Investors

As 2014 approached, investors taking an inventory of their savings relative to expected needs over time were faced with on abundantly clear problem in the financial marketplace. Investment securities available that paid a high rate of return, that and investor could be certain the money would be there on the date needed, were extremely rare. In large part this was because the government lowered interest rates to such low levels that typical savings vehicles such as CDs and Money Market accounts were paying interest rates below the rate of inflation. In other words, on a relative basis, people were earning money, usually through their job or business, putting it into a secure short-term savings account, and then indirectly paying the government through inflation to return the money at a later date for its intended use.

CDs and Money Market instruments became very poor savings options, but what other options do the majority of U.S. investors have? The monopolistic power of the government to hold interest rates low is a function not of supply and demand, rather, a function of the inter-working of the U.S. Treasury, the Federal Reserve and the U.S. Banking system all coordinating efforts to keep interest rates on the U.S. government debt at low levels. This was touted by President Obama when he took office as one of the primary methods he would use to keep the debt level from ballooning even as government spending levels increased. Most of the Americans who voted for him did not realize that the entire process was a disguised in-direct tax on their savings to fund a larger government.

The savings vehicles available for putting aside assets for long-term needs may have become more limited at the time; however, the needs across the population were not changed. Everyone has major life expenditures best handled by setting aside money in advance

AGE
25 – LARGE TICKET ITEMS LIKE HOUSE IN 5 YEARS
40 – RETIREMENT FOCUSED IN 25 OR LESS YEARS, PAYING CHILD EXPENSES LIKE COLLEGE
50 – RETIREMENT IN ABOUT 10 YEARS, PROBABLITY OF FIXED INCOME NEEDS RISING
60+ – MOST LIKELY IN NEED OF FIXED INCOME
MANY SHORT-DURATION NEEDS THROUGHOUT LIFE

rather than waiting until the time is near and funds are not available. These include house down payments, braces and college tuition for the kids, the unexpected need to cover an income drop due to job loss, and of course the need for funds when the time to retire arrives.

The practical reality is that people generally make sure that these needs are met first before they start putting funds aside into riskier investments which might not hold their value through time, even if the opportunity promises the possibility of "high returns." This human inclination is very healthy, and for many is instinctive. Most people realize that it is best to hold savings in assets that can readily convert into cash at the point in time they expect to need the money. Not following this rule for a fairly sizeable portion of your portfolio can introduce major risk to principle loss at the time when you need to cash in; even if the assets are deployed in risk-free U.S. Treasury securities. The reason that losses can arise can be understood by studying the mathematical concept known as duration.

Duration is a measure which shows how much a 1% change in market interest rates affects the principle value of a fixed income investment. The measure changes for a unique bond over time as it gets closer to maturity – the shorter the time frame to maturity, the lower the duration of the investment.

COUPON	BOND MATURITY IN YEARS					
& YIELD	1	2	5	10	20	30
2%	1.00	1.97	4.78	9.11	16.57	22.68
3%	0.99	1.96	4.68	8.71	15.17	19.97
4%	0.99	1.94	4.58	8.33	13.94	17.71
5%	0.99	1.93	4.48	7.98	12.85	15.82
6%	0.99	1.91	4.39	7.66	11.89	14.23
7%	0.98	1.90	4.30	7.35	11.04	12.89
8%	0.98	1.89	4.21	7.06	10.28	11.74
9%	0.98	1.87	4.13	6.79	9.60	10.76
10%	0.98	1.86	4.05	6.54	8.99	9.92

DURATION DECREASES

DURATION INCREASES

A very short-term investment of 1-2 years is not affected much by a 1% change in rates. Even if rates do change quickly, the investment will approach maturity much more quickly than a 30 year investment, so the principal change, whether up or down, is quickly reversed over the ensuing months.

The level of interest periodically paid on a bond also affects the impact that a change in interest rates will have on an investment. In general, the lower the coupon rate paid, the more a 1%

A 1% CHANGE IN YIELD PRODUCES X% MOVE IN BOND VALUE
WHERE X = DURATION STATED AS A PERCENTAGE
EXAMPLE: A 1% MOVE UP IN YIELD ON A 3%-30YR TREASURY
PRODUCES A 19.97% DECLINE IN BOND VALUE

movement in interest rates impacts a fixed income investment. This can be seen in the table above. As the coupon level increases on the left axis, the duration measure declines.

A simple example is useful in understanding the concept of duration. Consider a hypothetical investment in a 30 year U.S. Treasury Bond with a coupon of 3% at par value, meaning the security yields 3% at the time of purchase. In the interim, similar to what happened in May 2013, interest rates rise by 100 basis points. As shown in the table to above, the duration of a 30 year, 3% bond at the purchase point is 19.97. This means that the bond will fall in price by 19.97% in response to a 1% move up in market rates. Bonds prices can change due to other factors as well, primarily because of a change in credit risk, also known as risk of default.

Luckily for bond investors, all is not lost if rates go up and bond values fall. If the bond is intended to be held to maturity, then the value decline due to duration will be recovered when either rates fall or as the bond gets closer to maturity. In the case of a low coupon 30 year bond it might be a long time before the market value of the bond approaches par value again; but eventually it will unless the bond issuer defaults. The U.S government is not expected to default, so U.S. Treasury bonds are considered a proxy for the risk-free rate of interest, or at least the lowest risk asset in the market. Rarely will you see Treasury rates above the yield on bond securities of equal duration. The only exception to this rule is municipal bonds due to their favorable tax status. However, in the time frame from 2009-2013 Treasury rates were even below tax-free municipals primarily because the Fed was holding Treasury interest rates at the zero bound.

Stock investments also have a duration, although measuring it cannot be done as precisely as bond duration. Stocks have an implied duration which typically is assumed to equal the stock price earnings (P/E) ratio. Low P/E ratio stocks have lower duration. These stocks typically have higher dividend pay-out ratios and therefore react to market changes in interest rates in a very similar way to a fixed income coupon bond. A lower P/E ratio may also reflect that a stock has been beaten down in trading from a change in company performance, so do not assume a lower P/E, lower duration stock means lower risk. Homework for individual stock investments is always required. But generally, on a relative basis, a lower P/E ratio stock will show less volatility over time as rates rise compared to high P/E stocks. Stocks, however, react to rate changes on a slightly different heartbeat than bonds. Many times a rate rise happens when expectations of higher growth are present in the economy. In the GDP growth expectation case, lower P/E stocks react to rate increases much like bonds, whereas higher P/E stocks which are more growth driven do no exhibit the same decline in value. However, through time the rate change drags down the performance of high P/E stocks.

Investment Choices Poor for Average Investors

One of the aspects of the financial market that I preach about is that more investment products do not mean better options. In fact, for most investors the opposite is most likely the case. A false sense of safety can be created when an investor thinks they are diversifying their holdings by buying a green, blue and orange fund. The first point for investors is that diversifying more in a portfolio of already diversified investments of the same type and duration is pointless. Any break apart of an already diversified set of assets is nothing more than a reallocation of assets on the hope that on the margin the orange fund will somehow have a higher return than the blue one. However, the funds are all very highly correlated, assuming they are equity investment based.

The only way to truly affect the performance of a portfolio of diversified assets is to own non-correlated assets with different duration and trade into and out of assets at corresponding opportunistic peaks and valleys. Risky assets do not provide options at the <u>aggregate</u> level for much to be gained from trying to time the purchase of a group of mid-cap versus small cap versus large cap stocks. All that is really happening is a shift in the underlying risk of your portfolio. An interesting exercise, but for the most part the changes are just moving around market noise in your portfolio. Truly non-correlated assets to equity stocks over time tend to be short duration bonds and gold and at times longer duration bonds. The non-correlation comes primarily from the difference in security structure – bond contract versus common equity versus commodity – and the duration of the underlying asset.

TRAILING 12-MONTH RETURN ANALYSIS POST 1952 - JUNE 2013	2 YR T-BILL	3-5 YR T-NOTE	10 YR T-NOTE	30 YR T-BOND	20 YR MUNI	20-30 YR BAA	S&P500* CAGR	GOLD** CAGR
AVERAGE	5.64%	5.98%	6.48%	6.68%	5.56%	8.00%	8.70%	11.68%
MEDIAN	5.17%	5.02%	4.65%	4.83%	5.13%	6.87%	10.13%	6.04%
			DECREASING		12 MTH RETURN	INCREASING		
MAXIMUM	20.8%	30.1%	39.1%	59.9%	46.2%	44.7%	52.73%	197.14%
90% LESS THAN	9.8%	12.7%	16.0%	21.5%	17.1%	21.0%	28.6%	43.50%
75% LESS THAN	7.5%	9.1%	10.9%	12.6%	10.5%	14.5%	19.2%	23.00%
50% LESS THAN	5.2%	5.0%	4.6%	4.8%	5.1%	6.8%	10.1%	6.04%
25% LESS THAN	3.2%	2.1%	1.4%	-1.1%	0.0%	0.7%	-1.9%	-6.00%
10% LESS THAN	1.3%	-0.1%	-2.1%	-6.4%	-5.9%	-5.2%	-13.0%	-15.50%
MINIMUM	-0.5%	-5.9%	-10.1%	-28.1%	-19.0%	-20.6%	-44.78%	-36.47%
VARIANCE	0.13%	0.32%	0.65%	1.42%	0.95%	1.15%	2.64%	8.20%
STANDARD DEV	3.64%	5.69%	8.04%	11.90%	9.74%	10.72%	16.24%	28.64%

* S&P Returns Exclude Dividends ** Gold Returns Since April 1968

The return characteristics and volatility varies between stocks, bonds and gold. The table above summarizes the 12 month performance of a broad range of bonds, the S&P 500 since 1952 and gold since 1968. These are asset classes typically packaged as exchange traded funds (ETFs) through financial institutions for investors. A plethora of additional options are available in the market.

The variance, or volatility of each asset class, is the first feature that you should review. Stocks are considerably more volatile than bonds over time. Stock returns, however, do not necessarily increase in 1 for 1 proportion to their volatility. The CAGR on the stock market from 1953 through mid - 2013 as measured by the S&P 500 was 8.7%. Add to this a dividend component of approximately 1.8% depending on the fee level of the fund held, and on average the S&P 500 returns just over 10%. Through the same time period the 20-30 year BAA1 bond showed far less volatility and an 8% rate of return.

The primary variable driving bond volatility is duration risk due to interest rate changes. The longer-term 30 YR Treasury bond is more volatile than the BAA1 bond because it has a longer duration. However, the average rate of return on the 30 YR Treasury over the time period was lower attributed to its status as a "risk free" government bond.

Gold is also a very interesting asset class as the data shows. Over the time period since it began trading in open auction form in 1968, as an asset class it returns the highest CAGR. It also exhibited far greater variability than any of the other asset classes.

The table also highlights additional important information for investors. The first is the distribution of rates over time as a proxy for what an investor might expect as true fair rates of return in the future. Although by no means a given, the interest rate levels on U.S. government bonds in 2013 were at unsustainably low levels when compared to history. From 1953 through 2013, 50% of the time rates were close to 5% on almost all maturities of U.S. Treasuries. In 2013 the market "expectations" of fair trended toward a 4% yield on the 10 year T-Note and 5% on the 30 year T-Bond. Likewise, fair market interest rates on corporate long bonds were 1.5-2.0% greater than the equivalent maturity Treasury. This was not the case in 2013, and pointed to significant risk at the time of a flight from duration in the event interest rates began to revert to historical averages.

The average investor is inundated with more and more ETF options for buying assets in the modern financial marketplace. If the fragmentation of the market goes far enough, eventually an investor will get back to the point where they will need 20 different funds to get the diversification needed to equal the market as measured by the DOW or S&P 500. In other words, more options do not mean less risk.

One other aspect of exchange traded funds which make them more, not less risky, pertains to bond funds. Bonds when traded as index securities have a constant duration. If you buy a 10 year bond fund thinking that when you need the money in 10 years 100% of the principal value is certain to be there – think again. In ten years the fund value will depend greatly upon the level of interest rates on ten year bonds at that point in time. If rates are lower than when you purchased the investment, you should be in a position to sell at a gain. However, if rates are higher you will likely have to sell at a loss. If you had purchased the bond outright and held it to maturity, you would not have suffered any capital loss. Investment grade bonds, particularly U.S. Treasury bonds, provide no risk diversification advantage just because you hold more of them in a bond ETF. Diversifying away credit risk in an investment grade portfolio of bonds is also a relatively easy task with a properly structured bond ladder. I strongly recommend that investors buy bonds individually, <u>except in the case of non-investment grade </u>high yield bonds. In my opinion, buying individual high yield debt is a game only for true gamblers.

The lack of a maturity date makes bond funds very poor choices as savings vehicles for most investors. Duration mismatches across the U.S. population of investors is a real problem. The problem was being made worse in 2013 by zero bound interest rates which only heighten the volatility and loss levels in bond ETFs as rates began to rise. It doesn't take a brain surgeon to realize the impractical level of risk being assumed by an individual if they throw their savings into and investment account, allocate the funds on a 60/40 stock bond split, and assume they will withdraw the money as needed. No wonder the business talk shows continually referenced all of the cash "sitting on the side-lines" in 2013. Who wanted a piece of the action? Obviously not Wall Street or the U.S. government, as each was shifting risk through policy actions and investment product creation squarely back on the individual.

A more practical approach to portfolio management is available for investors interested in working toward true financial security over the long-term.

A Relative Approach to Portfolio Management

Why is there such a tendency of many investors to put away cash in more short duration assets while avoiding longer dated investments unless the chance of a pay-off is big? Seems like a very rational, irrational behavior. It stems from the fact that most people naturally place high value on satisfying their needs for security and lifestyle first before they embark on wealth creation through investing in stocks. An individual's biggest asset is typically his or her personal skill as a worker, manager or business owner. This skill set provides on-going cash flow to live on, and to put away savings for the future. In the truest sense, a job or small business is an equity investment that pays regularly scheduled dividends. If your job is disrupted, cash flow ceases.

Judgments to recover lost hours worked are not generally possible, with the exception of minor severance package agreements. The investment analog is that your company dividend was just cut-off.

Most people cannot live with the risk overhang of losing a job, so they set money aside. Based on this simple fact, the goal for most investors should be to create a portfolio which can generate cash flow equal to their job or business -

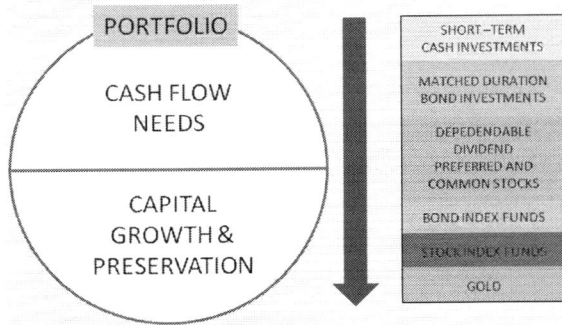

PORTFOLIO

CASH FLOW NEEDS

CAPITAL GROWTH & PRESERVATION

SHORT–TERM CASH INVESTMENTS

MATCHED DURATION BOND INVESTMENTS

DEPEDENDABLE DIVIDEND PREFERRED AND COMMON STOCKS

BOND INDEX FUNDS

STOCK INDEX FUNDS

GOLD

a lofty goal for many investors. But it should be the primary goal for most - second only to having enough cash on hand in the event of an emergency.

For most investors, the practical reality is that they are not able to generate the level of assets required to manage money in this fashion through their everyday trade or business. The drive to find the "homerun" investment is what causes the irrational aspect of otherwise rational investor behavior.

"CREATE A PORTFOLIO WHICH CAN GENERATE ENOUGH CASH TO COVER YOUR ON-GOING LIVING AND LIFESTYLE EXPENSES WITHOUT SELLING ASSETS"

Some investors start trying to make up the difference by taking a portion of their excess funds and speculating on stocks, usually with the help of margin debt, in the hope that a big pay-off will happen. For some the gamble pays off. However, for every one that wins, many more loose. I cannot make this point strongly enough.

The most important aspect of building a good cash generating portfolio is to have realistic expectations, be patient, and do not be afraid of higher quality longer duration investments as long as the coupon rate and yield are at historically average or above average relative rates. A good cash flow portfolio yielding 5% to 6% after tax or on a deferred tax basis will generate considerably higher levels of cash 15 to 20 years from now. In order for the cash flow to build, you need to utilize the "eighth wonder of the world" in your portfolio planning – compound interest. But you also need to make sure that you do not get stuck at rate levels that are historically too low.

INTEREST RATE ANALYSIS POST 1952 - JUNE 2013	FED FUNDS	2 YR T-BILL	3-5 YR T-NOTE	10 YR T-NOTE	30 YR T-BOND	20 YR MUNI	BAA
AVERAGE	5.1%	5.5%	5.8%	6.1%	6.3%	5.5%	7.9%
MEDIAN	4.8%	5.3%	5.5%	5.7%	5.8%	5.2%	7.8%
				ABOVE AVERAGE COUPON, LONG DURATION GREEN ZONE			
MAXIMUM	19.1%	16.5%	15.9%	15.3%	14.7%	13.3%	17.2%
90% LESS THAN	9.6%	9.5%	9.5%	10.1%	9.7%	8.0%	11.6%
75% LESS THAN	6.7%	7.2%	7.5%	7.7%	7.9%	6.6%	9.5%
50% LESS THAN	4.8%	5.3%	5.5%	5.7%	5.8%	5.2%	7.8%
25% LESS THAN	2.5%	3.5%	3.6%	4.0%	4.2%	3.9%	5.3%
10% LESS THAN	1.0%	1.6%	2.3%	3.0%	3.1%	3.2%	4.7%
MINIMUM	0.0%	0.2%	0.6%	1.5%	2.5%	2.3%	3.5%
				BELOW AVERAGE COUPON, LONG DURATION PROBLEMATIC			
STANDARD DEV	3.5%	3.1%	3.0%	2.8%	2.7%	2.3%	3.0%

For instance, in the summer of 2013, most long-term bonds were taking a beating due to the rising rate environment. Treasuries investments, particularly index funds, were particularly hard hit when it came to duration induced loss of principal. The table above gives an indication of why this happened. Treasury interest rates in May 2013 were at 2% on the 10 year T-Note and under 3% on the 30 year T-Bond. These rate levels were in the historical red zone. Rates were approaching the all-time low water mark, with only a 10% chance historically of being as low.

In the ensuing run-up in rates over the summer of 2013 the municipal bond market was re-priced as well, and the long-end of the curve for General Obligation Municipal Bonds approached 5%. If you have a taxable investment portfolio, which I recommend everyone have, then municipal bonds are one of the best options for safe, long-term income generating cash flow investments. In mid-2013, municipal bond rates actually approached levels on the long end of the curve experienced in the depths of the 2008 financial crisis. Plenty of opportunities were available to obtain 4%-5% after tax returns on bonds that in many cases were insured. As shown in the rate analysis table above, long-term municipal bonds with yields of 5% have been a relatively good buy.

The key in a low rate environment many times is to pick assets which have a high coupon rate, but are callable in the mid to intermediate term. These assets will trade at a short duration to call, and likely be priced close to par. Risk of change in price as rates rise is therefore more limited.

The main requirement for building a cash flow portfolio is a disciplined approach. Put money regularly into your designated cash flow account until the account reaches your target size requirement. Match the investment of the funds to when you will need to use the funds, and buy what the market is selling at a bargain through time. If your time frame is not long-term, don't stretch – but remember, most people need to plan for cash needs through the age of 80, not 60 or 65. The goal should be to build a portfolio of safe bond or near bond investments in assets such as energy, utilities and government obligation bonds.

At 2013 market interest rates most people need a portfolio of close to $1MM in investment grade, medium to long duration fixed income investments in order to produce $50,000 a year in income. Accumulating a portfolio of this size is a tall task for many to achieve. But, the strategy to save using a higher percentage of fixed income securities is the best path for most small investors because it avoids the ingrained tendency to "buy high and sell low" when playing the stock market. The fixed income part of a portfolio is not generally traded through time. Rather, assets are purchased with the intention of holding to maturity based on the needed duration and target income level which matches the investor's objectives. Building a sound portfolio of this nature cannot wait until you are 62 and retiring. You need to start early in life to lock down solid longer term bond investments that will keep paying handsomely for years to come.

Relative Size of Investment Portfolio Matters

Many are probably asking "what about capital growth, shouldn't that be my highest priority when I am young?" When pushed on this point I quickly point out that a person's job or small business is their main capital engine. Funding someone else's dreams with cheap capital before you have fulfilled your own is not usually the best use of funds. For workers owning in the money employee stock options, regularly cashing out and diversifying investment holdings is a good portfolio risk reduction strategy. You have enough invested in the company without linking your entire financial security to the firm. My best example is one I used at other points in the book about Nortel employees who lost major sums of capital they intended to use for retirement because they did not observe this rule in the late 1990s and 2000. I felt so strongly on this point that I cashed out and moved on to more fertile ground at the time. My position in the company was important; however, it was clear the company could not overcome the government regulatory changes that proved a fatal blow to the company in the years after my departure. These are risks that I could only diversify away by managing my own personal portfolio properly. The cashed out amounts of stock in Nortel first went to lowering my family's cash flow needs – such as lower mortgage payments, and secondly into longer duration assets which were invested in attractive interest rates at the time, and a portion that went into stocks in a diversified fashion.

Stocks are an important component of any portfolio for one reason – they are the best hedge against the eroding nature of government domestic policy, whether driven by fiscal spending or the Federal Reserve. The only question becomes how much can you afford to invest in the stock market?

If you can live off of a 1.8% dividend stream, and can stomach the ups and downs of the stock market without selling, then possibly a 100% stock position is an optimal path. But that $1M to produce $50,000 in cash flow in a long duration bond portfolio needs to be $$2.8M if invested in the S&P 500, assuming a 1.8% dividend stream.

In determining how much of your portfolio should be allocated to capital growth - size matters. Size matters because you need staying power in the event the market turns and you are not properly positioned. Many very wealthy people have large on-going cash needs. And I have come across many that did not keep track of

> "BUILD A RESERVE FOR LONG-TERM NEEDS WHICH WILL KEEP UP WITH ERODING FIAT CURRENCY ACTIONS THRU CAPITAL APPRECIATION"

just how much the jet and the yacht and all the other cash consuming toys were truly costing until a sudden collapse in the market triggered margin calls from their broker. At that point it was too late.

The example, the graphic below demonstrates the point of how the size of a portfolio can greatly shift the likelihood that an investor can rationally "afford" to be more heavily invested in potentially high capital appreciating investments. On a $2M portfolio, investing 75% of the funds in relatively safe long duration investments and the remainder in capital growth provides cash flow of about $80,000 per year. This would be a decent living for a retiree or a good supplemental account for an executive or business owner. Alternatively, if the level of assets rises to $10 million or even more, the needs for cash flow at least in most individual or family situations becomes less important as the shorter duration needs are easily met in almost any situation. The bigger the amount of funds in the portfolio, the bigger the problem becomes to find assets that can appreciate in value.

The majority of this book is dedicated to the capital appreciation segment of a portfolio – the stock market. Understanding why the market moves and how to take advantage of the moves is fundamental to being able to grow capital and build wealth. It also, however,

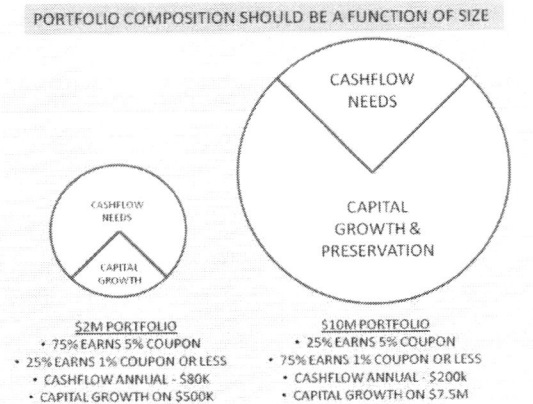

PORTFOLIO COMPOSITION SHOULD BE A FUNCTION OF SIZE

CASHFLOW NEEDS

CAPITAL GROWTH & PRESERVATION

CASHFLOW NEEDS

CAPITAL GROWTH

$2M PORTFOLIO
• 75% EARNS 5% COUPON
• 25% EARNS 1% COUPON OR LESS
• CASHFLOW ANNUAL - $80K
• CAPITAL GROWTH ON $500K

$10M PORTFOLIO
• 25% EARNS 5% COUPON
• 75% EARNS 1% COUPON OR LESS
• CASHFLOW ANNUAL - $200k
• CAPITAL GROWTH ON $7.5M

provides a solid foundation for understanding the dynamics in the fixed income market. The big difference between the two segments of the portfolio – the fixed income segment is not traded for capital gains. Investment grade bond investments are not meant to be opportunistic. Fixed income "savings" is a shock absorbing portfolio component that provides staying power even in the darkest moments for the market.

The capital appreciation segment of your portfolio, on the other hand, is subject to direct hits from the forces underlying the Theory of Financial Relativity. A stock portfolio can and should be managed to take advantage of the market discontinuity as peaks and lows are approached. The appropriate allocation to the fixed income versus capital growth segment of your portfolio is dependent on your "relative" situation.

Capital Growth – Stocks Relative to Bonds and Gold

This section of the book is dedicated to providing an understanding of how to periodically rebalance the capital growth component in your portfolio. The task of managing an equity growth portfolio for U.S. investors is really targeted at keeping up with or exceeding the country's nominal GDP growth level. This could be done by taking Warren Buffet recommended strategy of finding about 20 well managed companies in a diversified set of industries and taking a position in each, preferably at opportunistic buying points. Then, hold the company stock for the long-term. This path is best for very large dollar investors that can obtain controlling interests or highly preferential positions in companies. However, for the vast majority of investors, a diversified stock ETF that tracks the S&P 500 is just as effective.

Another key aspect of managing a growth portfolio is what level of cash or "reserve" equivalent asset do you keep on hand, and when do you increase and decrease reserves. No risk asset portfolio segment is likely to be fully 100% invested all the time. The question becomes, during the times the portfolio is underweight stocks, what should the money taken out of stocks be invested in. Optimally, as shown through historical data in this book, once the market hits a peak and the signals flash sell, all assets should be sold. And, when the market buy signal is given, a full return to stocks is warranted. However, except for the very small index fund investor, this trade is not possible. At best, large players may be able to raise 20-30% in cash leading up to a market correction. The rest of the portfolio must ride out the storm. The opportunity in a crisis led market downturn becomes assets sold at fire-sale prices to cover positions because the owner did not have enough staying power. These situations are the "blood on the street" opportunities that if your portfolio has staying power, you will be in a position to take advantage.

The next issue is, "What asset do you trade into when you sell an equity asset at the market peak?" The research in this book identified three suitable categories over time- short duration Treasuries – good in all cases - gold and long-duration Treasuries - good in certain defined cases.

When you closely examine the trading pattern of stocks, bonds and gold over time, it quickly becomes apparent that each of the asset classes trades on a different bio-rhythm. In the case of bonds, the bio-rhythm changes

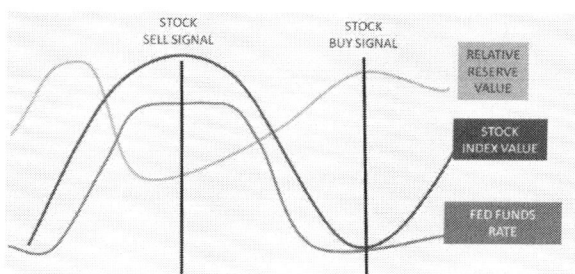

additionally by type of bond and the maturity date. The conceptual model to the left depicts how the market usually traded during the 13 stock market correction points examined in this book since the mid 1950s. As the stock market goes up after a recent low point, longer duration bonds hit a peak and begin to fall in value. As growth in the stock market endures fears of inflation heighten and short-term rates are boosted by the Federal Reserve raising the target Fed Funds rate. As the sell signal point in stocks is reached, the move down in value, up in yield on long duration Treasuries as well as the rise in rates on short duration Treasuries, provide two clear options for re-deploying cash from stock asset sales. These reserve options are depicted by the green line in the graphic.

Gold is an additional asset that frequently became a viable reserve option, particularly at times when either inflation was high or a sharp oil spike was triggering the market correction.

The weighting of the reserve level in a growth portfolio, therefore, should not be based on risk tolerance or trying to obtain some risk weighted market return. The decision on risk tolerance should be made based on the total level of assets allocated to the growth portfolio. In other words, how much can you afford to invest, and keep invested through thick and thin. Any assets not held in stocks in the portfolio should be viewed as reserves which are just waiting to eventually be deployed. In the case of Treasury-based reserves, they should be viewed as assets which pay a nominal rate to cover inflation risk. However, they bear significant duration risk the further out in maturity and the lower the interest rate they bear. On the other hand, gold is a reserve that has historically exceeded the average stock market return, but with far greater volatility. This makes gold a potential non-correlated growth asset class with special properties which can potentially take advantage of market discontinuities during cetain stock market corrections.

> OPTIMAL CAPITAL GROWTH PORTFOLIO RE-BALANCING CYCLE:
> - INCREASE SAFE-HAVEN RESERVES (TRESASURIES OR GOLD) AT STOCK MARKET PEAK
> - DURING MARKET CORRECTION RE-DEPLOY % OF RESERVES FIRST INTO LONGER DURATION RISK ASSETS RISK ASSETS FIRST
> - MOVE SECOND WAVE OF RESERVES INTO STOCKS AT COAST IS CLEAR SIGNAL
> - BEGIN UNDERWEIGHTING LONG DURATION BONDS AS FED HINTS AT TIGHTENING BY SHIFTING LONG DURATION BONDS INTO STOCK INDEX FUND
> - REPEAT CYCLE AT STOCK SELL SIGNAL
> - RESERVE CHOICE IS DEPENDENT ON WHETHER FED MUST RAISE RATES THROUGH THE CORRECTION OR WILL BE DROPPING RATES INTO MARKET DECLINE

The optimal cycle once a stock market correction starts begins by investors selling stocks and trading into some other asset, typically short duration T-Bills first. As the correction progresses, a shift begins as investors buy more conservative, but higher risk long duration assets like corporate bonds. As a result, the BAA1 / 30 YR Treasury bond spread typically shows a confirming signal ahead of a stock market low. Short duration cash or in certain cases gold reserves are used to buy up beaten down stocks as the market begins to recover. At some point in the upswing stocks usually get additional buying strentgth as long duration bonds are sold due to interest rate pressure. Eventually the cycle hits a peak again. The time span for the upswing in the cycle can range from 4 to 7 years. Probably not by coincidence, the peaks tend to coincide frequently with political elections, most often when the President changes from one party to another. The downturns, measured from optimal peak selling point to market low, have averaged 13 months in length.

The small 10-15% correctons have usually lasted less than a year, but the major recession corrections driven by sharp oil spikes since 1974 have shown time periods of up to two years for the market to clear.

Review of Historical Rebalancing Cycles

Three primary options exist for storing money in situations when you sell assets and do not intend to immediately redeploy the money into stocks. They include short duration notes or cash, long duration Treasuries of 5, 10 or even 30 year maturities, or gold. Each has different characteristics, and only one is a full-proof means of maintaining interim purchase power – the short term cash equivalent market.

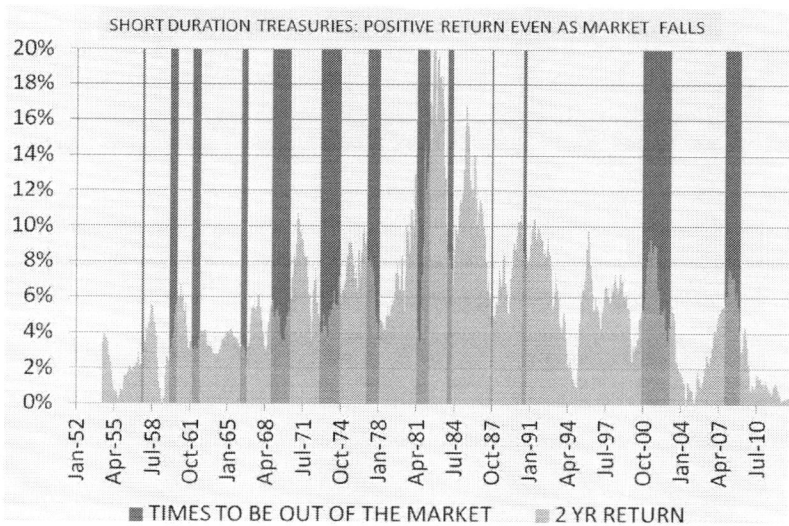

SHORT DURATION TREASURIES: POSITIVE RETURN EVEN AS MARKET FALLS

■ TIMES TO BE OUT OF THE MARKET ▓ 2 YR RETURN

In the graph above the return on the 2 year T-Bill is overlaid upon the optimal time periods to be out of the stock market. The 2 year return is the annual return including any capital gains or losses due to changes in interest rates. The return, therefore, is appropriately matched to the annual return on which the stock market corrections are judged. The red bars on the graph are times in which the market was undergoing negative, sometimes severely negative returns.

The beauty of the 2 Year T-Bill is that throughout the 60 year time period analyzed it never lost value in a correction time period in nominal terms. It held its value even when rates rose quickly in the 1970s. The short duration characteristic of the security make it a good choice in market corrections

221

because your chances of losing asset purchasing power are minimized, and you still gain a small rate of return in interest to cover inflation risk. The qualities of the 2 year from a duration standpoint are a likely reason that the 10 - 2 signal works so well in signaling market correction situations. The typical historical cycle shows the 2 year Treasury rate increasing as a market peak approaches, and then buyers rush in as they sell stocks and look for a place to park cash reserves for the expected 1-2 year market correction period.

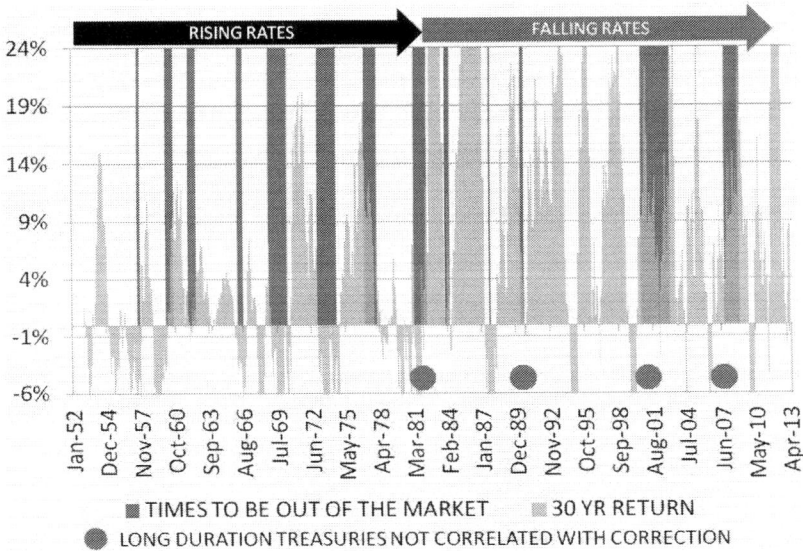

A second, but less effective alternative for storing funds which are generated from stock sales at a market peak is a longer duration Treasury bond. Duration risk may work against you in this trade, particularly in a rising interest rate environment. In general the risk becomes greater the further out in maturity you reach. In order to get a sense of just how great the risk can be, the annual returns on the 30 year Treasury were reviewed against the historical stock market correction cycle. Not surprisingly in the 1960s and 1970s, the long duration Treasury as a reserve was a very poor choice. As the stock market was falling in value, the long duration 30 year was falling in value as well. In some cases the relative decline in principal was equal or even greater in magnitude than stocks, such as in 1966, 1969 and 1974. These were time periods in which the Fed did not lower interest rates by purchasing government securities to add reserves as the stock market corrected. The Fed did not have the option to lower rates because inflation was on the increase during this time.

After 1980, the interest rate cycle for longer duration bonds began to be off-set from stock market returns. Long bonds began to sell-off during the growth phase of the stock market rise, with peaks (lowest price) in bond interest rates usually happening prior to the stock market peak. These time periods are marked in green in the above graph. The one exception was the 1987 market crash. From the early 1980s through the 2013 time period, long term interest rates were in a declining pattern owed to more subdued levels of consumer price inflation. This meant that the chances were good that in a stock market decline the Fed would enter the market and buy Treasuries to lower rates in the event of a market drop. There were also new buyers in the market other than the Fed, particularly in the 2008 crisis – foreign governments. The global reach of the U.S. dollar as a reserve currency meant that Treasury demand rose significantly as a safe-haven in the 2008 world liquidity crisis. Demand for Treasuries rose so much that the Fed balance sheet actually shows selling, rather than purchasing Treasuries in the middle of the 2008 crisis. Fed selling Treasuries into a major liquidity crisis which had the impact of tightening monetary conditions, rather than buying Treasuries to provide liquidity is an odd, but true fact. The Treasuries bought for safe-haven reasons by market participants were eventually sold off post the crisis, and the negative return in 2010 shown in the graph reflects the trailing result. The Fed re-entered with major quantitative easing purchase programs which benefited the long duration bond markets in 2011 and 2012.

The gold market is often referred to as a good place to preserve money in the event of a stock market crisis. The actual analysis of the performance, however, is mixed. The use of gold as a reserve as shown in the following graph tends to work well in market corrections that have a very strong foreign counter force pushing against the U.S. government and Federal Reserve policy. This counter force is usually exhibited through an oil price spike. Under these circumstances the return performance of gold is not correlated with the stock market decline as shown on the lower part of the graph.

Gold performed well as a safe-haven during the height of the inflationary 70s, but not in the 1969 downturn. The poor performance in the 1969 correction is likely due to the U.S. still being on the gold standard until August 1971, when the U.S. sold gold in times of crisis to foreign governments, increasing open market supply and lowering price. The lowering of U.S. gold reserves after the 1969 recession played a big role in the abandonment of the gold standard in 1971 as there was growing risk that the U.S. would suffer a run on its dwindling gold reserves relative to the amount of dollars outstanding.

GOLD AS A SAFE-HAVEN DEPENDS ON MARKET FORCE SCENARIO

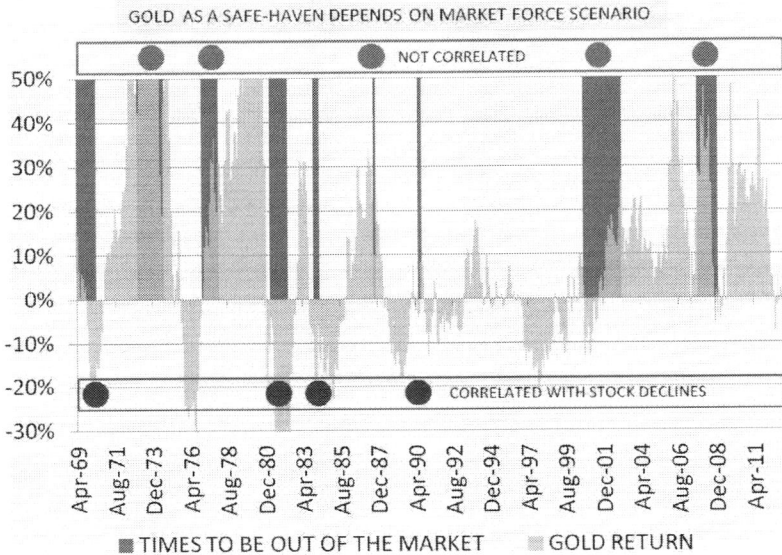

■ TIMES TO BE OUT OF THE MARKET   ■ GOLD RETURN

Gold also did not perform well in the early 1980s. This was a time period in which U.S. interest rates were at historical highs, and on a relative basis the return on the U.S. paper currency was higher than the expectation for gold. Predictably, the demand for the U.S. currency began to rise. When the market fell in the early 1980s, so did gold. However, interest rates remained high.

During a stock market correction the only predictably non-correlated asset to the risk asset sell-off is short duration T-Bills or cash. Gold is a good non-correlated alternative in scenarios where foreign forces are at odds with low U.S. interest rate and depreciating dollar policies. In cases where the dollar is strong due to high interest rates, gold is ineffective. Longer duration bonds are okay as a safe-haven when interest rates are in decline, as was the case from 1980 up through the 2008 crisis.

	T-BILL RATES		GOLD		
CORRECTION	PRIOR	DURING	PRIOR	DURING	BEST RESERVE CHOICE
1970	UP	UP	UP	DOWN	T-BILLS
1974	DOWN	UP	UP	UP	GOLD, T-BILLS
1976	DOWN	UP	UP	UP	GOLD, T-BILLS
1981	UP	DOWN	UP	DOWN	ANY DURATION TREASURY
1984	UP	DOWN	DOWN	DOWN	T-BILLS
1987	UP	STABLE	UP	STABLE	T-BILLS, GOLD
1991	UP	DOWN	DOWN	DOWN	ANY DURATION TREASURY
2001	UP	DOWN	DOWN	UP	ANY DURATION TREASURY, GOLD
2007	UP	DOWN	UP	STABLE	ANY DURATION TREASURY, GOLD

EPILOGUE

Closing this book with a statement about portfolio strategy and the rebalancing cycle as interest rates rise off the zero bound seemed the most fitting conclusion. Fitting because how the market would respond as rates rise from the zero bound was of premiere importance as this book was being prepared for publication in 2013. Fitting because the Federal Reserve was applying an extreme force into the market at the time, and the Theory introduced in this book is a guide on how to make sound decisions as the effects from the Fed force reverberate through the market.

The Federal Reserve became a very activist institution during the 2008 financial crisis, and it chose a path to continue extreme policies even after the crisis was over. When the Obama administration came into office, a Keynesian-based economic philosophy took over national government policy. It included increased government spending during the recession to try to raise aggregate demand, and the use of regulation to attempt to engineer intended economic results primarily focused on income redistribution.

The Fed's role in the Obama Administration economic policy framework was to keep interest rates low. Lowering interest rates to the zero bound is a form of price control, the primary intention for the control being to keep the interest expense on the U.S. National Debt from exploding to levels that would shut-off government spending programs. Zero rates also impose an in-direct tax on savers. As an in-direct tax on the wealthy, Keynes argued repressed interest rates force re-distribution of income. However, the review of the data from 2009 through 2013 empirically indicated the opposite as the stock market catapulted to new highs in direct correlation with lower rates.

The effectiveness of the policy is for economists to debate. The real issue for investors is to focus on dealing with market reality.

In order to maintain the overnight Fed Funds rate at zero in 2013, the Federal Reserve needed to keep adding reserves to the system. To negate the inflationary effect of the massive injection of reserves into the financial system, very strict bank lending regulations were put into effect. The U.S. banks were an integral part of an interest rate "price control" policy in 2013, just as they were in the 1940s, because they work with the Fed as the primary dealers for Treasury issuance. The real challenge for the low rate policy was the warping of market incentives that that the monopolistic market forces was causing. Five years into the policy the results were curtailed real economic growth, an upward movement of the stock market contrary to expected market behavior in poor economic situations, and a continual need for the Fed to supply dollar liquidity into the market in order to keep rates from rising.

There was an inherent financial market instability beginning to surface in 2013. On a relative basis the policy situation had a resemblance to the worst parts of two points in history, the late 1940s and the 1970s. On the one hand, the Fed was managing interest rates as if it was in post war 1940s. However, the economic scenario and government policy forces did not resemble the 1940s; they were more closely aligned with the 1970s. In the 1940s there was a current account *surplus* driven by demand for U.S. goods being utilized to re-build a war torn world. In the overall financial order, the foreign force was positive for the U.S. economy. Conversely, high current account *deficits* persisted from 2008 to 2013, as had been the case for decades. A megatrend was firmly entrenched to equalize wages on a relative basis between U.S. workers and the emerging world. In the overall financial order, this phenomenon is most directly correlated with the addiction to borrowing by the U.S. government from foreign sources to fund fiscal spending.

The government budget process slowed government spending in 2012 and early 2013, just as Truman did in 1946. However, on a relative basis the spending cuts made were not of similar magnitude. The real spending wildcard as of the writing of this book was the Affordable Care Act implementation in 2014. The Act is a strange beast economically. It is simultaneously a tax and spend and a government subsidy program that will need to be funded by increasing the National Debt. The tax and spend portion of the program is hard to decipher for most, but the Supreme Court gave approval legally for the government to implement a forced buying of an insurance product by the population because in the Court's view, it is a tax. Tax and spend programs are inflationary, particularly if they are monetized – see Chapter 8 if you need a refresher course. In the case of Obamacare the tax is the forced purchase of a product; the spending is immediate. The impact of this mandated scheme was perfectly anticipated by the Theory of Financial Relativity – prices on insurance went up, in some cases exponentially – 150% to 200% on average in some states. In NC, my wife and children had a policy that was $360 per month, and the new pricing increased to $860 per month. Taxing and spending left the door wide open for insurance companies to raise rates without any economic benefit.

When a new tax is implemented, particularly one that is as targeted as the Affordable Care Act, tax avoidance behavior is predictable. The avoidance actions in the economy were immediate in the job sector. In order for small businesses to avoid having to buy insurance for their workers at inflated prices, they began moving the workers to part-time status, a loop-hole in the law. This meant that workers not only would be working less, they would also have to pay the insurance bill themselves, or pay a tax penalty of 1% on their income level. In the first 6 months of 2013, 88% of the new jobs created were part-time workers according to the Bureau of Labor and Statistics, and there was a corresponding reduction in rate of growth in full-time workers. The trend halted in the 3rd quarter of 2013 because the tax penalty imposed on businesses that did not provide health insurance to full-time workers was deferred by Executive order beyond 2014.

The impact on individuals forced to buy the insurance product if it wasn't provided as a job benefit, was not fully known as 2014 came closer. The natural tendency of individuals was likely to avoid the mandate in some way, either refusing to buy the product and paying the penalty or cheating on their qualifications to receive a subsidy from the government to buy health insurance. The subsidy program was the fiscal spending wildcard in the socially engineered Obama administration economy as the country approached 2014. The Affordable Care Act created a subsidy program for a large portion of the U.S. population to buy insurance to pay for health care – if it was not provided by their employer. It is little wonder that employers quickly started reducing workers hours to make them part-time. The scenario reminded me of the many government led initiatives that caused disruptive force throughout my life – the Monetary Control Act of 1980, the 1982 Judge Greene MFJ decision breaking up AT&T, the Telecom Act of 1996, and various banking deregulation acts. All of these major government edicts eventually created forces which impacted the market, in some cases detrimental, in others not as cumbersome, but disruptive nonetheless. The Affordable Care Act was expected to be equally disruptive over time, and very likely to require much more government deficit spending than the meager estimates put forward by the CBO of $759 billion during fiscal years 2014 through 2019 when it was signed into law in March 2010[7]. The difference between an individual paying a 1% penalty on a $30,000 job, $300, and having to pay a much higher cost of $2400 – $3600 a year for a product which has no immediate benefit for a large part of the population is very large. It was already driving avoidance behavior in 2013, and for many, particularly the younger age group, the economic choice most likely would be to wait until they were truly sick to buy health insurance.

What did the mid 2013 scenario mean for investors? It meant that the Fed was facing a disorderly economy driven by incentives not to hire workers, increased taxation, and the possibility of even higher deficit spending than anticipated. It also meant the Fed was on the hook for supporting the government policies with low rates to an undeterminable point in the future. And it meant that normal interest rate signals were likely to be distorted if a break-down in the stock market was about to transpire. This was the reason the market became so fixated with the "Fed taper" as it became known in the business press in 2013. The "taper" was a made up media term to refer to the Federal Reserve lowering the amount of bond purchases (QE) it was making in the open market in its role of keeping U.S. Treasury interest rates low. The QE rate of change was being resorted to as a means of trying to understand whether the Fed was getting relatively tighter in its policy, since the government was telling the investing public through policy statements and testimony that the Fed Funds rate was not going to be raised until well into the future. However, the real and most observable measure of financial relativity is the interest rate market. If the Fed was distorting market activity through its actions, the force would be exhibited in some way. The first time the counter force to excessive QE was exhibited was in May 2013 when long duration bond rates rose in spite of the massive Fed buying program. Likewise, oil prices rose.

Zero bound interest rates are not sustainable forever in the United States, or anywhere else in the world, without some distorting effect. The market will

---

[7] http://www.cbo.gov/publication/44176

attempt to revert back to historical levels. In 2013 there were small but visible signs that the longer the zero-rate policy was maintained, the more volatile and disruptive the reversion to an orderly financial universe was likely to become. The reason this was happening can be explained by the essence of the Theory of Financial Relativity - domestic government institutions will not willingly exert a negative force on the market; however, foreign forces will do so if market imbalances become too great. Allowing rates to return to more typical historical averages should not be a negative force; however, in a world in which the U.S. stock market's relative value is an asset bubble directly linked to the size and ownership composition of the U.S. National Debt, popping the bubble is as simple as increasing the rate of interest paid on U.S. Treasuries. No politician in Washington wants to own this decision – so the problem perpetually festers until a crisis develops as it did in 2001 and 2008.

In this type of Fed and fiscal policy environment, one that is likely to be accompanied by rising interest rates, the stock correction cycles in the 1960s and 1970s become instructive relative points in history. A rising interest rate pattern usually involves long duration bonds moving lower in price, higher in yield, in correlation with the stock correction. Going into 2014 and beyond if government spending increases quickly and excessive banking reserves being put into the system as of 2013 are not

> "AS HISTORICAL RATES BEGIN TO RISE, SHORTER DURATION T-BILLS AND GOLD WILL BECOME THE BETTER CHOICE FOR PERSERVING CAPITAL INTO A CORRECTION"

withdrawn, the market will begin to exhibit the same tendencies as the 1970s. Eventually the Fed will have to react, but they are very likely to be late in pushing short rates higher. If this path is taken, the next major down-turn will be signaled by financial instability exhibited through rapidly rising long-term interest rates going into the crisis as well as a foreign force such as an oil price spike beyond the 2008 high of $140 per barrel or a sell-off of U.S. Treasury debt by foreign creditors. A strictly deflation led scenario also cannot be ruled out if GDP growth stagnates further, not unlikely given the economic incentive structure in the Affordable Care Act. Either scenario was possible as of the writing of this book. Both would eventually cause a stock market correction. The most unlikely relative outcome was the "hope" scenario, which required high growth in GDP triggered by closure of the trade gap. The foreign trading partners seemed entrenched in their position of holding on to the dollar trade surplus as a means of making sure they could continue to control their access to the U.S. market.

If you are selling stocks prior to a correction in years to come as the Fed raises rates from the zero bound, the only effective reserve will be short duration Treasuries or cash. Gold will be effective if government spending increases at a fast pace and the Fed remains accommodative for too long. The Theory of Financial Relativity predicts both excessive Fed accommodation and increased government spending are the most likely trajectory for domestic government forces as the country moves beyond 2013, followed by a foreign led reaction leading to a new relative valuation of the U.S. stock market.

Regrettably, the Theory cannot be used to predict the exact timing of a market breakdown many months or years in advance given the unpredictable human behavioral forces that eventually coalesce to tear down and then build the market back up. These forces can change in magnitude and direction at any time, particularly in conjunction with political events. The Theory is used to provide insight into why the market moves in a predictable relative way in response to these forces as pressure builds in the financial system. This insight gives a sound basis from which to guide your investing decisions within a reasonable amount of time leading up to decline in the market, and then in the eventual recovery. You do not need to take speculative investment positions in order to take advantage of an inevitable unfolding scenario. The best investment path is to understand the relative order in the financial universe, stay in-tune with the major market forces, and rebalance your portfolio in relation to the directional change in the overriding forces as the signals become clear.

John Maynard Keynes wrote, *"In the long run, we are all dead."*

For investors, *"**In the long run, all value is relative**."*

NOTE ABOUT SOURCES

The analysis and discussions presented in *Theory of Financial Relativity* rely on data drawn almost entirely from publicly available sources: The four web-sites primarily utilized to gather time series data dating from 1941 through 2013 include the St. Louis Federal Reserve Economic Research database known as FRED (http://research.stlouisfed.org/), U.S. Treasury Direct public debt on-line reports (www.treasurydirect.gov), the U.S. Department of Treasury Resource Center (www.treasury.gov) and the EIA (www.eia.gov).

Autobiographical sections of the book are compiled from memory and discussions with professional associates, friends and family. All accounts are personal recollections of events which I was directly involved.

Much of the discussion in the book about current invents is readily verifiable in contemporary business news web-sites such as CBNC, Bloomberg, Wall Street Journal, and The Financial Times. There were 70 years of history covered in the book in which the time series data reflecting major financial events that needed to be put into appropriate context. Fact checking of history was primarily done through the use of Wikipedia, a widely used on-line information resource. (http://en.wikipedia.org).

I strived to be as accurate as possible in the presentation of work and ideas which are the documented perspectives of other professionals and academics. The references to works which were used in the book are shown in the following bibliography.

BIBLIOGRAPY

Bell, John. *On the Einstein Podolsky Rosen Paradox*. Physics 1, 1964.

Bogle, John C. *Clash of the Cultures: Investment vs. Speculation*. New York: Wiley, John & Sons, Incorporated, 2012.

Buffett, Warren. *Tap Dancing to Work*. New York: Portfolio Hardcover, 2012.

Carmen M. Reinhart, Kenneth S. Rogoff. *A Decade of Debt*. NBER Working Paper, 2011.

Cooper, Andrew Scott. *Showdown at Doha: The Secret Oil Deal That Helped Sink the Shah of Iran*. The Middle East Institute, 2000

Friedman, Milton, and Rose D. Friedman. *Free to Choose a Personal Statement*. New York: Harcourt Brace Jovanovich, 1980.

Freidman, Thomas L. *The World is Flat: A Brief History of the Twenty-first Century*. New York: Farrar, Straus & Giroux, 2005.

Gilder, George. *Wealth and Poverty*. New York: Basic Books, 1981.

Graham, Benjamin. *The Intelligent Investor: A Book of Practical Counsel*. New York: Harper & Row Publishers, 1986.

Greenspan, Alan. *The Age of Turbulence*. New York: Penguin Group, 2007.

Greider, William. *Secrets of the Temple*. New York: Touchstone, 1987.

Hamilton, James D. *Causes and Consequences of the Oil Shock of 2007-08*. Brookings Papers on Economic Activity, Spring 2009.

Heisenburg's Uncertainty Paper of 1927.

Isaacson, Walter. *Einstein His Life and Universe*. New York: Simon and Schuster, 2007.

Keynes, John Maynard. Economic *Consequences of the Peace*. New York: Harcourt, Brace and Howe, 1920.

Meltzer, Allan, H. *Origins of the Great Inflation*. Federal Reserve Bank of St. Louis Review, March / April 2005.

Smith, Adam. *An Inquiry into the Nature and Causes of the Wealth of Nations*. 5th ed. London: Methuen & Co.,1904.

INDEX

ABOUT THE AUTHOR

Daniel Moore is the creator of FinancialRelativity.com, a web portal created for the purpose of tracking the status of financial markets and providing investment analysis and portfolio management insights to investors. Based on the systematic investment research, he writes about the market and publishes his views through internet market publications.

A graduate of Duke University's Fuqua School of Business in 1988, Dan has broad experience in company finance and investment portfolio management. Uniquely Daniel began his investment analysis work by building a Monte Carlo simulation computer model to assess fair market value of a business using publicly available financial data. The program was used in the MBA classroom from 1989-1991.

He manages a blog, publishing market viewpoints under the pen name Financial Market Vigilante. He currently resides in Durham, NC.

Made in the USA
Lexington, KY
12 January 2015